*The Uncertain Verdict*

# The Uncertain Verdict

*A Study of the 1969 Elections in Four Indian States*

*Ramashray Roy*

**University of California Press**
Berkeley, Los Angeles, London

University of California Press
Berkeley and Los Angeles, California

University of California Press Ltd.
London, England

Copyright © 1972, 1975
by Orient Longman Ltd.

Revised edition published in 1975
by the University of California Press
for sale in the United States, Canada and the United Kingdom

ISBN: 0-520-02475-3
Library of Congress Catalog Card Number: 73-78555

Printed in India
by Indraprastha Press (CBT), Bahadur Shah Zafar Marg,
New Delhi 110001

# *Foreword*

This study by Ramashray Roy is part of the programme of publications on the party system and electoral development in India planned by the Centre for the Study of Developing Societies. Earlier publications in this series are *Party System and Election Studies* (1967) and *Context of Electoral Change in India* (1969). The present publication is based on a detailed investigation of the mid-term elections held in 1969 in the states of Bihar, Punjab, Uttar Pradesh and West Bengal. Another work, *Citizens, Parties and Political Order,* which consists of analyses of the political implications of recent electoral behaviour, is now in press. A full-length study based on national sample surveys of the 1967 and 1971 elections, comparing the erosion of the Congress Party's strength in the former and its dramatic revival in the latter, will be sent for publication in the near future. While the Centre's research and publication programme covers a number of other areas of investigation in historical antecedents, social dynamics, psychological orientations and problem-oriented research on politics, its studies in mass political behaviour as galvanized through various elections will continue as part of its interest in understanding, on the basis of systematic empirical investigation, the emerging trends and issues in India's democratic functioning.

Ramashray Roy's interest in electoral behaviour and party system in India dates back to his earlier work on Bihar politics and on organizational components of grass-roots politics. He utilized the theoretical framework of factional alignments in a system of one-party dominance in a detailed analysis of selection of Congress candidates which was published through a series of articles in *Economic and Political Weekly* during 1966-67. He was responsible for the entire field work in Bihar for the Centre's national study of the 1967 elections. He directed the project on the 1969 mid-term elections in four states supported by the Indian Council of Social Science Research, the outcome of which is presented in this volume. He did the trend report on party system and elections for the ICSSR's *Survey of Research in Political Science* (forthcoming) and a preliminary analysis of data from the 1967 national election study of the Centre. The latter was published in *Perspectives* in 1971. He has also worked, along with other members of the Centre, on the analysis of aggregate data for the purpose of exploring regional and temporal patterns of socio-political reality. The results of this work will soon be published. Ramashray Roy is currently Director of Research at the Indian Council of Social Science Research, on loan from the Centre, where he will be developing the Council's data programme in the social sciences.

Delhi                                                                RAJNI KOTHARI

# *Preface*

The 1967 General Election constitutes a watershed in Indian politics. The electoral verdict considerably reduced the electoral strength of the Congress which had theretofore functioned as a sturdy prop of political stability. The failure of the Congress Party to win an effective majority in several states ushered in a period of shifting alliances among parties in opposition. These alliances formed governments, to be sure; however, several factors intervened to make them short-lived and tenuous. And, hence the 1969 mid-term poll in the four states.

The 1969 mid-term poll did not, however, succeed in producing a stable majority, and political uncertainty in these states continues even today to impede the process of development. Meanwhile, the frustration and the feeling of helplessness and impatience caused by continued uncertain electoral verdict and fragmented party system raise doubts about the viability of democratic institutions as an instrument of social change and effective government. Is democracy ill-suited for bringing about a rapid social change? Can it survive the corrosive impact of slowly accumulating disillusionment? Can it produce stable government to carry on the necessary programmes in order to satisfy aspirations aroused by the process of social mobilization?

These are some of the questions that need to be answered. For this, however, one has necessarily to take into account the conditions that sustain and preserve democracy. This requires that the characteristics of the political substratum, that is, political elites, the institutional framework, and the electorate—all these three essential dimensions—must be explored and examined. This study was not designed to undertake such a heavy task. It focusses on the electorate located in different milieus and, through an exploration of their attributes, examines the implications of differential configurations of these attributes for the sustenance and preservation of democratic institutions in the four states under study. Furthermore, it seeks in a modest way to furnish some materials that may help in understanding the complex process of interaction between socio-economic conditions, individual attributes and democratic development.

It need not be emphasized that a study like this draws heavily upon the accumulated knowledge that springs from diverse sources. My intellectual debts are too numerous to document here. The foot note references in the study represent only a partial public acknowledgement. Some of the other sources must, however, be recorded here. I am greatly obliged to the Indian Council of Social Science Research, Delhi, which through a generous grant, made this study possible. I am also indebted to my colleagues at the Centre for the Study of Developing Societies who combine in them the difficult roles of friends and critics. I am particularly grateful to Rajni Kothari, Gopal Krishna, D.L. Sheth, Ashish Nandy, H.R. Chaturvedi, R.K. Srivastava, N.K. Nijhawan, R. Chandidas and V.B. Singh for their many acts of kindness and encouragement. The credit for transforming the jungle of data into comprehensible tables must go to N.K. Nijhawan. I am also grateful to Jyotirindra Das Gupta for reading the first three chapters of this study. Needless to say that my gratitude to the numerous investigators who braved the hazards of field operation including that of *gherao* in West Bengal is immense. I am also thankful to M.K. Riyal for typing and re-typing the manuscript. Lastly, I must thank all the respondents who willingly gave their time to make this study a success.

It is enough to indicate the myriad source of my indebtedness. Whatever merits this study may have must be credited to these sources, while its shortcomings are entirely my own. This study represents no more than what Montaigne expressed long ago :

> Amongst so many borrowed things,
> I am glad,
> I can steal one,
> disguising and altering it
> for some new service.

Delhi　　　　　　　　　　　　　　　　　　　RAMASHRAY ROY

# Contents

|  | Page |
|---|---|
| Foreword | v |
| Preface | vii |
| List of Tables | x |
| List of Figures | xvi |
| *Chapter One* | |
| Introduction | 1 |
| *Chapter Two* | |
| Varying Contexts of Electoral Choice | 25 |
| *Chapter Three* | |
| Socio-Economic Background and Vote | 58 |
| *Chapter Four* | |
| Voters and Partisanship Variability | 99 |
| *Chapter Five* | |
| Political Profile of Voters | 148 |
| *Chapter Six* | |
| Political Comprehension and the Voter | 182 |
| *Chapter Seven* | |
| The Voter and the Political System | 219 |
| *Chapter Eight* | |
| Varieties of Electoral Behaviour | 258 |
| Appendix | 283 |
| Bibliography | 287 |
| Index | 291 |

# List of Tables

*Chapter Two*

| Table No. | | Page |
|---|---|---|
| 2:1 | Indices of Level of Development in Four States | 25 |
| 2:2 | Development Expenditure in Four States: 1968-69 | 26-27 |
| 2:3 | Average Number of Contestants in Four States: 1967-69 | 35 |
| 2:4 | Constituencies by Number of Candidates in Four States: 1967-69 | 36 |
| 2:5 | Losses and Gains by Parties in West Bengal: 1967-69 | 38 |
| 2:6 | Losses and Gains by Parties in Bihar: 1967-1969 | 39 |
| 2:7 | Losses and Gains by Parties in Uttar Pradesh 1967-1969 | 40 |
| 2:8 | Losses and Gains by Parties in Punjab: 1967-1969 | 41 |
| 2:9 | Shift in Voters' Party Allegiance: Punjab | 49 |
| 2:10 | Shift in Voters' Party Allegiance: Uttar Pradesh | 50 |
| 2:11 | Shift in Voters' Party Allegiance: Bihar | 51 |
| 2:12 | Shift in Voters' Party Allegiance: West Bengal | 52 |

*Chapter Three*

| | | |
|---|---|---|
| 3:1 | Socio-Economic Profiles of Voters | 62-63 |
| 3:2 | Socio-Economic Status and Voters by States | 68 |
| 3:3 | SES and Satisfaction of Voters with Past Financial Condition by States | 70 |

| Table No. | | Page |
|---|---|---|
| 3:4 | SES and Voters' Perception of Their Future Financial Condition by States | 72 |
| 3:5 | SES and Information of Voters by States | 76 |
| 3:6 | Voters' Personal Involvement in Election by States | 78 |
| 3:7 | Voters' and Electoral Interest by States | 79 |
| 3:8 | Partisanship and Voters by States | 82 |
| 3:9 | SES and Voters' Partisanship by States | 83 |
| 3:10 | SES and Partisanship of Voters by States | 85 |
| 3:11 | Environmental Pressures and Voting Decision (States Combined) | 89 |
| 3:12 | Considerations Influencing Voting Decision by States | 91 |
| 3:13 | SES and Timing of Voting Decision: All States | 92 |
| 3:14 | SES Level and Party Preference by States | 94-95 |

*Chapter Four*

| | | |
|---|---|---|
| 4:1 | Age and Voter Types | 108-110 |
| 4:2 | Place of Residence and Voter Types | 114 |
| 4:3 | Caste and Voter Types | 117-19 |
| 4:4 | Landownership and Voter Types | 122 |
| 4:5 | Education and Voter Types | 123 |
| 4:6 | Voter Types and Interest in Politics | 132-33 |
| 4:7 | Voter Types and Strength of Party Identification | 136-38 |
| 4:8 | Voter Types and Timing of Voting Decision | 140-42 |
| 4:9 | Voter Types, Campaign Participation and Satisfaction with MLA | 144-46 |

*Chapter Five*

| | | |
|---|---|---|
| 5:1 | SES and Information | 155 |
| 5:2 | Age and Level of Political Information | 157 |

LIST OF TABLES

| Table No. | | Page |
|---|---|---|
| 5:3 | SES and Political Interest | 159 |
| 5:4 | Age and Political Interest | 161 |
| 5:5 | Information and Political Interest | 163 |
| 5:6 | SES and Party Identification | 166 |
| 5:7 | Information and Party Identification | 170 |
| 5:8 | Political Interest and Party Identification | 172 |
| 5:9 | SES and Electoral Involvement | 174 |
| 5:10 | Age and Electoral Involvement | 176 |
| 5:11 | Information and Electoral Involvement | 177 |
| 5:12 | Party Identification and Electoral Involvement | 179 |
| 5:13 | Political Interest and Electoral Involvement | 180 |

*Chapter Six*

| | | |
|---|---|---|
| 6:1 | SES and Approval of Politics | 191 |
| 6:2 | SES and Issue-Orientation : Tax | 194 |
| 6:3 | SES and Issue-Orientation : Control on Industries | 195 |
| 6:4 | SES and Issue-Orientation : Private Property | 197 |
| 6:5 | SES and Leftist Orientation | 200 |
| 6:6 | SES and Acceptance of Democratic Institutions | 203 |
| 6:7 | SES and Perception of Party Differences | 205 |
| 6:8 | SES and the Perception of the Necessity of Parties | 207 |
| 6:9 | SES and Acceptance of the Rule of the Game | 209 |
| 6:10 | SES and Voters' Concept of Representatives' Role | 210 |
| 6:11 | SES and Voters' Concept of Representatives' Role | 211 |
| 6:12 | SES and Voters' Concept of Legislator's Role | 213 |
| 6:13 | SES and Voters' View on Defection | 215 |
| 6:14 | SES and Voters' View on Defection | 217 |

| Table No. | | Page |
|---|---|---|

*Chapter Seven*

| | | |
|---|---|---|
| 7:1 | SES and Election Victory Reflecting People's Wishes | 227 |
| 7:2 | SES and Legitimacy | 230 |
| 7:3 | SES and Obedience to Law | 232 |
| 7:4 | Caste and Political Efficacy | 234 |
| 7:5 | Education and Political Efficacy | 236 |
| 7:6 | SES and Level of Political Efficacy | 237 |
| 7:7 | Party Identification and Political Efficacy | 239 |
| 7:8 | Political Interest and Political Efficacy | 240 |
| 7:9 | Electoral Involvement and Political Efficacy | 242 |
| 7:10 | SES and Sense of Political Efficacy | 251 |
| 7:11 | Whether Connection Necessary for Contacting Officials | 252 |
| 7:12 | SES and Voters' Understanding of Politics | 253 |
| 7:13 | SES and Sense of Political Efficacy | 255 |
| 7:14 | Voters' Perception of Influence Potential of the People | 256 |

# List of Figures

Figure No.

| | | |
|---|---|---|
| 2.1 | The nature of party competition and party space in the four states | 55 |
| 2.2 | Retention capability of Congress and its attractiveness for fresh voters | 57 |
| 4.1 | Age and Congress vote in the four states: 1967 | 105 |
| 4.2 | Age and Congress vote in the four States: 1967-69 | 106 |
| 4.3 | Income and political interest | 126 |
| 4.4 | Education and political interest | 126 |
| 5.1 | Age and partisan strength in the four states | 168 |
| 8.1 | Casual linkages among political attributes | 277 |

# CHAPTER ONE

# *Introduction*

The relationship between a democratic polity and periodical elections for selecting rulers is intimate. It is true that in modern times even authoritarian regimes often take recourse to elections for the selection of rulers. However, the significance of elections is quite different in the two systems. While election in authoritarian regimes is meant to give a semblance of legitimacy through popular choice to what still remains an oligarchic process of political decision-making, its role in a democratic regime is more substantial in that it is the only means available for determining the mandate for governance. It is one thing to use elections as a formal ratification of the decisions taken by the ruling oligarchy, and quite another to make it the very basis of the determination of the composition of rulers. In a democratic regime, election itself decides who the rulers are going to be and how long they may continue in office. In authoritarian regimes, these vital decisions are taken outside of the democratic process and concealed from the scrutiny of those whose life is to be affected in several important respects by the decisions of the rulers.

Apart from the selection of rulers, the importance of popular elections lies in yet another factor. Elections serve not merely as a mechanism of safeguarding continuity but also as an instrument of change and of a redistribution of political power. The requirement that the entire adult population should participate in the selection of rulers has an important bearing on how political power is structured at a particular moment in the history of a democratic regime. This means the enmeshing of the political process with numerous interests—individual, group, sectional—that are heterogeneous and not infrequently incompatible. With a shift in the articulation of interest and a change in the perception of the relationship between the advancement of certain interests and the orientation of the ruling group towards these interests, the electoral outcome may bring about a complete change in the composition of the ruling elite with implications for future governmental policies and programmes. Thus, public opinion does frequently assert itself in bringing down one group of ruling elite and replacing it with another when governmental actions "stray far away from the effective balance of public opinion."[1] This happens even under conditions of the dominance of a single party, and much more so under a more competitive structure of power.

Though this change in the ruling group is in itself a reflection of a shift in the distribution of power, elections do in a real sense facilitate the process of structural shift in the distribution of power. Since majority rule is one of the basic operational principles of a democratic regime, number rather than privileges and social advantages determines the composition of the governing elite etc. The endowment of privileges does at times prove to be a potent factor in influencing others and, through indirect influence exerted on the public mind, frequently influences electoral outcome. However, when the antagonism between the privileged and the non-privileged is gradually perceived to be a critical element in social and political process, the non-privileged many may rise against the privileged few and demand effective share in political power when such a share is denied or obstructed.

As a matter of fact, the establishment of democratic principles as the guiding force of the ruling of men symbolizes, in a very real sense, the acceptance of claims of participation in political processes by social groups liberated from the shackles of economic dependence on the privileged groups. As a necessary consequence of the accomodation and incorporation of the rising socio-economic interests in the political process, two simultaneous processes come into operation: dispersal of power and integration of diverse socio-economic interests into the main stream of national political life. Periodical elections serve not only as the most appropriate means of recording popular verdict on the formation of government and thus of institutionalizing popular participation in political processes, but also, and even more importantly, they prompt and facilitate the development of "intermediate political structures" to articulate public policies,

---

1. Rajni Kothari, "Congress 'System' in India," *Asian Survey*, IV : 12 (1964), reprinted by Centre for the Study of Developing Societies, Delhi, *Party System and Election Studies* (New Delhi : Allied Publishers, 1967), p. 3.

# INTRODUCTION

mobilize public opinion and institutionalize political participation.²

The role of elections in implementing democratic principles or governance is crucial beyond doubt. Their impact on the politics of developing countries is all the more profound. The rigidity of social structure, the diversity of social groups, the inequality in the distribution of societal resources, the strangeness of democratic institutions, the strangle-hold of primordial loyalties—these and many other factors in fact impede the process of democratisation. If the rigidities inherent in the social structure do not easily yield to pressures of change, the aspirations of social mobility and the demand for political participation induced and accentuated by the modernization process cannot be shelved. A society launched upon the path of modernization must speedily attend to satisfying these aspirations and urges in order to escape upheavals caused by unrealized aspirations. And yet these are problems that cannot be solved in a short time. As a result, social tensions and conflicts are inevitably channelled into political processes.

At the political plane, the first need in the developing countries is to centralize political power in state authority and later to expand its scope to effectively grapple with multitudinous problems that attend the process of modernization. However, the adoption of democratic institutions initiates yet another process of dispersal of political power. One of the prime instruments for facilitating dispersal of power is, of course, the periodic elections. Through these elections the inert masses are politically activized and made aware of and conversant with the democratic rules of the game. It is through elections, again, that social rigidities impeding a speedy resolution of the participation crisis are overcome and neutralized. But before a final solution to the participation crisis³ is achieved and democratic institutions take firm root, the involvement of the inert mass in shaping the course

---

2. For an extensive theoretical discussion of this process and its relevance to the Indian case, see Rajni Kothari, *Politics in India* (Boston : Little Brown & Co., 1970).
3. For a discussion of the participation crisis in developing countries, see Lucian Pye, *Aspects of Political Development* (Boston : Little Brown & Co., 1966).

of political development through periodical elections may well upset the intricately balanced consensus of the system and its mechanism for the distribution of power, making all the more difficult for the centralized political authority to carry on its tasks of nation-building. The wakened giant now wields a powerful weapon to chastize those who ignore his preferences and reward those who pamper his vanities.

The power to chastize as well as to reward is, of course, a reflection of the majesty of popular sovereignty. However, the giant of the sovereign mass is like a broken mirror reflecting multitudinous images, divergent perspectives, differential articulation of orientations and interests, and uneven capabilities. To expect a consistent and well-integrated formulation of policies and programmes to be undertaken and implemented by the centralized political authority is, therefore, unrealistic. And yet the mass of voters does in a very significant way affect the course of political development in the developing countries. Whatever impact popular elections may have on what the government does or does not do, the one crucial consequence emanating from periodical elections is what Robert A. Dahl calls the transition from "cumulative inequality" to "dispersal of inequality."[4] The convergence of traditional privileges and acquisition of political power in the modern era slowly gives way to a disjunction between privileges and power.

It is through this transformation of structural shift in the distribution of power that political processes and governmental efficacy are shaped, modified and structured. That such a transformation has serious consequences for the political system can be appreciated from the changes it brings about in the party system. Like many developing countries, India too started its post-independence political career under the beneficial canopy of dominant one-party system where other parties did exist but were unable to effectively challenge the monopoly of power enjoyed by the Indian National Congress. While in the initial period, Congress was able to contain the prevailing socio-economic divisions in the country, articulate and define political consensus, and provide stable government for implementing systemic goals,

---

4. See Robert A. Dahl, *Who Governs* (New Haven : Yale University Press 1961).

it was increasingly beset with the problem of maintaining internal harmony and preserving electoral strength from getting depleted in each subsequent election.[5] While the growing heterogeneity in its ranks is a prime cause of its inability to protect its monopoly of power, it is by no means the only cause.

"Party systems originate in the patterns of cleavage and alignment among social forces. Different relationships among social forces and different sequences in the development of cleavages among them give rise to different types of party systems."[6] Given this intimate linkage between the nature of social cleavages and the type of party system, it is but natural that the transformation of latent socio-economic cleavages into manifest political conflicts should profoundly influence the development of the party system in India. Committed to the task of nation-building through social, economic and political reconstruction, the Congress party had to mobilize popular support for realizing systemic goals, on the one hand, and to consolidate and extend its support base for stabilizing its hold on political power, on the other. This inevitably led, first, to growing heterogeneity in the Congress ranks and, second, to he reassertion of social diversity in the form of clashing socio-economic interests some of which were still struggling for recognition and rewards. For various reasons, the Congress Party found it increasingly difficult to weave such heterogeneity and clashing perspectives into a coherent whole and was therefore exposed to nibbling from both within and without. As a result, Congress increasingly lost its electoral strength and, in 1967, failed in several of the States to obtain the requisite majority to be able to form a government.

A sharp decline in the Congress dominance is one of the consequences of the electoral process in India. It is true that

---

5. For a characterisation of the system of one-party dominance and the changes that have come over it, see the two publications of the Centre for the Study of Developing Societies, *Party System and Election Studies* (New Delhi : Allied Publishers, 1967) and *Context of Electoral Change in India* (New Delhi : Academic Books, 1969).
6. Samuel P. Huntington, "Social and Institutional Dynamics of One-party Systems" in Samuel P. Huntington and Clement H. Moore, eds., *Authoritarian Politics in Modern Society : The Dynamics of Established One-Party Systems* (New York : Basic Books, Inc., 1970), pp. 9-10.

this has brought in its wake political instability as reflected in a quick turn-over in coalition ministries caused by ideological and programmatic differences, clash of personalities, and a large incidence of shifts in party affiliation on the part of elected legislators. However, it is only a belated manifestation at the political level of the process of socio-economic plurality, producing the tendency towards a dispersal of political power beyond the confines of the dominant party. And yet this cumulative outcome of the electoral process threatens to endanger the carrying out of developmental programmes so essential for modernizing the society. If stability of the political regime is an essential ingredient of nation-building, the functioning of the electoral system has decidedly given rise to a multi-party system incapable of providing a stable government in several Indian states. And it is also doubtful now whether such political instability in the states will for long allow a stable government at the centre. Already the ruling party at the centre and several states has, after the split in the Congress party in August 1969, been reduced to a minority government forced to depend on its survival on the support of diverse parties. If the next election to Parliament scheduled to be held in March 1971 reinforces the present situation or brings about further deterioration, the one strong basis of stability would be removed.

The crucial role of elections in determining a structural shift in the distribution of power with all its implications for the functioning of the political system brings into sharp focus the question of the viability of democratic institutions as an instrument of facilitating the task of nation-building. If the continued instability of a political regime is likely to wreck development efforts, the consequent frustration of popular aspirations for a better life may produce a widespread feeling of disaffection, apathy and alienation striking at the roots of the legitimacy of the political regime. This is, in turn, likely to incline popular sentiments in favour of some kind of auhoritarian regime. In view of this, it is essential to explore in depth the factors that impinge on the functioning of the political system in India.

It should at the very outset be pointed out that democratic institutions in India have enjoyed only a short existence and it cannot legitimately be expected that support for them in the public mind is widespread and deep-rooted. As empirical studies of democracy indicate, the robustness of democratic institutions depends on three interrelated phenomena. First, there must exist a cadre of political activists who are committed to democratic principles and compete among themselves for capturing political power *within the confines of* democratic rules of the game. Second, there must be available an institutional structure that facilitates articulation of divergent public policies and promotes smooth transformation of inputs into appropriate systemic outputs. And, lastly, there must exist a generalized commitment to democratic values and norms on the part of the general public. This last condition is important inasmuch as, in the last analysis, it is the responsibility of the general public to exercise effective control over political activists in order to prevent them from straying too far from the path of democratic principles.

This study is concerned with exploring the extent to which people in India manifest in their attitudes and behaviour the internalization of democratic principles. In the remainder of this chapter we outline in operational terms our theoretical concerns as they grew out of the basic theme stated above. In the remaining chapters of this report we make use of data collected in four Indian states—Bihar, Punjab, Uttar Pradesh (U.P.) and West Bengal (W.B.)—through a sample survey immediately after the mid-term poll held in 1969. Before proceeding to answer the issue raised here, it would be worthwhile to (a) discuss the theoretical framework that informs our inquiry; (b) specify the particular concerns that motivated this inquiry; and (c) state the methods used to operationalize and investigate these concerns.

Viewed from the perspective of political development in India, our inquiry seeks to grapple with the relationship between the functioning of the electoral system, the developing patterns of the party system and the performance capability of the political system. This is neither accidental nor arbitrary. Despite the wide currency of the trend of partitioning social reality into convenient but often misleading analytical compartments, it must be asserted that social phenomena are interlinked and, through this interlinkage, are bound together in a chain of reciprocal influence structure. Take for example, the case of political parties or party system. It is universally recognized that political parties are the cornerstone of not only democratic political systems but also of authoritarian and autocratic political systems. However, the centrality of political parties for the successful functioning of a democratic regime cannot be exaggerated. It is through parties that the centre and the periphery are joined together in a meaningful relationship and politics receives some order and organization. This mediatory function of parties exposes them to two different kinds of influences to which they must respond. Yet a large part of literature on parties is devoted to examining the structure and functions of parties as if they are discrete and autonomous social groupings.[7]

It does not need any demonstration to assert that the performance capability of a political system is dependent not only on how parties are organized and on how they function and interact among themselves. In an even more important sense, it is dependent on how parties themselves are shaped by the interaction between dynamic components of the society reflecting themselves in electoral competition. The elitist bias that the electorate passively responds to whatever stimulus political elites and activists choose to direct towards it must be dismissed as being too simplistic.[8] As Key argues,

> ....electoral victory cannot be regarded as necessarily a popular ratification of a candidate's outlook. The voice of the people is but an echo. The output of an echo chamber bears an inevitable and invariable relation to the input. As candidates and parties clamour for attention and vie for popular support, the people's verdict can be no more than a selective reflection from among the alternatives and outlooks presented to them.[9]

The conception of the electorate as an echo chamber, although

---

7. For such an approach to parties in India, see Myron Weiner, *Party Politics in India* (Princeton, New Jersey : Princeton University Press, 1957); *Party-Building in a New Nation* (Chicago : Chicago University Press, 1967). For a statement of the approach suggested here, see *Context of Electoral Change, op. cit.*
8. For a fuller discussion of this point in Indian context, see Ramashray Roy, "Elections, Electorate, and Democracy in India," *Perspectives*, a supplement to *Indian Journal of Public Administration*, XVII : 4 (Oct-Dec, 1971).
9. V. O. Key, Jr., *The Responsible Electorate* (Cambridge, Massachusetts : Harvard University Press, 1966), p. 2.

an improvement over the narrow and restrictive conception in the elitist theory of democracy of the electorate as passive, is deficient in that it still conceives of the electorate simply as musical cords producing tunes played by the political artist. It is true that "even the most discriminating popular judgment can reflect only ambiguity, uncertainty, or even foolishness if those are the qualities of the input into the echo chamber."[10] Yet the ambiguity of popular verdict cannot legitimately be attributed to the quality of the input. The ambiguity is much more the result of the individual voter's differing perspectives and motivations entering into the voting act. These motivations do not necessarily have to be political or concerned with burning topics of public issues. Once we recognize this, we have also to appreciate that the output of the echo chamber is related not only to the input that political elites channel into it but also to the structure of relevance rooted into the subjective reality of individual voters functioning as a basis for endowing certain meaning to objective reality.

This should make us aware of two important factors. First, considering the fact that voters are influenced in their voting act by what we refer to as their relevance structure, we have to take into account the context in which voting decision is made. Second, the voters' decision has to be included as a crucial variable which moulds and shapes the pattern of party competition and thereby the parties themselves. To take the second first, it is as a consequence of voters' decision in particular elections that change in the relative strength of different parties occurs. That reduction or increase in the strength of the ruling party is associated with the nature of evaluation which the voters make of its performance is understandable. What is not quite understandable is the fact that the relative power position of parties in opposition should also undergo changes. We are not concerned at this moment with why this should happen. What concerns us here is the fact that voters think it appropriate to transfer their allegiance from one party to another and, by doing so, bring about a change, sometimes very drastic, in the fortunes of different parties.

The occurrence of this phenomenon in, say the United States

---

10. Key, *loc. cit.*

of America was long noted by Key and well recorded by other scholars subsequently.[11] Key, for example, talks of "critical elections" when a large-scale defection of voters from one party to another takes place. Although most of the defectors, it is suggested, go back to the party of their first allegiance—an argument very difficult to prove conclusively—the fact remains that such a desertion takes place and affects the fortunes of different parties. This shift can be viewed from different perspectives.[12] First, although periodical shifts in voters' allegiance to the party of their preference is a continuous phenomenon there exists under the swift stream of restless voters the hard core of calm and serene voters with deeper loyalties. It is the voters falling in the latter category that, many argue, contribute to the stability of a political system. The argument is very attractive but at the same time dubious. Starting from a position of stability as the prime value, one can very well condemn the shifters as rocking the system and jeopardizing the realization of values that primarily only stability can assure. One must, however, be on one's guard lest the argument favouring stability should be utilized to bolster up the claim of a regime fast losing its legitimacy. As Wendell Phillips observes,

> Republics exist only on the tenure of being constantly agitated... Every government is always growing corrupt....A republic is nothing but a constant overflow of lava...The republic which sinks to sleep, trusting constitutions and machinery, to politicians and statesmen, for the safety of its liberties, never will have any.[13]

If republics keep on the right track because of the prospects of

---

11. V.O. Key, Jr., "A Theory of Critical Elections," *Journal of Politics*, XVII (1955), pp. 1-18, Duncan McRae Jr. and James A. Meldrum, "Factor Analysis of Aggregate Voting Analysis," in Mattei Dogan and Stein Rokkan, eds., *Quantitative Ecological Analysis in the Social Sciences* (Cambridge, Mass. : The M.I.T. Press, 1969), pp. 487-506; and Philip Converse, "Survey Research and the Decoding of Patterns in Ecological Data," in *ibid.*, pp. 459-485.
12. For a discussion of variation in party strength see, Maurice Duverger, *Political Parties,* trans. by Barbara and Robert North (London : Methuen & Co. Ltd., 1961), chap. 11.
13. Quoted in Richard Hofstadter, *The American Political Tradition* (New York : Vintage Books, 1959), pp. 138-139.

their being periodically shaken, shifters must, then, be given the credit of keeping the republic on the right track. The firm voters, i.e., voters that do not shift their allegiance, are after all partisans and cannot be expected to evaluate objectively and dispassionately the performance of the parties of their preference. As studies of American voting behaviour show, the stronger the allegiance of the voter to his party, there is little or no possibility of his transferring his allegiance to another party.[14] By the same token, the stronger the sense of identity, the smaller the likelihood of dispassionate consideration of public issues. If the firm voters lend stability, the shifters offer a check on the autocratic tendencies bred by the stability and long tenure of a slowly degenerating party in power.

Interesting in this regard is to note that the very domination enjoyed by a party bears within itself the seeds of its own destruction. Referring to Hatscheck's law[15], Duverger points out that:

...on the one hand, the exercise of power compels a party to attenuate its programme and not to fulfil completely the promises made to its elector; a certain proportion of them are therefore naturally disappointed and led to transfer their votes to the opposing party; on the other hand, the activity of government naturally gives rise to disagreements within the majority party;...Thus exercise of power involves a process of disintegration of the party, weakening it to the advantage of its rival.[16]

In view of this recurring process of disintegration, the espousal of the cause of stability is therefore a plea to keep a disintegrating party in power.

The variation in the electoral strength of political parties is therefore an index of the varying temperature characterizing the political atmosphere. Viewed from another perspective,

---

14. See, for example, Philip Converse, "Information Flow and the Stability of Partisan Attitudes," in Angus Campbell, et al, *Elections and the Political Order* (New York : John Wiley & Sons, Inc., 1967), pp. 136-157.
15. This law was advanced in *Englische Verfassungsgeschichte* (Berlin, 1913) and discussed in Duverger, *op. cit.*
16. Duverger, *op. cit.*, pp. 300-1. For a discussion on this point in Indian context, see Ramashray Roy, "Dynamics of One-party Dominance in an Indian State," *Asian Survey*, July 1967.

shifting party loyalty may be treated as necessary shocks that immunize the political system from the traumatic experience of violent change. As we indicated earlier, shifts in the electoral strength of different parties are like weathercocks strongly indicating the change in political climate. In a very significant way, these shifts reflect a divergence between the "factual order"[17] and the normative order. Since the continued legitimacy of the political regime depends on the degree to which its functioning is adjusted to the obtaining reality in the society, periodical electoral shifts are warnings sent out to political rulers to take note of the growing divergence between the factual and the normative. If these warnings transmitted through the electoral mechanism are ignored for long, and the gap between the factual and the normative remains unbridged, the accumulation of discontent, articulated and blown up into gigantic proportions by parties in opposition, may flare up into a revolutionary holocaust consuming in its rage the institutional fabric of society. The shifts in voting therefore constitute a necessary corrective mechanism for sloth, inefficiency, and unresponsiveness of the government induced by long tenure in power.

It can, however, be argued that in the developing countries where problems of nation-building have priority over others, shift in party allegiance may, by fragmenting the structure of party system, usher in a period of political instability and thereby jeopardize nation-building efforts. The weight of this argument must be accepted. In countries like England and the U.S.A. where a two-party system is a well-established political tendency, shifts in voters' party allegiance do not prove dysfunctional inasmuch as when one party is voted down another is put in power to carry on the business of government. In contradistinction to this, most of the developing countries have, under the influence of national movement for freedom, come to be governed by one dominant party. The post-freedom politics in these countries has, however, been characterized by a proliferation of parties springing from the multiplicity of primordial groupings and ideological orientations. A shift in voters' political

---

17. David Lockwood, "Some Remarks on 'the Social System'," in N.J. Demerath and Richard A. Peterson, eds., *System, Change and Conflict* (New York : The Free Press, 1967), p. 285.

preference means, in essence, a shift away from the dominant party without producing any viable alternative. As a result, one-party dominance is, in many of these countries, being gradually replaced by a multi-party system. What is even more important, stable majority is giving way to a make-shift, shifting casual majority which can be disrupted any moment by a coalition partner. The quick turn-over in government makes it difficult, if not quite impossible, to sustainedly carry on developmental activities. In consequence, nation-building activities suffer.

The validity of this argument is confirmed by the experience of many of the developing countries. One, however, wonders whether a multiplicity of political parties can really be treated as the cause of political instability and therefore of retardation of political development. We should consider in this regard the fact that in several of the developed countries (especially in continental Europe) a multi-party system exists and the business of government is carried on by a coalition government. And yet coalitions do remain stable and prove effective in discharging their responsibilities. This should make us alert to the pitfalls inherent in any simplistic correlation between the number of parties and the stability or instability of political regimes. We should in this regard take into account the West German tradition adopted by major coalition partners not to use power for annihilating their junior partners. A look at the recent Indian experience in coalition governments will immediately make it clear that no such tradition informs the working of coalitions in India.

This brings us to discuss the role of democratic traditions in the unfolding of political tendencies in a society. Theorists of political development take delight in pointing to the lack of democratic tradition as a crucial factor in what Eisenstadt calls the "breakdown of modernization" in the developing countries. To a very large extent this argument carries weight. It should not be forgotten that democratic institutions are adopted institutions in the developing countries and have to grow in an alien soil heavily inundated with what sociologists refer to as particularistic, ascriptive and functionally diffuse criteria of social organisation and distribution of power. The successful functioning of democratic institutions is, on the contrary, postulated upon the universalistic criterion of equality between citizens. As a matter of fact, the classical conception of democracy posits the idea of a body of citizens which is alert, informed, objective and actively participant.[18] According to this conception, the individual is analytically split up into two personalities. While one personality symbolizes the ordinary man of the world concerned more with the existential problems of his living, the other part, that of citizen, is much more exalted and represents a person who rises above the petty concerns of his living and participates in making decisions pertaining to public affairs in a dispassionate and disinterested manner.

It will, however, be unfair to characterize this splitting as simply analytical. Implicit in this distinction is the value premise that enjoins the citizens to behave in accordance with the assumptions informing the analytical framework. Trouble starts when certain behavioural norms appropriate for the role of a citizen are deduced from these value premises. When articulated at the behavioural level, the democratic imperatives mean that a citizen ought to be sufficiently informed, actively participant and dispassionately interested in public affairs. In other words, a democratic regime must be peopled with active *demos*. Viewed in this way, the analytical assumptions also become evaluative standards for judging the merits of democracy.

As empirical studies of democratic regimes show, the classical conception of democracy is based on an erroneous notion of the subject-cum-citizen role of the individual. Citizens have been found to be neither well-informed nor active nor objective. And yet, democracy implies that leaders must be responsible and responsive to the people and public opinion. The people are required to exercise a controlling function by selecting the rulers. It is also well recorded that while doing so they are not usually moved by the distinction between the subject and the citizen.[19] Analysts of democracy have, therefore, postulated three conditions referred to earlier for sustaining and preserving democracy.

All these three factors are, however, either lacking or too

---

18. For a sophisticated analysis of democratic theory see Giovanni Sartori, *Democratic Theory* (Calcutta : Oxford and IBH Publishing Co., 1965).
19. For a conceptualisation of this distinction see Gabriel Almond and Sidney Verba, *Civic Culture* (Princeton : Princeton University Press, 1963).

# INTRODUCTION

delicate to survive the intense interplay of clashing interests based on primordial loyalties in developing countries. Too many democratic regimes have succumbed to the corroding impact of unrestrained parochialism to throw in doubt the proposition that adopted democratic institutions would take firm roots without receiving any indigenous sustenance. But how is this sustenance derived? Here again we tread an unknown territory. The democratic principles can be likened to a position strongly suggested for fighting a virus but without any knowledge as to how to prepare it. Recently several scholars have, dulled by the bewitching but highly misleading potency of correlation coefficients, pointed out that if only we had a high rate of industrialization, urbanization and education and far-flung network of mass media, the fate of democracy could be saved.[20] We need not go here into the merit of this wisdom, except to point out that such a thought is hardly reassuring for those in the developing countries who are struggling to actualize these highly rated achievements through democratic processes without having any democratic tradition.

We should have thought that the ambitious study conducted by Almond and Verba[21] would help us here. However, relying solely on cross-sectional analysis based on survey research in five highly rated as well as not too highly rated democracies, the authors do not achieve anything beyond proposing certain taxonomic categories of citizens and typifying democracies on the basis of such a taxonomy—a fallacious and misleading reasoning by any means.[22] Moreover, culture is never static and its dimensions all fixed for ever. To study a society at one point in time and to make inferences about it as if these characteristics had been there and will continue to persist is quite naive. What assumes central importance in the context of developing countries is the question that directs our attention to the processes through which democratic institutions crystallize and become relevant structure for ordering political life.

---

20. See among others, S.M. Lipset, *The Political Man* (Garden City, N. Y. : Dubleday and Co., 1960), chap. 2; Daniel Lerner, *The Passing of the Traditional Society* (Glencoe : The Free Press, 1958).
21. *Op. cit.*
22. On this point see, Erwin K. Scheuch, "Social Context and Individual Behaviour," in Dogan and Rokkan, *op. cit.,* pp. 133-134.

Put this way, our interest must focus on the development of the sense of citizenship in the developing countries. As a minimal requirement, this means "some subordination of private to public interest and private to public decision."[23] To put it differently, becoming a citizen means transcending parochial ties and forging a link with the political community at large, on the one hand, and the recognition of the superior claim of this community over the different claims of individual in certain areas, on the other. It also means that in the areas where the claims of the community are recognized to be superior, the individual must submit to decisions made by competent authorities representing the community at large. This development of a civic sense is predicated upon a structural transformation overarching several facets of this process. In the first place, the diverse people must first be bound together in a political community by a sense of belongingness. Now, this involves identifications at two levels. At one level, the individuals placed in different life situations, ethnic and economic groups, cultural traditions and geographical units must transcend the innumerable dividing lines that separate them and forge an identity equivalent to a sense of common destiny although differentiated on the basis of separate destinations. This can be termed as horizontal identity transcending geographical boundaries and social divisions that weave a diverse people in a political community. This identity is often equated to national integration.[24] This identity is, as Weilenmann suggests, consequent upon the experiencing of a a particular segment of reality by several people (or groups) from the same vantage point.[25] However, this experience can

---

23. Reinhard Bendix, *Nation-Building and Citizenship* (New York : John Wiley & Sons, 1964), p. 19.
24. The vastly increasing literature on political development and comparative politics points to the centrality of national integration for political development. For a critique and an alternative formulation see, Jyotirindra Das Gupta, "Language Diversity and National Development", in J.A. Fishman, et al, *Language Problems of Developing Nations* (New York : John Wiley & Sons, 1968) and Ramashray Roy, "Social Diversity, Economic Development and Political Integration," (Mimeo.)
25. Hermann Wilenmann, "The Interlocking of Nation and Personality structure", in Karl W. Deutsch and W.J. Foltz, eds., *Nation-Building* (New York : Atherton Press, 1963), p. 39.

never encompass the totality of the human existence since it is differentiated on the basis of different factual ordering for different individuals. This means that the forging of identity does not eliminate conflict generated by diversity and that such an identity requires a focal point even if it is partial.

In the case of countries where social and cultural diversity is uninformed by the tradition of effective central political authority, the necessity of a focal point is all the more obvious. At another level, therefore, the development of vertical political ties is essential for providing the basis for identity. These ties must be woven around the existence of a central political authority which symbolizes the coming into being of a political community. The political authority represents the body politic and exercises on its behalf prerogatives that are associated with a political community. Since the exercise of such an authority is on behalf and for the preservation and benefit of the community, the individual members must submit to the decisions made by the central political authority. "Implicitly more than explicitly, the members of a political community consent to that subordination in an exchange for certain public rights."[26] Thus the relationship between the "rulers" and the "ruled" can, for the sake of convenience, be characterized as based on some kind of agreement that enjoins the latter to comply to the *dictate* of the former in exchange of certain benefits. This implicit agreement (or, understanding or goodwill) becomes the basis of vertical integration joining not only the "rulers" and the "ruled" but also the "ruled" *inter se*. The integration of the "ruled" is important for the growth of citizenship inasmuch as it is based on some kind of coalescence of interest and represents a combination that over-arches the various differences dividing the "ruled". In other words, it is such a coalescence of interests that submerges primordial divisiveness and brings into force secularizing tendencies.

In the second place, the implicit agreement regulating the relationship between the "rulers" and the "ruled" is not enough of a condition for the exercise of political authority. The rulers in their arrogance of power may flout the agreement; institutions may become fossilized so that they do not adequately reflect the changing reality; and political activists may get smug thinking

---

26. Bendix, *op. cit.*, p. 19.

the changing contours of political landscape to be temporary aberrations. As a result, norms of behaviour established long ago may not provide appropriate guidelines for action in the changed factual order and therefore the relationship between various groups in a political system may come to be characterized by tension and conflict. The appropriateness of institutional structure and political processes is dependent on the degree to which the political regime succeeds in transforming chaotic impulses for change into a new consensus. Neiburg's distinction between legality and legitimacy[27] becomes relevant in this regard. Legality means an attempt to resolve conflicts on the basis of existing consensus which is no longer in consonance with the demands of changed situation. Insistence on strict adherence to the rules of the game can, therefore, be nothing more than a facade to the privileged group's attempt to make its privileges secure and endow stability to norms that no longer reflect the real bargaining relations between groups. The adherence to legality, therefore, is likely to aggravate a conflict situation rather than solve it. In contradistinction to this, *legitimacy* symbolizes the bridging of the gap between the "normative" and the "factual" on the basis of accommodating conflicting interests and renewal of consensual basis of the regime. Legitimacy can be preserved only by "the success of the state institutions in cultivating and meeting expectations, in mediating interests and aiding the process by which the values of individuals and groups are allocated in the making, enforcement, adjudication, and general observance of law."[28] Legitimacy, therefore, insures establishment of order in the midst of change and change in the midst of rigid order. Legitimacy of the political regime is thus the corner-stone of a political community.

It should, however, be noted that legitimacy and its renewal characterize all politics. This defines the relationship between the "rulers" and the "ruled". In a democratic polity, however, an individual is more than what is connoted by the term "ruled";

---

27. H.L. Neiburg, "Violence, Law, and the Informal Polity." *The Journal of Conflict Resolution,* XIII : 2 (June 1969).
28. Neiburg, *op. cit.,* p. 197. For a discussion of this in the context of Indian experience, see Ramashray Roy, "Social Diversity, Economic Development and Political Integration." (Mimeo.)

he is, at the least, a citizen who participates in the selection of rulers, and possibly more. As we indicated earlier, at the level of the citizen at least a generalized understanding of and commitment to democratic principles is a *sine qua non* of a successful democracy. In view of this, a syndrome of the citizen's attributes, such as, the level of his political information, his involvement in public affairs, partisanship and sense of efficacy, identified in voting behaviour studies, merits our consideration. It does not, however, mean that each of the citizens in a democratic polity would conform to the classical model of the citizen. A differential configuration of these attributes characterizes the body of citizens. One important question, therefore, relates to why such a differential configuration takes place and what is its implication for the functioning of a democratic polity.

Social scientists working in the field of voting behaviour have generally confined themselves to explaining this differential configurations in terms of usual socio-economic and experiential variables, such as, sex, age, class, campaign experience, etc. This raises an important question. Can it be legitimately assumed that similarity on any of these attributes will have a homogeneous impact on voters' attitudes, orientations and dispositions? More serious in this regard is the tendency towards what Scheuch characterizes as a preference "to use data on individual behaviour (such as mobility aspirations) to account for higher-order phenomena (such as the rigidity of a social system)."[29] To put it differently, the extensive use of survey research, based on the delineation of certain properties of individuals in order to draw inferences about certain geographical units, such as, a country, or analytical categories, such as, a social order, raises the important question of whether this is a legitimate exercise. As Scheuch remarks, "...there appears to be a tendency among the newer behavioural political scientists to rely on individual measurement and in so doing to commit what we termed the individualistic fallacy."[30]

---

29. "Social Context and Individual Behaviour," *op. cit.*, p. 133.
30. Erwin K. Scheuch, "Cross-National Comparison Using Aggregate Data: Some Substantive and Methodological Problems," in Richard Merritt and Stein Rokkan, eds., *Comparing Nations* (New Haven : Yale University Press, 1966), p. 158.

Equally hazardous is to infer patterns of individual behaviour from the analysis of aggregate data relating to some geographical unit. The likelihood of what Robinson long ago characterized as "ecological fallacy"[31] is always present in such an exercise. Rechristening it as "group fallacy", Scheuch suggests that this fallacy "..results from the difference between units of observation and units of inference. The danger of committing this fallacy is always present when the unit to which the inference refers is smaller than the unit either of observation or counting.[32]

Apart from these methodological issues involved in the proper delineation of the unit of observation and the unit of inference, there is yet another problem that needs to be considered in respect of theory construction on the basis of sample surveys.

This is the problem of social context and its impact on individual motivation and behaviour. Without denying the usefulness of survey research as a tool for exploring the attitudinal determinants of behaviour, it can readily be admitted that it is poorly suited to explore the importance of context and process. As Marvick and Bays observe, "Political phenomena occur in 'domains'—that is, organized social entities. Survey methods lift a panel of respondents 'out of context' to form a representative 'sample' of some larger universe".[33] With its emphasis on representative samples from large and heterogeneous universes, survey research fails to account for the profound influence that immediate environment exerts on individual motivation and behaviour.

Also important in this connection is the fact that, in addition to ignoring the varying contexts of human behaviour, survey research is conducted on the erroneous assumption that everywhere individuals encounter the same set of stimuli that prompt them to respond. What Marvick and Bays have to say on this

---

31. W.S. Robinson, "Ecological Correlations and Behaviour of Individuals." *American Sociological Review*, 15 (1950), pp. 351-57; see also Austin Ranney, "The Utility and Limitations of Aggregate Data in the Study of Electoral Behaviour," in Austin Ranney, ed., *Essays on the Behavioural Study of Politics* (Urbana : University of Illinois Press, 1962), pp. 91-102.
32. Schevch, in Merritt and Rokkan, *op. cit.*, p. 164. (Italics omitted.)
33. Dwaine Marvick and Jane H. Bays, "Domains and Universe : Problems in Concerted Use of Multiple Data Files for Social Science Inquiries," in Dogan and Rokkan, *op. cit.*, p. 533.

# INTRODUCTION 21

point is well-worth quoting:

> ...people live in organized settings or "domains" within the larger universe sampled. In the individual's environment, interaction and sequence are often known to be coercive determinants of conduct. Yet these considerations are attenuated in survey research. Individuals are treated as the basic universe. In voting studies, those interviewed in a cross-section survey live in different communities and neighbourhoods. They are stimulated by dissimilar campaign developments, despite mass media communications. They face election day "choices" that are cast in particular terms by the conscious campaign efforts of local organized rival party groups—each trying to tailor the electioneering to the audience immediately at hand.[34]

The lifting up of the individual from "his habitat, both mundane, non-political rounds of activities and his occasional politicized moments," make for a great weakness in theories that claim to explain the motivating forces of human behaviour.

> ...National surveys, by drawing from a very dispersed sample of respondents..., have been unable to account systematically for the effects of social context in which a person finds himself, his immediate environment, on his political choices. The effects of local community structure or locally based formal organizations cannot be deduced from data that ignore these variables.[35]

The relevance of context for political choice cannot be doubted. However, to restrict the meaning of context to local community structure, as Segal and Meyer do, is to make the fallacious assumption that the local community is immune to influences impinging upon it from outside.[36] It is also tantamount to arguing that the objective conditions obtaining at the local level determine individual actions totally. It does not need to be demonstrated that quantum of knowledge of the individual

---

34. Marvick and Bays, *op. cit.*
35. David R. Segal and Marshall W. Meyer, "The Social Context of Political Partisanship," in Dogan and Rokkan, *op. cit.*, pp. 219-20.
36. On this point, see, Kevin R. Cox, "The Spatial Structuring of Information Flow and Partisan Attitudes," in Dogan and Rokkan, *op. cit.*, pp. 157-185.

determines the magnitude of his linkage with the outer world. It follows from this that the greater his access to the sources of knowledge, the greater will be his autonomy from the influences flowing from his immediate environment. To put it differently, it is true that the nature of objective reality is to a greater extent the determinant of subjective reality. However, it should also be emphasized that the individual has his own subjective image of manifest reality and it is this subjective reality that is the seed-bed of action.[37] It is, therefore, apparent that the analysis of voting behaviour even when placed in appropriate immediate contexts falls short of a desirable analytical model.

To sum up our discussion, we pointed out earlier that in the context of developing countries, the central theme for exploration in voting behaviour studies must be the growth of a sense of citizenship. It is through the flowering of the sense of citizenship that both horizontal and vertical integration can be expected to occur. It is also through this that the all-powerful pull of primordial loyalties is expected to be weakened. It does not, however, mean that primordial loyalties can ever be wiped out.[38] What is does mean is that the phenomenon of what Max Weber calls "coalescence of interests" acquires greater spread and relevance for political processes. The voter's norms, although derived to a great extent from his environment, acquire also secular moorings. However to really get at his intentions and actions, one must take into account all relevant forces that impinge on it. The context or the nature of manifest reality is one of them, and the structure of differential attributes, both social and attitudinal, is the other.

This study focusses on the mid-term elections held in February, 1969 in four of the Indian states and purports to explore the factors that impinge on the behaviour of voters in these

---

37. On this subject see, Gerald A. Gutenshwager, "Social Reality and Social Change," *Social Research*, XXXVII : 1 (Spring 1970), pp. 48-70; see also, Peter L. Berger and Thomas Luckmann, *The Social Construction of Reality* : *A Treatise in the Sociology of Knowledge* (Garden City : Doubleday & Co., Inc., 1966).

38. On this point see Edward Shils, "Primordial, Personal, Sacred and Civil Ties : Observations on the Relationship of Sociological Research and Theory," *The British Journal of Sociology*, VIII: 2 (1957), p. 130.

states.[39] As we will see later, these four states differ in the way in which political forces have come to be aligned. As such, the nature of contextual factors including political must be taken into account while discussing voters' attributes. For the purposes of this study, however, it is not possible for us to go into it in greater details; nor do we propose to organically link contextual factor with other dimensions of study.[40] We do, however, indicate in some details (Chapter Two) the differential characteristics of these four states. Against the back-drop of these characteristics, we explore other dimensions of this study using states as our controlling variable. We then go on to discuss the relationship of socio-economic variables with the vote (Chapter Three).

In regard to the growth of citizenship we identify several variables that are central to such a growth. The extent to which voters identify themselves with different political parties is an index both of stability and change, reflecting the ongoing process between the formal and informal politics. It is of interest then to identify the partisans, the shifters and the indifferent voters and ascertain their attributes (Chapter Four). The other characteristics relate to political profiles of the voters. This includes the extent to which voters are interested and engage in political activities (Chapters Five). In the next two chapters we discuss the legitimacy of democratic institutions as seen through the voter's eyes and their sense of efficacy. In the last chapter we round up our discussion by drawing implications for the political system in the four states.

The data for this study was collected through post-election sample survey carried on in the four states.[41] In all, 1309 voters were interviewed. The state break-down of our respondents is as follows; Bihar=340; Punjab=292; Uttar Pradesh=428; West Bengal=249.

---

39. The Centre for the Study of Developing Societies also carried out a sample survey of the 1967 general election. For an analysis of this study, see various articles in *Asian Survey*, X : 10 (October 1970).
40. A systematic exploration of the model discussed above is under hand and will be presented at some future date. For a preliminary report, see Ramashray Roy, "Patterns of Political Instability : A Study of the 1969 Mid-Term Elections," *Economic and Political Weekly*, VI: 3-5, (January) 1971, Annual Number, pp. 289-306.
41. For sample selection, see Appendix.

## CHAPTER TWO
# *Varying Contexts of Electoral Choice*

From West Bengal in the north-east to Punjab in the north-west stretches perhaps one of the most fertile land masses in the world. This plain, rich in fertility and endowed with minerals in the east, can be characterized not only as the granary but also as the industrial lifeline of India. It is thus a meeting ground of agricultural tradition and industrial innovation. Forming only about 21 per cent of the total land area of India—U.P., 113,654 sq.m., (9.2 per cent); Bihar, 67,196 sq.m. (6 per cent); West Bengal, 33,928 sq.m. (a little less than 3 per cent) and Punjab, 47,205 sq.m. (3.8 per cent)—the plain contains about 40.8 per cent of Indian population—U.P., 73,746,401 (16.8 per cent), Bihar 46,455,610 (12 per cent), West Bengal 34,967,634 (8 per cent), and Punjab 20,306,812 (4 per cent).[1]

The distribution of tradition and innovation is, however, uneven. If the two ends of the plain are fairly industrialized and therefore prosperous, the middle of the plain is predominantly agricultural with stagnant economy. This is reflected in the unequal rates of literacy and differential patterns of urban growth. West Bengal tops with 29.3 per cent of literacy followed by Punjab (24.2 per cent), Bihar (18.4 per cent) and U.P. (17.6 per cent). Similarly, in the case of urbanization, West Bengal records 24.45 per cent, Punjab 20.13 per cent, U.P. 12.85 per cent and Bihar only 8.43 per cent.

The differential pattern of growth in the four states is also reflected in their differential position on the composite index of development (Table 2:1). West Bengal again ranks highest on the index followed by Punjab, Uttar Pradesh and Bihar in that order. Given this, however, variations in the direction of development and the hierarchical patterns of economic activities from one state to another can be observed. Note, for instance, that in West Bengal the core of economic life consists of secondary, i.e., manufacturing activities. Given this core, the extent

---

1. Based on 1961 Census.

TABLE 2 : 1
**Indices of Level of Development in Four States**

| Index of Development | West Bengal | Punjab | Uttar Pradesh | Bihar |
|---|---|---|---|---|
| Agriculture | 1.1197 | 1.0979 | 1.0722 | 0.9930 |
| Secondary Activities | 1.4961 | 1.1160 | 0.9642 | 1.0517 |
| Tertiary Activities | 1.2984 | 1.1043 | 1.0149 | 0.9868 |
| Non-Agriculture | 1.4053 | 1.1424 | 1.0635 | 1.0366 |
| Urbanization | 1.4449 | 1.2022 | 1.2124 | 1.0758 |
| Composite | 1.5298 | 1.2227 | 1.0231 | 0.9148 |

*Source :* Paul and Subramanyan.

of urbanization in Bengal is the highest in India.[2] Associated with these twin phenomena is also the greater degree of tertiary activities. The growing pace of industrialization also acts as a greater catalyst for agricultural development since the creation of necessary inputs for such a development becomes possible. Punjab follows more or less the same pattern except for the fact that the index of urbanization is higher than other indices in the State.

In contrast, Uttar Pradesh and Bihar present altogether a different picture. In Uttar Pradesh, for example, the degree of urbanization outstrips development in other fields. Note particularly the fact that secondary economic activities are less developed in comparison to other areas. If industrialization has lagged behind, agricultural development is not also very high in Uttar Pradesh. In comparison, tertiary activities are quite extensive leading to the inference that urbanization in U.P. is mainly the function of expanding administrative machinery in addition to commercial activities. Almost the same pattern obtains in Bihar. There are, however, some notable variations. Firstly, the level of growth in the primary sector is higher in Uttar Pradesh than that in Bihar. Secondly, Bihar ranks higher than Uttar Pradesh in industrialization. Given this, however, Bihar lags behind Uttar Pradesh in overall development.

---

2. To be precise, Delhi records the highest degree of urbanization (2.2460); however, Delhi is a case by itself.

TABLE 2 : 2

Development Expenditure in Four States; 1968-69 (in Crores Rs.)

| Items | Bihar[1] 55.427 | | Punjab[2] 14.043 | | Uttar Pradesh 87.393 | | West Bengal 42.886 | |
|---|---|---|---|---|---|---|---|---|
| | Total | Per Capita[3] | Total | Per Capita | Total | Per Capita | Total | Per Capita |
| 1 | 2 | 3 | 4 | 5 | 6 | 7 | 8 | 9 |
| Education | 24.35 (29.4)[4] | 4.39 | 36.58 (38.1) | 26.05 | 58.44 (35.6) | 6.69 | 43.83 (36.6) | 10.22 |
| Medical & Public Health | 14.07 (17.1) | 2.54 | 12.31 (12.8) | 8.77 | 23.88 (14.8) | 2.73 | 21.40 (17.9) | 4.99 |
| Agriculture, Veterinary & Cooperation | 18.22 (22.1) | 3.29 | 14.28 (14.9) | 10.17 | 20.13 (12.2) | 2.30 | 19.11 (16.0) | 4.46 |
| Rural & Community Development | 8.32 (10.1) | 1.50 | 3.40 (3.5) | 2.42 | 8.58 (5.2) | 0.98 | 4.53 (3.8) | 1.06 |
| Irrigation | 1.09 (1.3) | 0.20 | 7.30 (7.6) | 5.20 | 8.24 (5.0) | 0.94 | 3.78 (3.2) | 0.88 |
| Civil Work | 3.93 (4.8) | 0.71 | 8.86 (9.2) | 6.31 | 15.05 (9.2) | 1.72 | 7.81 (6.5) | 1.82 |
| Industries & Supplies | 2.70 (2.5) | 0.37 | 3.20 (3.3) | 2.28 | 1.36 (0.8) | 0.16 | 5.10 (4.3) | 1.19 |

| 1 | 2 | 3 | 4 | 5 | 6 | 7 | 8 | 9 |
|---|---|---|---|---|---|---|---|---|
| Others | 10.30<br>(12.7) | 1.86 | 10.17<br>(10.6) | 7.24 | 28.69<br>(17.2) | 3.28 | 14.13<br>(11.7) | 3.39 |
| Total | 82.35<br>(100.0) | 14.86 | 96.10<br>(100.0) | 68.44 | 164.37<br>(100.0) | 18.80 | 119.69<br>(100.0) | 27.91 |

*Source :* Indian Oxygen Ltd. *India : A Statistical Outline* (3rd. ed.), p. 105.

[1]Figures immediately below each state represent 1968-69 estimated population (in millions).
[2]Undivided Punjab.
[3]Calculated on the basis of estimated population for the year 1968-69.
[4]Figures in parentheses indicate percentage to column totals.

The differential patterns of the structuring of economic activities and the direction of development are very well reflected in the distribution of per capita national income in these states. West Bengal (Rs. 464.62) and Punjab (Rs.451.31) enjoy much higher per capita income than Uttar Pradesh (Rs. 297.35) and Bihar (Rs. 220.69). This initial disparity has further consequences for economic growth in these states. Lacking the requisite wherewithals or, endowed with only a very meagre resource base, the underdeveloped states are handicapped in canalizing adequate input for obtaining a faster rate of economic growth. In the meantime, the increase in population and the rising expectations far outstrip whatever developmental benefits are created out of meagre resources. In contrast, the developed states, because of the economic advantage they enjoy, can very easily quicken the pace of economic development.

The differential patterns of development inputs are clearly reflected in Table 2:2 which presents information on developmental expenditures in the year 1968-69 in these states. If we take into account per capita expenditure on developmental activities, Punjab ranks the highest (68.44) followed by West Bengal (27.91), Uttar Pradesh (18.80) and, last, Bihar (a meagre 14.86). It is clear from this that even though West Bengal has the highest per capita income among the four states, it spends less than, say, Punjab. Given this difference, however, all the four states spend a large part of their developmental fund on education: Punjab 38.1 per cent; West Bengal 36.6 per cent; Uttar Pradesh 35.6 per cent; and Bihar 29.4 per cent. Translated in terms of per capita expenditure on education, Punjab retains its first position (26.05) followed by West Bengal (10.22). Uttar Pradesh (6.69) and Bihar (4.39) record very low per capita expenditure on education.

If we characterized expenditure on education and medical and public health as welfare expenditure, West Bengal with 54.5 per cent tops the list and Bihar again comes last with 46.5 per cent. Punjab and Uttar Pradesh spend almost the same proportion of their resources on welfare activities. It is interesting to note that, except Bihar, all the three states spend about half of their development resources on welfare activities. In per capita term, however, Bihar spends about Rs. 7, Uttar Pradesh Rs. 9, West Bengal about Rs. 15 and Punjab about Rs. 35.

When we come to what can strictly be termed as developmental expenditure, percentage-wise, Bihar seems to be spending most on development in agriculture and other allied fields followed by West Bengal, Punjab and U.P. in that order. If we take per capita expenditure as an index, the order is substantially reversed. Punjab with per capita expenditure of Rs. 10.17 comes first followed by West Bengal (Rs. 4.46), Bihar (Rs. 3.29), and U.P. (Rs. 2.30). In the industrial field, Punjab again spends the highest (Rs. 2.28) and U.P. the lowest (Rs. 0.16).

It should, however, be emphasized that per capita income distribution is a poor index of the standard of welfare of the people in general. Notwithstanding the fact that West Bengal enjoys the highest per capita income, its developmental expenditure is pretty low compared to, say, Punjab. One probable reason for this is that the non-traditional economy in West Bengal is heavily dominated by non-Bengalees. As a consequence, a large part of the earnings is exported. This is true to a large extent also of Bihar. However, except in Punjab, the proportion of expenditure on developmental activities is very low in West Bengal, Bihar and U.P. Since expectations have been rising faster than outputs, it is not unreasonable to suppose that the degree of relative deprivation experienced by the people living in these states must be quite high. If this is true, a higher magnitude of political unrest in these states can also be expected.

We can look at it from a different angle. One of the measures of economic distress is the degree of unemployment in these states. It is interesting to note that in West Bengal one out of 52, in Punjab one out of 264, in U.P. one out of 625 and in Bihar one out of 682 persons of working age is unemployed.[3] Consider also the fact that the magnitude of industrial disputes is highest in West Bengal (one out of 11 workers involved in industrial disputes in 1966) and lowest in Bihar (one out of 29). Punjab (one out of 10) and U.P. (one out of 13) are nearer both to West Bengal and the Indian average (one out of 12 for the year 1966).[4]

All this points to the association between insufficient level of development and widespread unrest. With growing economic

---

3. Based on the 1961 Indian census figures.
4. Based on IOL, *India : A Statistical Handbook, op. cit.,* Tables J-3 (p. 65) and K-1 (p. 69).

activities in the non-traditional sectors, people become mobile and exposed to influences and experiences that induce them to aspire for a better standard of living. Frustrated in their attempts to move up in the social hierarchy, most of them turn against the existing power structure and engage in the attempt to change it.[5] The discontent is bound to be reflected in political processes and must affect electoral choices as they are the most effective way of changing political rulers.

This is enough to show the differential patterns of economic situation in the four states. We now turn to delineating some of the political tendencies operating in these states. Since the 1967 general elections, politics in West Bengal, Bihar, Uttar Pradesh and Punjab have been characterised by the following features: a sharp decline in Congress dominance; an ensuing political instability as a result of quick turn-overs in coalition ministries caused by ideological and programmatic differences; a clash of personalities and an extensive change of party affiliation by legislators; and the imposition of President's rule.[6]

The expectation that the electorate, tired of political instability and uncertainties which hampered developmental activities in these states, would exercise the franchise in a way that would ensure stable government in these states was not fulfilled. Not only did Congress sustain further losses in all the states except Uttar Pradesh, no other single party succeeded in obtaining an absolute majority in any of the state legislatures. Ministries were formed in these states, to be sure. Their continued tenure is, however, doubtful.

It is of interest, therefore, to explore what the mid-term poll results portend in terms of (a) prospect of political stability in these states; and (b) the noticeable trends in the development of the party system. Since the mid-term polls symbolise the culmination of an unfolding political process, it is essential to review in brief the events that led to the mid-term polls in these states. We therefore present (1) a brief sketch of the pre-poll

---

5. For a detailed examination of this theme, see "Social Diversity, Economic Development and Political Integration," *op. cit.*
6. Haryana also manifested these characteristics, but discussion is confined here to the four states that went to the polls in February, 1969. Similarly, Nagaland and Pondicherry are beyond the scope of this study.

political situation in the four states; (2) an analysis of the mid-term elections results; and (3) a discussion of the implications of the results for political stability in these states and for the developing party system.

The Indian party system, described as a "dominant one-party" system, does not preclude competition, because minor national or regional parties constantly pose a threat to the dominant party; but it does make competition unequal. Being weak, the opposition parties do not provide an immediate alternative to the dominant party. Instead, it devolves on them "to constantly pressurize, criticise, censure and influence and, above all, exert a latent threat"[7] in order to keep the ruling party on the right track.

With oppostion parties performing the role of pressure groups, the interactions and interrelationship inside the dominant party assume a crucial importance. The heterogeneity of its support base promotes a multiplicity of factions which compete among themselves for the control of party organisation and, through it, endeavour to capture governmental power. Since alternation in the party system is absent, the continuance of the dominant party in power proves to be instrumental in holding the country together, providing viable government, legitimising democratic institutions and implementing developmental goals. There is, however, an ever-present possibility of disintegration of the dominant party before viable alternatives have firmly emerged to avoid the chances of political instability.

That this possibility is not unreal is indicated by the growing incoherence in Congress, manifested in subordination of party goals to personal and sectional goals, fractionalization of the party structure into factions, intense intra-party conflict marked by unrelenting postures, and "balkanisation" of power relations.[8] The growing incompatibilities in the party have led to depletion of the leadership ranks and a massive erosion of popular support, resulting in the decline of party dominance.

If the dominant party has registered a decline, opposition

---

7. R. Kothari, "The Congress 'System' in India", in *Party System and Election Studies,op. cit.*, p. 2.
8. The split in the Congress Party in August 1969 is a necessary result of their characteristics.

parties are still fragmented and localised. The sharpness of their ideological differences, tendency to maintain their separate identities and intra-party conflicts hamper the growth of vigorous and strong opposition parties. In fact most of the "national" opposition parties are only local or regional.[9] In addition to being confronted with the organisationally more resourceful and well-entrenched Congress Party, they have also to contend with local parties which claim voters' support on parochial and traditional considerations. Characterised by ideological chauvinism as well as heterogeneity, propelled by a sense of maintaining their separate identity, and mesmerised by the idea of enjoying unshared political power, opposition parties do not find it possible to pool their resources except on an *ad hoc* basis.

Even if coalitions are forged, they remain uneasy, marked by tensions. Opportunistic in nature, they disintegrate under the burden of internal incompatibilities. The recent events leading to the imposition of President's rule in all the four states illustrate this.

In 1967, when Congress failed to get an absolute majority in the four states,[10] coalition ministries were installed in three of them. The exception was U.P., where Congress, with the support of seventeen independent and four opposition legislators, formed the government to be replaced eighteen days later by a coalition government headed by Charan Singh, who left Congress along with his seventeen supporters. Thus, by April, 1967, each of the four states was governed by coalition governments composed of a multiplicity of opposition parties representing almost all shades of political ideology. In U.P. the coalition consisted of eight political parties, in Bihar of eleven, in Punjab of seven and in West Bengal of fourteen parties. It is to be noted that independent legislators were associated with coalition ministries in all the four states. The radical left,[11] such as the Communist Party

---

9. The Bharatiya Jana Sangh, for example, displays some strength only in U.P., Rajasthan, Madhya Pradesh and Bihar. The Swatantra Party, once a strong contender for power, has almost come to its demise.
10. In West Bengal, Congress secured 127 out of 280 seats, in Bihar 128 out of 318, in UP 199 out of 425, and in Punjab 47 out of 104.
11. In 1965, when the Communist Party of India split, the right-wing or pro-Moscow faction retained the name and the left-wing or pro-Peking faction became the Communist Party of India (Marxist).

of India (Marxist), the extreme right like the Swatantra Party, communal parties, such as the Akali Dal, and moderate parties of different nomenclatures—all found a place in the united fronts.

It is true that the united front in each state formulated a minimum programme to guide the working of the government; but sooner or later the coalition ministries were to fall a prey to a clash of interests among their various constituents and the ever-shifting loyalties of some of their key men as well as numerous legislators.[12]

In U.P. threats of resignation, matched in many cases by actual resignations, followed in quick succession, paralysing the functioning of the government. In disgust, the Chief Minister resigned on February 17, 1968. After efforts to elect a new leader had failed, President's rule was imposed on February 25, 1968.

In West Bengal, the United front suffered from grave internal dissensions due to industrial and agrarian disputes and a threat to law and order. A crisis in October, 1967, created by the Chief Minister's threat to resign, was patched up. However, one of the cabinet ministers along with seventeen other legislators defected from the United Front, reducing it to a minority. Confronted with the refusal of the ministry either to resign or to test its majority in the legislature at an early date, the Governor dismissed the ministry on November 21, 1967. The new ministry, headed by P.C. Ghosh, a defector, and supported by Congress was also confronted with defections on the issue of selection of Congressmen for ministerial posts and in protest against coterie rule in Congress. President's rule was imposed on February 20, 1968.

In Punjab, too, the United Front ministry, which continued till November, 1967, fell because of defections and a minority government with the support of Congress was installed. However, Congress was badly divided on the issue of support to the ministry. The ministry fell on August 21, 1968, when Congress withdrew its support and President's rule was imposed.

Bihar presented an extreme case, where defection and counter-defection affected the fate of three ministries between March

---

12. For a detailed treatment, see S.C. Kashyap, *The Politics of Defection : A Study of State Politics in India* (Delhi: National Publishing House, 1969).

1967, and June, 1968. As many as 82 legislators defected at least twice, some four times. The confusing political situation was finally brought to an end on June 29, 1968, when President's rule was imposed.

Their experience with united fronts made opposition parties wary of entering into alliances for the mid-term poll. It was only in West Bengal and Punjab that some kind of united front was brought into being. In West Bengal, twelve parties entered into an alliance and Akali Dal and Jana Sangh forged another alliance in Punjab, later joined by CPI (M). In Bihar, also, the half-hearted Lok Tantrik Dal - PSP - SSP alliance came into being; and the Bharatiya Kranti Dal and the Swatantra Party reached an understanding to minimise conflicts between them during the poll. Apart from the difficulty of forging alliances, parties contesting the poll proliferated. In Bihar 22 parties entered the election battles, in West Bengal 25, in U.P. 27 and in Punjab about a dozen parties. A similar trend is noticeable in the number of candidates.

Before examining the mid-term election results in detail, let us review some of the trends thrown up by previous elections. There is no doubt that Congress has registered a steady decline in the percentage of votes polled in the last four general elections. In West Bengal, Congress polled 38.42 per cent of the votes in 1952, recorded a rise in 1957, but since then a steady decline in its share of votes ensued. The same happened in Punjab. In Bihar and U.P. there is a steady decline in Congress votes without any relief. Another noticeable feature is the sharp decline in the Congress votes in the fourth general elections.

The steady decline in Congress votes over the years is paralleled by the continuing fragmentation of opposition parties. In none of the general elections in West Bengal did the six opposition national parties poll between themselves more votes than Congress. In Bihar and U.P., these parties taken together polled between 44 and 47 per cent of votes in 1962 and 1967. In Punjab they polled only a little more than 20 per cent in each of the last two general elections. In addition, the Swatantra Party seems to have declined to the verge of disappearance in all four states. In Punjab, the real challenge to Congress dominance has come from a communal and local party, Akali Dal, whereas in Bengal such a challenge is spearheaded by the CPI (M), which leads a united front of twelve parties representing small splinter groups composed of ideologically chauvinistic parties, Congress defectors and local and communal parties. If in West Bengal and Punjab opposition has crystallised to a great extent in single parties, it remains as fragmented and diffuse as ever in Bihar and U.P.

One clear indication of the trend towards polarisation or diffusion of opposition to Congress is the average number of candidates contesting in each constituency. As Table 2:3 indicates, in U.P., West Bengal and Punjab the average number of contestants has dropped since 1967, whereas it increased in Bihar. However, both in U.P. and Bihar the average number of contestants remains very high compared to West Bengal and Punjab.

TABLE 2:3

Average Number of Contestants in Four States : 1967-69

| Year | Uttar Pradesh | Bihar | West Bengal | Punjab |
|------|---------------|-------|-------------|--------|
| 1967 | 7.09 | 6.37 | 3.78 | 4.62 |
| 1969 | 6.80 | 6.79 | 3.67 | 4.44 |

Yet another index of polarisation or diffusion is to verify the number of contestants in each of the constituencies. Table 2:4 shows two distinct patterns : one in U.P. and Bihar, where multi-cornered contests greatly outnumber two-, three- and four-cornered contests; the other in West Bengal and Punjab, where a large number of contests fall within the range of two- to four-cornered contests.

In the case of West Bengal and Punjab, then, polarisation of political forces has taken place, whereas in the case of U.P. and Bihar, fragmentation of opposition parties continues to be a fact. This must be taken into account in predicting the future course of development in the party system in these two types of states.

Turning to the 1969 election results, one general feature that emerges relates to the decline in the number of seats won by

## TABLE 2 : 4

### Constituencies by Number of Candidates in Four States : 1967-69

| Number of Candidates | Uttar Pradesh | | Bihar | | West Bengal | | Punjab | |
|---|---|---|---|---|---|---|---|---|
| | 1967 | 1969 | 1967 | 1969 | 1967 | 1969 | 1967 | 1969 |
| 2 | 2 | 1 | 2 | 2 | 36 | 66 | 1 | 17 |
| 3 | 29 | 17 | 14 | 6 | 106 | 81 | 8 | 17 |
| 4 | 46 | 46 | 37 | 40 | 67 | 56 | 20 | 23 |
| 5 | 49 | 67 | 66 | 51 | 44 | 53 | 24 | 19 |
| 6 | 72 | 79 | 68 | 62 | 18 | 17 | 19 | 13 |
| 7 | 69 | 73 | 53 | 52 | 5 | 5 | 11 | 10 |
| 8 | 51 | 60 | 28 | 40 | — | 1 | 10 | 3 |
| 9 | 35 | 45 | 25 | 27 | 3 | — | 7 | 2 |
| 10 | 25 | 9 | 15 | 18 | 1 | — | 2 | — |
| 11 | 15 | 15 | 3 | 9 | — | — | 2 | — |
| 12 and more | 32 | 13 | 7 | 11 | — | — | — | — |
| Total | 425 | 425 | 318 | 318 | 280 | 279* | 104 | 104 |

*Details for one constituency not available.

Congress in all the four states except U.P. The Congress losses in West Bengal and Punjab have proved to be gains for CPI(M) and Akali Dal respectively. In U.P., Congress lost heavily to Bharatiya Kranti Dal, a party made up mostly of Congress defectors. In Bihar, no single party became the beneficiary of the Congress losses. Apart from this general trend, patterns of losses and gains of different parties differ from one state to another. We therefore turn to analysing state election results.

To take West Bengal first: it is evident from Table 2:5 that out of 127 seats that Congress won in 1967, it could retain only 30 seats. It lost 41 seats to CPI(M), gaining only five seats from it. Next to the CPI(M), CPI wrested thirteen seats from Congress and lost only one seat to it. In other words, parties representing leftist ideologies have been the principal beneficiaries of voters' dissatisfaction against Congress. No doubt other parties, such as the Bangla Congress, Forward Bloc, SSP and PSP, have also benefitted from Congress losses; but their gains in comparison to the Communist parties' are meagre. The two Communist parties account for 54 seats, the other four parties for only 25. The major gain (eleven seats) accruing to Congress is that from the Bangla Congress, indicating that about one-third of the Congressmen who left Congress on the eve of the 1967 general election were rejected by the voters.

Another interesting fact that emerges from the table concerns the degree to which different parties have been able to consolidate as well as extend their position in the state. That Congress has lost much of its ground in West Bengal is beyond doubt. It could retain only a little over 23 per cent of seats captured in the 1967 general election. A little more than 45 per cent of seats won by Congress in 1969 are new acquisitions. In contrast, the two Communist parties, CPI and CPI(M), seem not only to have consolidated their gains in 1967 but also to have extended their support base considerably. CPI(M) retained 37 out of 43 seats won in 1967 and captured 43 new seats. The CPI retained fifteen out of sixteen seats won in 1967 and captured fifteen new seats. The cases of Bangla Congress, the Forward Bloc and SSP are similar. While the Bangla Congress has remained static, the other left parties, the Forward Bloc and the SSP, gained further ground. All this shows that the major contest for power in West Bengal is between Congress and the Communist parties.

TABLE 2 : 5

Losses and Gains by Parties[1] in West Bengal : 1967-1969

| 1969 losses<br>1969 gains | Congress | CPI(M) | CPI | Bangla Congress | Forward Bloc | SSP | PSP | Independents | Total |
|---|---|---|---|---|---|---|---|---|---|
| Congress | 30 | 41 | 13 | 11 | 8 | 4 | 2 | 18 | 127 |
| CPI(M) | 5 | 37 | — | — | — | — | — | 1 | 43 |
| CPI | 1 | — | 15 | — | — | — | — | — | 16 |
| Bangla Congress | 11 | — | 1 | 22 | — | — | — | — | 34 |
| Forward Bloc | 2 | — | — | — | 11 | — | — | — | 13 |
| SSP | 2 | 1 | — | — | 1 | 5 | — | — | 7 |
| PSP | 1 | 2 | — | — | — | — | 3 | — | 7 |
| Others[2] | 1 | — | — | — | 1 | — | — | 1 | 2 |
| Independents | 2 | — | 1 | — | — | — | — | 27 | 31 |
| Total 1969 | 55 | 88 | 30 | 33 | 21 | 9 | 5 | 47[3] | 280 |

[1] In Tables 5, 6, 7 and 8 the following abbreviations are used : AKD—Akali Dal; BKD—Bharatiya Kranti Dal; CPI—Communist Party of India; CPI (M)—Communist Party of India (Marxist); PSP—Praja Socialist Party; RPI—Republican Party of India; SSP—Samyukta Socialist Party.
[2] Others—Jana Sangh and Swatantra.
[3] Includes Independents 11 and ten other parties 36.

TABLE 2 : 6

Losses and Gains by Parties in Bihar : 1967-1969

| 1969 gains \ 1969 losses | Congress | SSP | Jana Sangh | CPI & CPI(M) | PSP | Other parties and Independents | Total |
|---|---|---|---|---|---|---|---|
| Congress | — | 20 | 15 | 11 | 11 | 24 | 128 |
| SSP | 30 | 26 | 2 | 1 | 1 | 8 | 68 |
| Jana Sangh | 10 | 1 | 8 | 1 | — | 6 | 26 |
| CPI & CPI (M) | 9 | 2 | 4 | 11 | — | 1 | 28 |
| PSP | 8 | 1 | 1 | 1 | 6 | 1 | 18 |
| Other Parties[2] and Independents | 14 | 2 | 4 | 3 | — | 27 | 50 |
| Total 1969 | 118 | 52 | 34 | 28 | 18 | 68[1] | 318 |

1 Includes Janta Party 14, Forward Block 1, Bharatiya Kranti Dal 6 and Other Parties 25.
2 Includes Swatantra.

TABLE 2 : 7

Losses and Gains by Parties in Uttar Pradesh : 1967-1969

| 1969 losses / 1969 gains | Congress | Jana Sangh | SSP | PSP | Swatantra | CPI & CPI (M) | RPI | BKD | Independents | Total |
|---|---|---|---|---|---|---|---|---|---|---|
| Congress | 82 | 23 | 20 | 1 | 1 | 3 | — | 59 | 10 | 199 |
| Jana Sangh | 67 | 17 | 1 | — | 2 | 1 | — | 9 | 1 | 98 |
| SSP | 22 | 3 | 8 | — | — | — | — | 8 | 3 | 44 |
| PSP | 6 | 1 | 1 | — | — | — | — | 3 | — | 11 |
| Swatantra | 6 | 1 | — | 1 | 2 | — | — | 2 | — | 12 |
| CPI & CPI (M) | 9 | 1 | — | — | — | 1 | — | 3 | — | 14 |
| RPI | 3 | 1 | 1 | — | — | — | — | 5 | — | 10 |
| Independents | 16 | 2 | 2 | 1 | — | — | — | 10 | 6 | 37 |
| Total 1969 | 211 | 49 | 33 | 1 | — | — | — | 99 | 20 | 425 |

TABLE 2 : 8

Losses and Gains by Parties in Punjab : 1967-1969

| 1969 gains \ 1969 losses | Congress | AKD | Jana Sangh | CPI & CPI (M) | Others | Independents | Total |
|---|---|---|---|---|---|---|---|
| Congress | 12 | 24 | 5 | 3 | 1 | 2 | 47 |
| AKD | 11 | 14 | — | — | — | 1 | 26 |
| Jana Sangh | 5 | — | 3 | — | 1 | — | 9 |
| CPI & CPI (M) | 5 | 1 | — | 2 | — | — | 8 |
| Others[1] | 2 | 1 | — | — | 1 | — | 8 |
| Independents | 3 | 3 | — | 1 | 1 | 2 | 10 |
| Total 1969 | 38 | 43 | 8 | 6 | 4 | 5 | 104 |

[1] Others include RPI, SSP, PSP and Swatantra.

Bihar presents a slightly different picture. It is true that the Congress share of seats was reduced from 128 in 1967 to 118 in 1969, but this loss is not as heavy as in West Bengal, where it lost a total of 72 seats. Moreover, its loss has not meant a gain for a single party as is the case in West Bengal. As is evident from Table 2:6, if Congress lost 81 seats to different parties, it gained 71 seats from them. Congress was able to retain a little over 36 per cent of seats, that is 47 out of 128 seats won in 1967, a performance matched only by the SSP and surpassed only by the CPI (which retained about 40 per cent of seats won in 1967). The Jana Sangh and PSP, on the other hand, could retain only about a third of the seats won in 1967. Also, only the Jana Sangh performed better in 1969 than in 1967.

Congress has gained most from the SSP, capturing 30 seats and losing only 20 seats to it. In the case of the Jana Sangh, Congress wrested ten seats from it and lost fifteen seats to it. Considering that the Congress ranks were considerably depleted by two major defections, one before the 1967 general election and the other in March, 1968, when some key Congress leaders left the party, Congress performance in Bihar does not seem to be that disappointing. Moreover, as the table reveals, opposition to Congress is still fragmented. The decline in Congress dominance in Bihar has not benefitted any single party. Not only have the opposition parties to contend with the superior organisational strength of Congress; they have also to squander their strength by fighting among themselves. If we add to it the fact that they have a lower capacity for consolidating their gains, the frustration inherent in the situation becomes apparent.

In U.P., however, the situation of Congress is somewhat brighter. Considering that two major defections occurred in the span of two years, it is to the credit of Congress that it won twelve seats more in 1969 than it had in 1967. Moreover, it was able to wrest back a large number of seats lost to opposition parties in 1967. For example, it took 67 seats from the Jana Sangh, yielding only 23 seats to it. Likewise, Congress gained more from other parties than it lost to them (see Table 2:7). Gains apart, it is only in U.P. that Congress succeeded in retaining a little over 41 per cent of seats captured in 1967.

If Congress increased its strength, other parties suffered losses. For example, the Jana Sangh strength was reduced by half, the SSP lost eleven seats, the PSP eight seats, the Swatantra seven seats, the CPI eight seats, and the Republican Party of India was completely wiped out. In addition, the table reflects the minimal capacity of opposition parties to consolidate their gains. The relative weakness of the opposition parties is indicated by the fact that a fresh entrant into the electoral battle like the BKD secured more seats than the total number of seats secured by the six national opposition parties. It should also be pointed out that the BKD made major inroads into Congress territory and won 59 seats previously held by Congress. It seems that the opposition parties were sandwiched between two parties, Congress and BKD, with a broader base and wider mass appeal, and in consequence lost to them.

Punjab is another state where polarisation of political forces has gone farther ahead. About 78 per cent of the total number of seats was captured by only two parties—Congress and AKD. However, Congress' strength was reduced from 47 in 1967 to 38 in 1969, while that of the AKD increased from 26 in 1967 to 43 in 1969. Other opposition parties have either remained stationary or suffered loss of strength. The one beneficiary of the mid-term polls has been the AKD, which captured 43 seats, eight more than the Congress share and seventeen more than its own share in 1967. It retained fourteen seats out of the 26 won in 1967 and captured 24 seats previously held by Congress, yielding eleven seats to it.

The decline in Congress strength is obvious. Its share of 47 seats in 1967 came down to 38 in 1969. It should be pointed out, however, that in terms of the percentage of votes polled, Congress has a decided advantage over other parties. It polled 37.74 per cent of votes in 1967 and 39.28 per cent in 1969. The inverse relationship between votes polled and seats won, then, must be due to the reduction in the number of contestants and the communal appeal of the AKD.

We can now ask the question: what does all this signify in terms of the development of the party system in the states and its implications for the stability of the political regime in these states? In order to answer this question three factors must be taken into consideration: the number of contestants, vote differentials between major contestants, and the internal dynamics of parties or groups of parties.

As was indicated earlier, political parties have proliferated over the years in these states. Notwithstanding several exceptions, the proliferation of parties, a persistent trend all over India, tends to distribute votes among several contestants without concentrating real strength in one of the contestants. This tendency can be checked, however, if the contesting parties, either through merger or adjustment of seats, succeed in reducing the number of contestants. This was achieved only in West Bengal and Punjab. U.P. and Bihar present a different pattern. Not only has the proliferation of parties gone farther, there is also no indication that different opposition parties will find it easy to reduce the number of contestants.

In addition, the pattern of opposition to Congress differs from one state to another. In West Bengal, it is spearheaded by left parties, particularly the radical left, such as the CPI(M). In Bihar, it is mainly the socialist forces that offer some opposition to Congress. However, there is a parallel trend in the strengthening of rightist forces represented by the Jana Sangh. In U.P., opposition to Congress is divided between rightist forces represented by the Jana Sangh, and the BKD, a personality party with rightist orientations. In Punjab, it is a parochial party drawing its support mainly from one community that has challenged the dominance of Congress. One interesting fact is the localised nature of major opposition in each of the states. The AKD, for example, has little prospect of extending its support beyond its habitat.

One thing is clear. While in West Bengal and Punjab there is a tendency towards the possibility of alternation in the party system, this tendency is obstructed in U.P. and Bihar by the fragmentation of opposition parties. It is quite premature to assert either that alternation in the party system in West Bengal and Punjab is a firm tendency or that Congress has been permanently eclipsed. In these two states more than 70 per cent of constituencies can be characterised either as competitive two-party (50.7 per cent in West Bengal and 37.5 per cent in Punjab) or marginal two-party (26.1 per cent in West Bengal and 29.8 per cent in Punjab).[13] If this is indicative of the trend towards

---

13. For a definition of these terms, see Goyal, O.P., and Hahn, H., "The Nature of Party Competition in the Five Indian States," *Asian Survey*, VI : 10 (October 1966).

alternation, it also, by the same token, negates any prediction of the demise of Congress in these states.

The possibility of alternation is dependent upon the nature of intra-party and inter-party relationships. Congress has buckled increasingly under the pressure of its own internal contradictions. So long as opposition remains diffuse and divided, internal constraints do not affect, to any considerable degree, its prospect for victory in electoral battle. But the moment opposition parties forge a united front, its winning capability is reduced considerably.

It does not necessarily follow that opposition parties or any combination of them are free from internal contradiction. In the case of united fronts it has been amply demonstrated that such a unity is, at best, short-lived. The anti-Congress feelings become instrumental in forging a united front against Congress, but once the coalition comes into power, ideological and programmatic differences, rivalry for the first position and personal jealousies make it difficult for coalition partners to pull together.

Another fruitful way of looking at the likely developments in the party system in these states is to examine the degree to which each of the parties succeeds in retaining the allegiance of voters who have been habitually voting for it. As was argued earlier, the dynamics of electoral competition are a crucial factor in determining the shape of parties. For one thing, through the operation of the phenomenon of "partisan conversion", i.e., shift in the party preference of the voter, parties lose or gain strength. Particularly in an open polity relying on electoral mechanism for recruiting leaders, parties trying for political power must woo the voters and transform their allegiance into electoral victory. If no shift occurred, party structure would become very rigid; the party knocking at the gates of power would for ever be denied entry into the precincts of power. Given the centrality of partisan conversion to the functioning of democracy, the fact, however, remains that large-scale desertions occur only at critical points in time reducing drastically the strength of the major party. At other periods desertions do take place but at a slower pace and without unduly disturbing the balance of power. In the midst of this ongoing process of change, parties, however, retain a hard core of supporters. Without it, parties may find it difficult to survive against the corroding influence of electorates' antipathy. Even if they manage to survive, their influence on the course of political development will only be marginal.

In the second place, granting that the movement of voters from one party to another does take place, can it be assumed that this movement is haphazard? To put it differently, is it appropriate to believe that voters transfer their allegiance from one party to another without taking into account either their own predispositions and political preferences or the attributes of different parties contesting for their support? Common sense would suggest that some kind of selection must be operating at the voter level in terms of which party to prefer once the process of disillusionment with the party of allegiance reaches its apex. The anchoring of political preference in a particular election must be viewed in terms of voters' conception of the relative position of parties in party space. This conception of party space will usually vary from one voter to another because of the differences in life situations. In addition, the very definition of party space will usually conform to certain political orientations of the voters. It will be quite unusual for a voter, for example, to switch his allegiance from a rightist party to a leftist one but quite normal to move away from a centrist party to a party either on the left or on the right.

In other words, the switch in party allegiance will normally conform to the voters' perception of ideological distances between political parties as they relate to their own political perspective, their conception of the instrumental relevance of different parties and the pressure of political climate prevailing in their environment. This does not exhaust the range of factors that impinge upon voters' choice. Nor is it implied that these different factors are homogeneous in their influence. What is really emphasized is the fact that the voters' concept of party space is actually the range of possibilities which defines the probable paths of their movement in that space with the direction of such a movement being determined primarily by the degree of ideological articulation of the voters and certain other contextual factors. This movement is seldom erratic; certain patterns can be discerned which remain consistent.

Our concern then is two-fold. In the first place, we want to know the extent to which different parties succeed in retaining the allegiance of their supporters. To put it differently, we are interested in identifying, even though very crudely, the retention of support capability of different parties amidst the flux of shifting allegiances. In the second place, we are also interested in ascertaining the direction of shift in voters' allegiance. An exploration of these two factors will give us some idea not only of how deeply rooted parties are in different milieus but also of directions of change in their electoral fortunes. To explore these dimensions, we use a simple measure derived by cross-tabulating our respondents' choice of parties in 1967 and 1969 elections.[14]

In terms of retention capability, Congress seems to be well entrenched in Punjab inasmuch as 78.2 per cent of voters who voted for Congress in 1967 also voted for it in 1969. The second well-entrenched party in Punjab seems to be the Communist Party of India (CPI). Note, for example, that its retention capability comes to 72.5 per cent, i.e., second to Congress. The third in rank is the residual category, —"other parties and independents"—primarily the AKD, a communal party.[15] In other states, however, the retention capability of the Congress gradually declines till it reaches the low water mark of only 44.3 per cent in West Bengal. In the case of U.P. too—supposedly a Congress stronghold—Congress manifests only 53.8 per cent of retention capability. In contrast, other parties show a much better record. The rightist parties, primarily Jana Sangh in this instance, demonstrate more than 80 per cent of retention capability. Also,

---

14. It should be pointed out that the 1967 vote of our respondents is based on recall and, therefore, exposed to all the weaknesses that recall data are subject to. Although we have at our disposal recall voting data for previous elections, in view of the probability of a greater margin of error because of lengthening time span, we think it safer to restrict ourselves to just two elections.
15. We must, however, interpret these figures with caution. As the Appendix shows, both Congress and Communist voters are over-represented while those of Akali Dal are under-represented. Similarly in West Bengal, Congress voters are under-represented while SSP voters are over-represented. In U.P. it is the rightist voters that are over-represented. It should, however, be noted that this gives us a better rationale to observe the twin phenomena of partisanship strength and direction of shift since most of our respondents come from areas that can be safely characterized as party strongholds. It does, however, vitiate our inference about parties that are located in an alien environment.

the Socialist parties, mainly the SSP, manifest greater retention capability than Congress. In Bihar, among the rightist parties, mainly the Jana Sangh seems to be much more stable than any other party. However, because of the very small number of respondents falling in this category, the percentage may be a poor indicator of retention capability. The Socialist parties rank next with 60 per cent with Congress recording only 53.8 per cent of retention capability. It is in West Bengal that Congress seems to have lost much ground that was assiduously conquered by the Congress leaders—through bossism informed by corruption and chicanery. Note, for example, that as much as 56 per cent of Congress voters deserted it in 1969. The Socialist, mainly the SSP, seems to have a much stronger partisan base (91.7 per cent) than even the Communist parties, mainly the CPI (M) —(67.3 per cent). Also indicated is the fact that the purely local parties that mushroom the political scene in West Bengal are well-entrenched there since their retention capability is even greater than that of the Communist parties.

Given the varying patterns of retention capability of different parties in different states, the one fact that sharply emerges from these tables pertains to the central position of Congress in the party system in each of these states. That its support base is diffuse, cross-cutting all social divisions is quite clear. It is also clear that if it loses support to almost all parties, it also attracts voters from parties with different ideological colourations. In Punjab, for example, it lost 12 per cent of voters to the Communists but gained about 16 per cent from them (Fig. 1). Similarly, it lost 8.5 per cent to the Akali Dal and independent candidates but gained about 15 per cent from them. Likewise, the Akali Dal lost more both to Congress and Communists than it gained from them. It will be apparent from this, that voter's movement from one party to another does not exactly conform to ideological distances between the party. If it were not so, it will be very difficult to explain why supporters of an ideological party like the CPI shift their allegiance to a party which is exclusively a regional and communal party. The explanation lies in the fact that three parties project three different images and perspectives. If Congress projects an image of a party of consensus bringing about changes through accommodation and the widening of the circle of participation, the Communist

TABLE 2 : 9

Shift in Voters' Party Allegiance : Punjab

| 1967 \ 1969 | Congress | Communists | Others & Independents | Ref; DK; N.A. | Inap. | Total |
|---|---|---|---|---|---|---|
| Congress | 111 (78.2) | 17 (12.0) | 12 (8.5) | — | 2 (1.4) | 142 (48.6) |
| Communists | 11 (15.9) | 50 (72.5) | 7 (10.1) | — | 1 (1.4) | 69 (23.6) |
| Rightists | — | — | 3 (100.0) | — | — | 3 (1.0) |
| Others & Independents | 4 (14.8) | 7 (25.9) | 16 (59.3) | — | — | 27 (9.2) |
| Ref; DK; NA. | 3 | 2 | 2 | 2 | — | 9 (3.1) |
| Inap. | 18 (42.9) | 16 (38.1) | 5 (11.9) | — | 3 (7.1) | 42 (14.4) |
| Total | 147 (50.3) | 92 (31.5) | 45 (15.4) | 2 (0.7) | 6 (2.1) | 292 (100.0) |

TABLE 2 : 10

Shift in Voters' Party Allegiance : U.P.

| 1967 \ 1969 | Congress | Communists | Rightists | Socialists | Others & Independents | Ref; DK; N.A. | Inap. | Total |
|---|---|---|---|---|---|---|---|---|
| Congress | 105 (53.8) | — | 6 (3.1) | 10 (5.1) | 44 (22.6) | — | 30 (15.4) | 195 (45.6) |
| Communists | — | — | — | — | — | — | — | — |
| Rightists | 2 (7.1) | — | 23 (82.1) | 1 (3.6) | — | 1 (3.6) | 1 (3.6) | 28 (6.5) |
| Socialists | 3 (10.0) | — | — | 48 (60.0) | 5 (16.7) | — | 4 (13.3) | 30 (7.0) |
| Others & Independents | 6 (17.6) | — | — | — | 28 (82.4) | — | — | 34 (7.9) |
| Ref; D.K.; N.A. | 12 (32.4) | — | 1 (2.7) | 4 (10.8) | 10 (27.0) | 6 (16.2) | 4 (10.8) | 37 (8.6) |
| Inap. | 26 (25.0) | — | 8 (7.7) | 12 (11.5) | 20 (19.0) | 4 (3.8) | 34 (32.7) | 104 (24.3) |
| Total | 154 (36.0) | — | 38 (8.9) | 45 (10.5) | 107 (25.0) | 11 (2.6) | 73 (17.1) | 428 (100.0) |

TABLE 2 : 11

Shift in Voters' Party Allegiance : Bihar

| 1967 \ 1969 | Congress | Communists | Rightists | Socialists | Other parties & Independents | Ref; DK; N.A. | Inap. | Total |
|---|---|---|---|---|---|---|---|---|
| Congress | 79 (50.3) | 12 (7.6) | 18 (11.5) | 23 (14.6) | 9 (5.7) | 1 (0.6) | 15 (9.6) | 157 (46.2) |
| Communists | 4 (11.1) | 24 (66.7) | — | — | 5 (13.9) | — | 3 (8.3) | 36 (10.6) |
| Rightists | — | — | 6 (85.7) | — | — | — | 1 (14.3) | 7 (2.1) |
| Socialists | 2 (3.8) | 7 (13.5) | 1 (1.9) | 38 (37.1) | 1 (1.9) | — | 3 (5.8) | 52 (15.3) |
| Other parties & Independents | — | — | — | — | 1 (100.0) | — | — | 1 (0.3) |
| Ref; DK; N.A. | 4 (13.3) | 8 (26.7) | 1 (3.3) | 7 (23.3) | 3 (10.0) | 3 (10.0) | 4 (13.3) | 30 (8.8) |
| Inap. | 16 (38.1) | 3 (5.3) | 2 (3.5) | 111 (3.5) | 8 (14.0) | 3 (5.3) | 14 (24.6) | 57 (16.4) |
| Total | 105 (30.9) | 54 (15.9) | 28 (8.2) | 79 (23.2) | 27 (7.9) | 7 (2.1) | 40 (11.8) | 340 (100.0) |

TABLE 2 : 12

Shift in Voters' Party Allegiance : West Bengal

| 1967 \ 1969 | Congress | Communists | Rightists | Socialists | Others & Independents | Ref; DK; N.A. | Inap. | Total |
|---|---|---|---|---|---|---|---|---|
| Congress | 39 (44.3) | 23 (26.1) | 1 (1.1) | 16 (18.2) | 6 (6.8) | — | — | 88 (35.3) |
| Communists | 10 (19.2) | 35 (67.3) | — | — | 3 (15.8) | — | 4 (7.7) | 52 (20.9) |
| Rightists | 1 (100.0) | — | — | — | — | — | — | 1 (0.4) |
| Socialists | 2 (50.6) | — | — | 33 (91.7) | 1 (2.8) | — | — | 36 (14.5) |
| Others & Independents | 4 (13.8) | 1 (3.4) | — | 2 (6.9) | 20 (69.0) | — | 2 (6.9) | 29 (11.6) |
| Ref; DK; N.A. | 2 (20.0) | 3 (30.0) | — | 1 (10.0) | 2 (20.0) | 2 (20.0) | — | 10 (4.0) |
| Inap. | 4 (12.1) | 9 (27.3) | — | 7 (21.2) | 10 (30.3) | — | 3 (9.1) | 33 (13.3) |
| Total | 62 (24.9) | 71 (28.5) | 1 (0.4) | 59 (23.7) | 42 (16.9) | 2 (0.8) | 12 (4.8) | 249 |

parties identify themselves with a radical transformation of the social order ensuring a better living standard for the poor and downtrodden. The Akali Dal, in contrast, claims to be the spokesman of the Sikh interest and espouses purely regional and parochial political orientations. If due to certain changes in the milieu there occurs any shift in the salience of these perspectives, one party gains at the expense of others.

In U.P., on the other hand, one obtains a different picture. The triangular contest in Punjab gives way to a quadrangular one in which the extreme left tendency has only a marginal role (both CPI and CPI (M) taken together polled a little over 3 per cent of popular votes in U.P. in 1969). The electoral contest takes place among a bifurcated centrist tendency represented by Congress and Bhartiya Kranti Dal (BKD), a moderate left of the centre tendency represented by the PSP and the SSP, and a rightist tendency in the form of Jana Sangh. One interesting point pertains to the fact that in 1969, Congress gained much more support from voters voting for other parties than it lost to others. This does not, however, hold true in the case of the relationship between Congress and other parties (mainly the BKD). As will be seen, BKD captured a larger territory from Congress than what it yielded to Congress. It is important in this regard to note than the BKD is a splinter party which broke away from Congress after the formation of the first Congress ministry in U.P. in 1967. As such, it offered a rallying point for disgruntled elements in the Congress. Second, the movement of voters from the right side of the party space to the left or *vice versa* is non-existent. And, lastly, the BKD has also made some dent in the support base of the socialist parties leading to the inference that it attracts disgruntled voters both from Congress and Socialist parties by injecting in U.P. politics an element of regional and parochial considerations.

In Bihar, the party space is cluttered by a proliferation of political parties forming a cluster of five distinct political tendencies. The largest incidence of partisanship conversion is noticeable in the case of Congress. Note, for example, that Congress has lost more votes to Socialist parties than what it got in exchange. Also it has lost much ground to the Jana Sangh and regional and local parties without getting anything in return. It is only in the case of the Communist parties that Congress has gained more than it has lost to them. Noticeable also is the fact that despite a complex cross-boundary movement of the voters, the salience of ideological distinctions for the voters' choice of the party is quite clear. The voters of right persuasion have not, it will be seen, crossed over to vote either for the Socialist or the Communist parties. The reverse is also true. Note also that there is discernible a movement of voters from Socialist parties to Communist parties, but the reverse movement does not take place.

West Bengal presents yet another pattern. The proliferation of political parties *sans* the rightist parties is a function mainly of ideological chauvinism and unrestrained pursuit of power by major left parties. The centrist tendency represented by Congress is being eroded on all sides. However, the phenomenon of partisanship conversion affects all parties. Only in the case of Socialist and Communist parties can it be seen that there occurs no movement of the voters from one to the other. This is interesting in view of the fact that due to the almost complete elimination of rightist political tendencies from West Bengal, Congress represents one extreme of ideological pole with Socialists falling in the middle of the continuum. Since its share of popular vote is small (a little over 3 per cent), the danger of its being wiped out by the ruthlessness and volatility of West Bengal politics reinforces partisanship.

Our survey, then, clearly indicates the differential configucation of political forces in different states, the varying degrees of retention capabilities manifested by different parties, and the variegated nature of party space in these states. We will round up our discussion by presenting one other interesting tendency that is associated with retention capability. It needs no demonstration to suggest that parties contesting for power not only have to consolidate their support structure but also to extend it over unconquered territories. In addition, they have to win over the up-coming generation of new voters in order to compensate for losses due to mortality and other causes. In other words, parties have to go on renewing in addition to consolidating their support base. Viewed from this perspective, one of the indicators of the robustness of a particular party can be the degree to which it attracts new voters.

It should at this point be indicated that several factors may

VARYING CONTEXTS OF ELECTORAL CHOICE    55

account for the party preference of new voters. First, it must depend on the political orientation of the new voters themselves. Their perception of different political inclinations and their

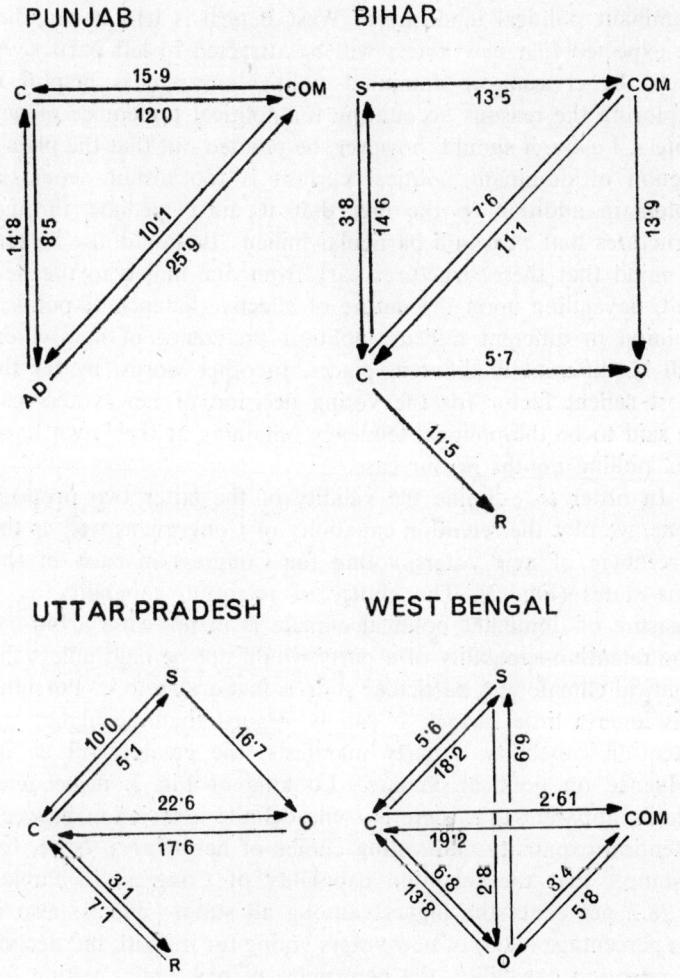

FIG. 2.1 **The nature of party competition and party space in the four states**
Abbreviations :   C—Congress;          S—Socialist parties;
                  Com—Communist parties;   AD—Akali Dal;
                  O—Other parties;     R—Rightist parties

interest in and involvement with political activities are some of the factors that decide the direction of their political preference. Second, given the subjective variations from one new voter to another, what is of importance for us is the kind of political climate that obtains in a particular state. If, for example, the dominant political tendency in West Bengal is left, it can then be expected that new voters will be attracted to left parties. As such the concept of dominant political current is helpful in exploring the reasons accounting for political preference of new voters. Lastly, it should, however, be pointed out that the phenomenon of dominant political current is too distant from the voters in addition to the fact that it must mediate through structures that exist in a particular milieu. It should also be kept in mind that these structures vary from one milieu to the next and, depending upon the nature of effective balance of political opinion in different milieus, political preference of new voters will be different in different places. In other words, by far the most salient factor for the voting decision of new voters can be said to be the political tendency obtaining at their own level, i.e., polling booths in our case.

In order to examine the validity of the latter two propositions, we plot the retention capability of Congress as well as the percentage of new voters voting for Congress in each of the four states (Fig. 2). The choice of retention capability as a measure of dominant political climate is in no sense arbitrary. The retention capability of a party would not be high unless the political climate in a particular state is favourable to it. Pursuing this logic a little further, it can be argued that the higher the retention capability a party manifests, the greater will be its influence on political climate. Looking at Fig. 2, it becomes readily apparent that there is some definite association between retention capability and voting choice of new voters. Note, for instance, that the retention capability of Congress in Punjab is 78.2 per cent—the highest among all states—and so also is the percentage (42.9) of new voters voting for it. With the decline in retention capability, the percentage of new voters voting for Congress also declines. To be specific, in U.P. retention capability comes down to 53.8 per cent and with it the percentage of new Congress voters also declines (25 per cent). In Bihar there is a slight upturn in the trend, but the general pattern continues

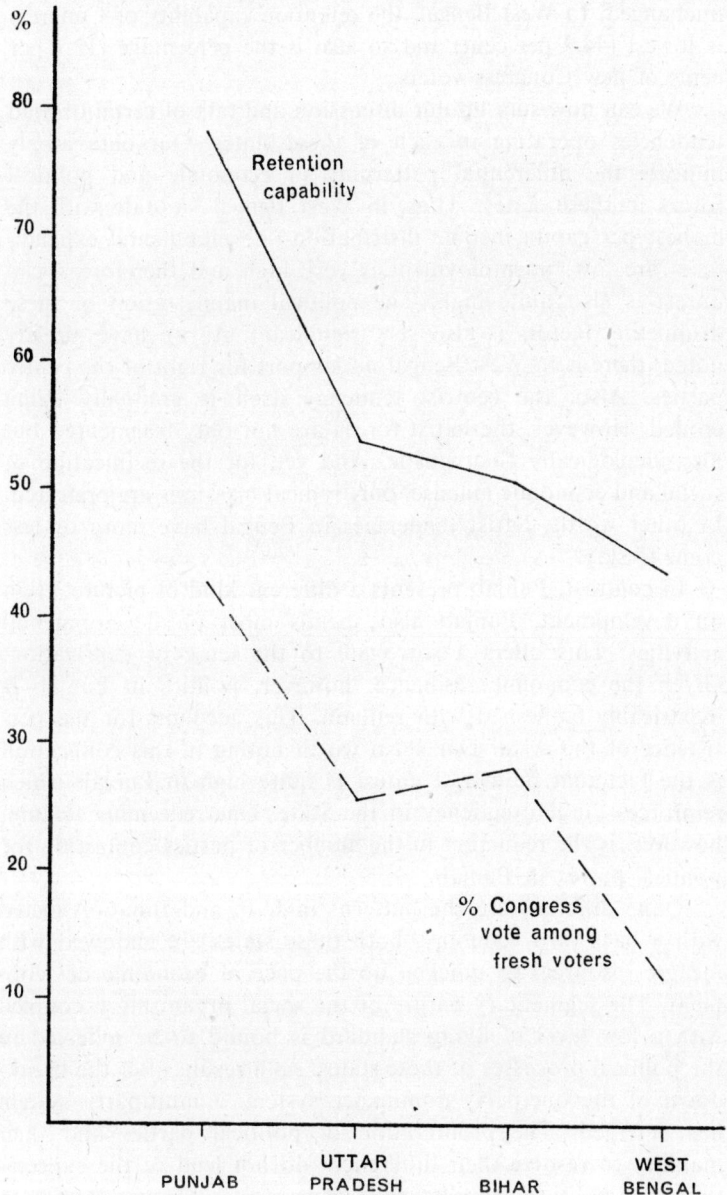

FIG. 2.2 Retention capability of Congress and its attractiveness for fresh voters

unchanged. In West Bengal, the retention capability of Congress is lowest (44.3 per cent) and so also is the percentage (12.1 per cent) of new Congress voters.

We can now sum up our discussion and talk of certain broad tendencies operating in each of these states. Our data amply indicate the differential patterning of economic and political forces in these states. Thus, in West Bengal—a state with the highest per capita income distribution—developmental expenditures are low, unemployment is very high and therefore social unrest is also quite high. The political manifestation of these disquieting factors is also very significant. As we have already noted, there is in West Bengal no support for right of the centre parties. Also, the centrist tendency itself is gradually being eroded. However, the leftist forces are not only fragmented but also ideologically chauvinistic. And yet, for the rectification of social and economic malaise, only radical measures are preferred. In other words, leftist tendencies in Bengal have more or less come to stay.

In contrast, Punjab presents a different kind of picture. High on development, Punjab also spends most on developmental activities. This offers a surrogate to the sense of deprivation. Given the economic resilience, however, politics in Punjab is inextricably enmeshed with religion. This accounts for the persistence of the Akali Dal. Also worth noting in this connection is the fact that industrial unrest is quite high in Punjab which reinforces the left tendency in the State. One redeeming feature, however, is the reduction in the number of parties contesting for political power in Punjab.

Quite different are the patterns in U.P. and Bihar. Afflicted with a backward economy, both these states are endowed with meagre resources to quicken up the pace of economic development. The segmentary nature of the social organization coupled with a low level of living standard is bound to be reflected in the political processes of these states. As a result, after the breakdown of the one-party dominance system, a multiparty system has emerged. The proliferation of political parties and their inability to resolve their differences do not lead to the expectation that political stability will ensue.

# CHAPTER THREE

# *Socio-Economic Background & Vote*

It is customary in voting studies to make an extensive use of socio-economic background variables, such as age, income, occupation, education, etc. for different purposes. At one level, these variables are used as background data in order to illustrate the social variation of voters located in different regions. At another level, they are treated as explanatory variables for explaining variations among voters on some chosen dimensions pertaining mainly to political attitudes and voting patterns. The assumption underlying such an approach is that similarity of life situation induces or promotes similar political orientations which, in turn, influence voting behaviour. Needless to say, this is tantamount to the Marxian argument that considers socio-economic structure as determining the superstructure of political orientations and institutions. We have already shown that such an assumption is fallacious and theoretically untenable. There is no reason to believe that similarity of life situation, especially when geographical and other barriers prevent communication among voters scattered in various regions, would invariably result in similar behaviour pattern.

Our own experience shows[1] that background variables are poor predictors of either political variables or voting behaviour. The predictive poverty of socio-economic variables becomes all the more apparent when these variables are taken singly and cross-tabulated with selected dependent variables. While we do not dispute the importance of background variables for the act of voting, the cross-tabulation of a singled-out background variable with any dependent variable is not likely to bear any significant fruit. The reason for this is very simple. The "umbrella" categories conceal within them quite a number of other cross-cutting identities pulling a voter in several directions.

---

1. Reference here is to various sample surveys conducted by the Centre for the Study of Developing Societies, Delhi. When analysed, they show poor relationship between background variables and political variables.

Whether or not the voter is in fact pulled in different directions is again a question not easy to answer. However, it can convincingly be argued, as Sarlvik does, that the conditioning factors (i.e., background variables) affect behaviour only through the mediation of other factors which are themselves causally related.[2]

In view of these considerations, it is theoretically proper to treat background variables as conditioning factors. To be more precise, they should be treated as causal agents not in themselves, but rather as convenient means of marking off how much of some more substantive process is in fact operating. That background variables taken singly are possibly the weakest predictors is beyond doubt. This does not, however, mean that as conditioning factors they are not relevant for explaining differential patterns of voting behaviour. When summated in a composite score or combined with other predictor variables, background information yields satisfying results.

In this chapter we utilize socio-economic and other experiential information on our respondents to illuminate the way voters located in different life situations cast their votes in different states. We begin, first, with a general discussion of the socio-economic profits of voters in each state. This is followed by a discussion of some of the antecedents that impinge on the act of voting. We are particularly interested in such factors as considerations that entered into the voting act, the nature of group pressure on voting decision, the timing of voting decision, etc. Lastly, we turn to discussing the pattern of voters' choice and their socio-economic antecedents. We will be more often using summated socio-economic status scores[3] to highlight the voting choice and other relevant variables. Wherever necessary and

---

2. See B.O. Sarlvik, "Socio-economic Determinants of Voting Behaviour in the Swedish Electorate," *Comparative Political Studies,* II : 1 (April 1969), p. 99.

3. Our SES index is derived from three socio-economic variables, viz., education, caste, and income in the case of city-and-town-dwellers and land ownership in the case of rural voters. It would have strengthened the index if occupations were included in it. Unfortunately, we do not have any reliable prestige scores of occupations such as that of NORC. However, it is our belief that the three factors included in the index amply compensate for this. We scored the three factors on an integer

theoretically interesting, tabulations of certain dependent variables against single socio-economic information are also presented.[4]

In table 3:1 are presented some socio-economic attributes of our respondents in four states. The table makes it quite clear that the profiles of voters differ in many crucial respects from one state to the next. In terms of rural-urban stratification of respondents, the largest number of urban voters (31.72 per cent) is from West Bengal which is quite in keeping with the high rate of urbanization there. It is, however, surprising that as much as 20.59 per cent of our respondents come from the urban areas of Bihar as compared to only 17.81 per cent in Punjab. As a matter of fact, the proportion of urban respondents from Punjab is slightly lower than that in U.P. also. In terms of age distribution, younger voters constitute the largest proportion in each state varying between about 45 per cent in U.P. and 54 per cent in Bihar. In contrast, the older generation voters constitute about one-fourth in Bihar and West Bengal while their proportion shoots up to one-third in Punjab and U.P. This has certain consequences for the functioning of the electoral system. As Converse argues:

> ...the partisan stability of voting behaviour tends to accumulate quite notably over the adult years of participation in the electoral process. It is little wonder that with monotonous regularity in country after country, major shifts in electoral outcomes are found to have arisen very disproportionately in the youngest cohorts of the electorate. New voters are flexible/unstable, and much more responsive to new events than are other voting cohorts.[5]

If the validity of this argument is accepted, it, then, logically follows that the larger the proportion of young voters, highly fluctuating will be the election outcome. This argument is

---

scale and divided total scores into high, medium and low after deciding upon the cut-off points on the basis of our judgement and marginal distributions.

4. It should be indicated at this point that we have at our disposal a large amount of processed data. However, lack of space does not permit us to discuss them all. We present in this study only those aspects of voting behaviour which are most salient.

5. Philip E. Converse, "Of Time and Partisan Stability", *Comparative Political Studies*, II : 2 (July 1969), p. 143.

## TABLE 3 : 1

### Socio-economic Profiles of Voters (in per cent)

| Attributes | Bihar (N=340) | Punjab (N=292) | U.P. (N=428) | W.B. (N=249) |
|---|---|---|---|---|
| Rural | 79.41% | 82.19% | 81.54% | 68.28% |
| Urban | 20.59 | 17.81 | 18.46 | 31.72 |
| Total | 100.00 | 100.00 | 100.00 | 100.00 |
| *Age (in years)* | | | | |
| Below 21 | 4.40 | 1.70 | 0.90 | — |
| 21-25 | 15.00 | 22.60 | 19.60 | 18.10 |
| 26-35 | 34.40 | 26.70 | 24.30 | 34.20 |
| 36-45 | 20.90 | 16.10 | 19.60 | 22.90 |
| 46-55 | 11.80 | 15.10 | 17.30 | 14.00 |
| 56— | 13.50 | 17.80 | 18.30 | 10.80 |
| Total | 100.00 | 100.00 | 100.00 | 100.00 |
| *Caste* | | | | |
| Upper | 29.40 | 10.30 | 18.50 | 26.50 |
| Middle | 35.60 | 55.40 | 45.00 | 35.80 |
| Low | 19.70 | 20.90 | 10.50 | 28.90 |
| Schedule Castes and Tribes | 15.00 | 13.40 | 25.50 | 8.80 |
| N.A. | 0.30 | — | 0.50 | — |
| Total | 100.00 | 100.00 | 100.00 | 100.00 |
| *Income (per month Rs.)* | | | | |
| Less-than 50 | 22.00 | 8.90 | 15.20 | 21.30 |
| 51-150 | 45.60 | 45.60 | 47.20 | 44.60 |
| 151-450 | 27.10 | 32.50 | 26.20 | 21.30 |
| 451 — | 3.20 | 7.20 | 5.80 | 8.00 |
| N.A., D.K. | 2.10 | 5.80 | 5.60 | 4.80 |
| Total | 100.00 | 100.00 | 100.00 | 100.00 |

| Attributes | Bihar (N=340) | Punjab (N=292) | U.P. (N=428) | W.B. (N=249) |
|---|---|---|---|---|
| *Land Owned* | | | | |
| Less than ½ acre | 39.50 | 39.80 | 33.20 | 48.20 |
| More than half but less than 5 acres | 38.50 | 23.60 | 41.60 | 42.20 |
| More than 5 acres but less than 10 acres | 12.90 | 12.30 | 13.30 | 6.80 |
| More than 10 acres | 8.50 | 24.30 | 11.20 | 2.40 |
| N.A. | 0.60 | — | 0.70 | 0.40 |
| Total | 100.00 | 100.00 | 100.00 | 100.00 |
| *Education* | | | | |
| None | 47.60 | 49.40 | 56.50 | 30.50 |
| Upto Primary | 29.10 | 29.10 | 25.20 | 22.90 |
| High School with some college but no degree | 20.60 | 20.50 | 16.40 | 38.20 |
| Degree and above | 2.40 | 1.00 | 1.40 | 7.60 |
| N.A. | 0.30 | — | 0.50 | 0.80 |
| Total | 100.00 | 100.00 | 100.00 | 100.00 |
| *Occupation* | | | | |
| Professions | 5.90 | 5.50 | 4.70 | 14.80 |
| Skilled-unskilled workers | 18.20 | 31.80 | 20.30 | 20.50 |
| Business | 3.80 | 5.50 | 6.50 | 4.00 |
| Cultivators | 50.90 | 43.80 | 52.80 | 38.20 |
| Agricultural labour | 17.10 | 11.30 | 13.60 | 15.70 |
| Unemployed D.K., N.A. | 4.10 | 2.10 | 2.10 | 6.80 |
| Total | 100.00 | 100.00 | 100.00 | 100.00 |

predicated upon the assumption that crystallization of partisanship is dependent mainly upon two factors. In the first place, young voters entering the electoral arena for the first time will not have developed any firm partisanship. Partisanship is an acquired trait and "significant increments of political learning are visible over almost the whole course of the adult participation in the electorate."[6] The more experience of electoral battles the young voter has, the more habituated he becomes to a competitive party system. Also, through experience and learning, he comes to be identified with one or the other of the competing political parties. However, as long as this habituation process remains incomplete and partisan loyalties do not become deep-rooted, electoral support will have numerous capricious overtones.

In the second place, the learning process is reinforced by the transmission of appropriate political orientations from the parents and other older family members to voters of the younger generation. This is, in essence, the process of political socialization. As a child learns socially relevant norms of behaviour in the family, so does he also learn regime relevant political norms there. Numerous studies of voting behaviour underscore the fact that people tend, to a large extent, to vote for the party supported by their parents in the preceding generation.

Looking back at the table, it is noticeable that all the four states in our sample are characterized by a quite significant degree of political instability brought about by capricious electoral outcomes. It may be that this instability bears some crucial relationship to the preponderance of young voters in these states Note, for example, that close to one-fifth of the total sample in each state has the experience of only one election (1969) and one-fourth to one-third of the sample in each state has voted in only two or three elections. It is, therefore, most likely that voters of the younger generation have yet to develop firm party loyalties.[7] It can be asked: Does not the transmission effect operate in the case of these states? Since the proportion of voters of the older generation ranges between one-fourth to one-third in these states, does not the young voter inherit political loyalties and orientations from the preceding generation? This question becomes all the more important in view of the fact that while most of the people of the older generation had participated in the struggle for freedom most other still carry the memories of those days when the Congress party occupied the central position in the political firmament.

---

6. *Ibid*, p. 142.
7. We return to this point in Chapter 4.

Three considerations lead us to conclude otherwise. In the first place, as I have reported elsewhere,[8] our analysis of the 1967 election study reveals that political discussion takes place in the family of only about 15 per cent of respondents. This means that quite a large proportion of Indian voters is socialized politically outside the family setting. That is to say, intergenerational transmission of political loyalties does not take place in the majority of the cases. In the second place, it should be remembered that with education taking great strides, the people of younger generation manifest a higher level of educational attainment than their parental generations. As such, the younger generation enjoys much more autonomy of decision than ever before. And, lastly, it may be true that most of the voters of the older generation may have very firm party loyalty leaning, particularly towards Congress. It is very difficult to transmit such loyalty to the younger generation since it has been increasingly exposed to incompetence and degeneration of the Congress party. As such, it is very difficult to bequeath Congress partisanship to the voters of the younger generation.

In terms of caste stratification, the dominance of upper castes in Bihar and West Bengal is apparent. Punjab and also U.P. to a large extent, manifest a somewhat symmetric distribution of caste groups. More important in this respect is the unbalanced income distribution not only among but also within states. Taking mean income as a measure of inequality between states, Punjab has the mean income of Rs. 195, West Bengal Rs. 185, U.P. Rs. 166.7 and Bihar Rs. 148.4. What is more important, in terms of within-state variation in income distribution, our sample reveals the highest incidence of income inequality in Bihar and West Bengal. In Bihar, for example, 67.6 per cent of our respondents have incomes below the mean, that is, below Rs. 148. In West Bengal, about 66 per cent of our respondents fall in the income category of Rs. 0-150. U.P. too does not show any the less inequality in income distribution inasmuch as in terms of overall pattern, it is closer to West Bengal than to Punjab which exhibits lesser inequality in income distribution—an inference reinforced by the fact that the largest proportion of respondents (32.50 per cent) fall in the income category

---

8. See my "Electorate, Elections, and Democracy in India," *op. cit.*

of Rs. 151-450. Given these variations, however, the fact remains that more than 50 per cent of our respondents in each state have meagre income.

Another way of looking at the inequality in the access to social resources particularly in the rural areas is to examine the distribution of land holdings. Due to certain historical factors,[9] higher social status has come to be associated with greater control over economic resources and, as a consequence, considerable political power. We shall presently discuss the differential configuration of these factors; for the moment our interest lies in examining the pattern of land distribution in each of the states. As can be seen from Table 3:1, the percentage of our respondents with less than half an acre of land is largest (48.20 per cent) in West Bengal and smallest (33.20 per cent) in U.P. In both Punjab and U.P. this proportion comes down to 39.80 and 33.20 per cent, respectively. If we add to it the category of those with more than half but less than five acres of land, the heaviest concentration of uneconomic holdings is in West Bengal (90.4 per cent), followed by Bihar (78 per cent), U.P. (74.8 per cent), and Punjab (63.4 per cent). Another interesting feature concerns the concentration of larger land holdings in each state. In Punjab, for example 36.6 per cent of our respondents possess more than five acres of land. The picture changes considerably in U.P. (24.5 per cent), Bihar (21 per cent) and West Bengal (9.2 per cent). This suggests the inference that while in West Bengal, Bihar and, to some extent, U.P., poverty as measured in terms of land distribution is general, in Punjab there is a large gap between affluent landed gentry and poor farmers.

The over-all impact of general and extensive poverty is reflected in educational attainments and occupational structure in each of these states. After all, to take advantage of modern education and thereby get access to non-traditional occupations, one needs to be financially well-off. Viewed from another perspective, modern education and non-traditional occupations are the prime agents of mobility in a static society. With increased

---

9. For detailed discussion of this aspect, see B.B. Mishra, *The Indian Middle Classes : Their Growth in Modern Times* (London : Oxford University Press, 1961).

mobility, exposure to the greatly variegated outer world brings into operation modernization tendencies and, consequently, change. An examination of these attributes of our voters would help us to determine the extent to which modern elements have penetrated their lives.

An examination of Table 3:1 indicates that the highest degree of illiteracy occurs in U.P. (56.50 per cent) followed by Punjab (49.4 per cent). That Bihar should exhibit a lesser degree of illiteracy (47.60 per cent) than Punjab is unexpected. What is, however not unexpected is the lower incidence of illiteracy in West Bengal (30.50 per cent). Along with this, West Bengal surpasses other states in the area of higher education. Note, for example, that the percentage of respondents with high school and some college education is largest (38.20 per cent) here as compared to other states—Bihar and Punjab 20.60 and 20.50 per cent, respectively, and U.P. 16.40 per cent. Similarly, West Bengal again has more degree holders, i.e., university educated persons, (7.60 per cent) than any other state.

The pattern of educational achievement is clearly reflected in the occupational structures of our respondents. Note, for example, that the percentage of professionals is highest in West Bengal (14.80 per cent) as compared to other states: Bihar (5.90 per cent), Punjab (5.50 per cent) and U.P. (4.70 per cent). In contrast to this, U.P. has the heaviest concentration of cultivators (52.80 per cent) followed by Bihar (50.90 per cent), Punjab (43.80 per cent) and West Bengal (38.20 per cent). This suggests that absentee landlordism may be quite widespread in West Bengal as compared to other states. It is also interesting to note that Punjab has the largest percentage of non-agricultural workers.

We have so far presented some information on the socio-economic background of our respondents in the four states. The variables are too numerous and their relative distribution too uneven from one state to the next to allow any illuminating over-view of the universe. As Blalock points out, "With so much information it would be exceedingly difficult for any but the most photographic mind to grasp intuitively what is in the data. The information must somehow or other be boiled down to a point at which the researcher can see what is in it; it must be summarized".[10] In what follows we present a summated index of socio-economic status and its distribution in each of the four states.

TABLE 3 : 2

Socio-Economic Status and Voters by States (in per cent)

| State<br>SES | Bihar<br>(N=340) | Punjab<br>(N=292) | U.P.<br>(N=428) | W.B.<br>(N=249) |
|---|---|---|---|---|
| High | 22.4 (76)* | 20.9 (61) | 17.8 (76) | 24.5 (61) |
| Medium | 41.8(142) | 50.7(148) | 44.2(189) | 50.2(125) |
| Low | 35.0(119) | 28.0 (82) | 36.7(157) | 24.5 (61) |
| NA | 0.8 (3) | 0.4 (1) | 1.3 (6) | 0.8 (2) |
| Total | 100.00 | 100.00 | 100.00 | 100.00 |

* Figures in parentheses indicate the total number of cases in a particular category. Since they remain unchanged, they are not given in other tables.

As is evident from Table 3:2, the heaviest concentration of respondents scoring high on the SES index is in West Bengal (24.5 per cent) followed by Bihar (22.4 per cent), Punjab (20.9 per cent) and U.P. (17.8 per cent). In contrast, the heaviest concentration of respondents with low status is in U.P. (36.7 per cent) and Bihar (35.0 per cent). Punjab and West Bengal have 28.0 and 34.5 per cent, respectively, of low statused respondents. As a corollary, the size of middle class is larger in Punjab (50.7 per cent) and West Bengal (50.2 per cent).

Before we take up the discussion of certain factors that impinge on voting decision, we would like to present some information on how the voters evaluate their past economic situation and with what kinds of hopes and fears they look at their future financial position. Underlying this is the assumption that one of the factors responsible for alienation from the political regime is rooted in the

---

10. Hurbert M. Blalock, Jr., *Social Statistics*, (New York : McGraw-Hill Book Co., Inc. 1960), p. 4.

level of relative deprivation that characterizes different people. As a matter of fact, the level of relative deprivation is supposed to be the prime cause of confict and violence.[11] By relative depriviation is meant the gap between the level of aspiration and that of capability of realizing aspiration. It should, however, be pointed out that a direct relationship between relative deprivation and conflict and violence cannot be presumed since a person placed in an anomalous situation can opt for any one of three available choices. He may either find a rational way out of the anomaly; or he may grow apathetic; or he may jump the boundary and be involved in conflict.[12] Which course the individual will eventually take depends upon his own personality structure as well as on the prevailing nature of societal norms and institutional arrangements.

This is not to detract from the importance of the concept of relative deprivation as a source of either alienation from the political regime or of opposition to it. Democratic theory posits that either of the eventualities—i.e., a large scale alienation or active opposition—is destabilizing. If extensive alienation encourages a rich crop of ideologies and political self-aggrandizers, active opposition eats away the vitals of a democratic system. It is, therefore, of importance to ascertain the degree to which voters in each of the four states take a dim view of their past and future. As a crude measure of deprivation, we present our respondents' own evaluation of how they have fared financially in the past and with what hopes and fears they look to the uncertain future. In Tables 3:3 and 3:4 we present information on these two counts.

As will be seen from Table 3:3, the heaviest concentration of those who think that their financial situation in the last few years has been getting worse is in Bihar. In West Bengal, the situation is not different from Bihar in any substantial sense inasmuch as 38.2 per cent of our respondents evaluate their past financial situation in a worse light. In contrast, the situation in Punjab and U.P. is quite similar. Note, for example, that

---

11. See, for example, Ted Gurr, *Why Men Rebel* (Princeton : Princeton University Press, 1970).
12. On this point see Kenneth Boulding, *Conflict and Defence : A General Theory* (Harper Torchbooks, 1963).

TABLE 3 : 3

SES and Satisfaction of Voters with Past Financial Condition by States (in per cent)

(Q: During the last few years has your financial situation been getting better, worse, or has it stayed the same ?)

| States | Bihar | | | | Punjab | | | | U.P. | | | | | W.B. | | | |
|---|---|---|---|---|---|---|---|---|---|---|---|---|---|---|---|---|---|
| Responses SES | Better | Same | Worse | Total | Better | Same | Worse | Total | Better | Same | Worse | NA | Total | Better | Same | Worse | Total |
| High | 19.7 | 36.8 | 43.5 | 76 100.0 | 70.4 | 23.0 | 6.6 | 61 100.0 | 46.1 | 28.9 | 23.7 | 1.3 | 76 100.0 | 32.8 | 31.1 | 36.1 | 76 100.0 |
| Medium | 24.6 | 34.5 | 40.9 | 142 100.0 | 36.5 | 43.9 | 19.6 | 148 100.0 | 39.9 | 35.6 | 22.9 | 1.6 | 188 100.0 | 15.2 | 45.6 | 39.2 | 125 100.0 |
| Low | 19.3 | 34.5 | 46.2 | 199 100.0 | 13.4 | 50.0 | 36.6 | 82 100.0 | 36.9 | 33.1 | 26.8 | 3.2 | 157 100.0 | 23.0 | 39.3 | 37.7 | 61 100.0 |
| N.A. | 33.3 | 33.3 | 33.3 | 3 100.0 | — | 100.0 | — | 1 100.0 | 14.3 | 28.6 | 57.7 | 2.1 | 7 100.0 | — | 50.0 | 50.0 | 2 100.0 |
| Total | 21.8 74 | 35.0 119 | 43.2 147 | 340 100.0 | 37.0 108 | 41.4 121 | 21.6 63 | 292 100.0 | 40.3 173 | 33.5 143 | 24.1 103 | 9 | 428 100.0 | 21.3 53 | 40.6 101 | 38.2 95 | 349 |

only 24.1 per cent and 21.6 per cent of respondents in U.P. and Punjab, respectively, admit that their past financial situation has been worse.

Leaving aside inter-state comparison, the state patterns are in themselves interesting. In Bihar, for example, only 21.8 per cent of our respondents admit that their financial position had been getting better in the past. We are not concerned with whether or not this is in fact true; what is of importance is the voters' subjective feelings about it. It is also interesting to note that the dissatisfaction with the past financial situation is quite widespread. The difference in socio-economic status does not make any difference in how our respondents in Bihar evaluate their past financial situation. Dissatisfaction with financial condition seems to be pervasive. One can, however, detect a slight variation: people of medium status seem to be much less unfavourably evaluating their past financial condition than either those with high status or those with low status.

West Bengal presents a similar situation to that of Bihar but with one crucial difference. If in Bihar it is medium statused people that seem to be more satisfied than high or low statused people, in West Bengal the reverse is true. It is mostly the people in the middle range of status hierarchy that are dissatisfied with their past financial situation. In Punjab and U.P., a different situation obtains. There seems to be a very close connection between the level of status one enjoys and his satisfaction with his financial condition. Note, for example, that both in Punjab and U.P., the percentage of those who claim that their financial condition has been getting better declines appreciably with each drop in the status hierarchy. This pattern is, however, much more consistent in Punjab than in U.P.

If a sizeable number of our respondents seem dissatisfied with their past financial situation, what about their future hopes? In many respects, the trends observed earlier are reversed. Note, for example, that only 22.1 per cent of respondents in Bihar, 18.5 per cent in Punjab, 14.1 per cent in West Bengal and 7.5 per cent in U.P. think that their financial condition will get worse in the next few years. Given this, however, the salience of status for optimistic orientation towards the future holds true in both Punjab and U.P. That is to say, the higher the status of an

TABLE 3 : 4

SES and Voters' Perception of Their Future Financial Condition by States (in per cent)

| States | Bihar | | | | | Punjab | | | | | U.P. | | | | | W.B. | | | | |
|---|---|---|---|---|---|---|---|---|---|---|---|---|---|---|---|---|---|---|---|---|
| Responses / SES | Better | Same | Worse | D.K & N.A. | Total | Better | Same | Worse | DK & NA | Total | Better | Same | Worse | DK & NA | Total | Better | Same | Worse | DK & NA | Total |
| High | 38.2 | 25.0 | 27.6 | 9.2 | 76 / 100.0 | 75.4 | 13.1 | 9.8 | 1.6 | 61 / 100.0 | 77.6 | 10.5 | 6.6 | 5.2 | 76 / 100.0 | 55.7 | 14.8 | 18.0 | 11.1 | 61 / 100.0 |
| Medium | 48.6 | 21.8 | 14.8 | 14.8 | 142 / 100.0 | 55.4 | 19.6 | 15.5 | 9.5 | 148 / 100.0 | 66.7 | 20.1 | 7.9 | 5.3 | 189 / 100.0 | 64.8 | 12.0 | 15.2 | 8.0 | 125 / 100.0 |
| Low | 31.1 | 34.5 | 26.9 | 7.6 | 119 / 100.0 | 37.8 | 26.8 | 29.3 | 6.1 | 82 / 100.0 | 59.2 | 26.8 | 7.6 | 6.4 | 157 / 100.0 | 47.5 | 26.2 | 6.6 | 19.7 | 61 / 100.0 |
| NA | 76.7 | — | 33.3 | — | 3 / 100.0 | — | — | 100.0 | — | 1 / 100.0 | 50.0 | 33.3 | — | 16.7 | 6 / 100.0 | 50.0 | — | 50.0 | — | 2 / 100.0 |
| Total | 137 / 43.3 | 91 / 26.8 | 75 / 22.1 | 37 / 10.9 | 340 / 100.0 | 159 / 54.5 | 59 / 20.2 | 54 / 18.5 | 20 / 6.8 | 292 / 100.0 | 281 / 65.7 | 90 / 21.0 | 32 / 7.5 | 25 / 5.8 | 428 / 100.0 | 145 / 58.2 | 40 / 16.1 | 35 / 14.1 | 29 / 11.6 | 249 / 100.0 |

individual, the more likely is he to be favourably oriented to the future.

Given the fact that a large number of respondents articulate their depressing past, what implication does their optimistic estimation of the future[13] have for the political system in general and the functioning of the electoral system in particular? It may mean that most respondents feel quite confident that they can really have control over their future in terms of bettering their financial condition. This, however, would not be true if objective conditions surrounding the individual are depressing and disorderly. Indirectly, then, the prevalence of optimism reflects both a self-confidence at the individual level and the individual's favourable perception of political regime as capable of maintaining propitious conditions for sustaining individual efforts towards making good. It should, however, be emphasized that, very broadly speaking, this is largely a phenomenon characterizing people located in high and medium status categories.[14]

In terms of the functioning of the electoral system, the import of our data may lie in the fact that since optimism signifies at least a minimal level of propensity to overcome environmental impediments in order to succeed in the efforts of making good, electoral choice may largely hinge upon the perception of immediate anomalies. Also, since a large contingent of young voters are present in the electorate and since their purtisanship level is very low, the admixture of these two elements is bound to lead to capricious electoral outcomes.

The electoral choice is, however, not solely dependent on the individual's age or his sense of optimism. Inspite of the claim frequently made that he is sovereign as far as electoral choices are concerned, his voting decision is influenced by several factors. Worth mentioning in this connection are factors, such as, the evaluation of the electoral system *per se,* his attachment

---

13. That this optimism is a recurrent factor in the Indian context can be ascertained from Roy, "Social Diversity, Economic Development, and Political Integration," *op. cit.,* pp. 82-3.
14. It may be argued that perhaps too much is read in it. Possibly so, but, as we shall see later, there exists quite a large degree of acceptance and legitimation of political institutions.

to parties and candidates, social pressures operating on the individual, etc. As Berelson suggests,

> For many voters political preferences may be considered analogous to cultural tastes.... Both have their origin in ethnic, sectional, class, and family traditions. Both exhibit stability and resistance to change for individuals, but flexibility and adjustment over generations for the society as a whole. Both seem to be matters of sentiment and disposition rather than 'reasoned preferences'. While both are responsive to changed conditions and unusual stimuli, they are relatively invulnerable to direct argumentation.... Both are characterized more by faith than by conviction and by wishful expectation rather than careful prediction of consequences.[15]

It does not, however, mean that elections are treated as rituals to be piously attended to every few years when elections are held. Elections are occasions when the electorate is aroused from its hibernation, so to say, and asked to give expression to its accumulated satisfaction or dissatisfaction with things in general and the political regime in particular. As Sartori rightly points out, "the average voter does not act, he reacts."[16] And through his reaction, he often demands a heavy toll of those who initiate and supervise the implementation of policies. However, in order to react, he must evince at least a generalized interest in and knowledge of things that affect his life. It is our contention that higher the social status of a voter, greater will be his stake in the functioning of the electoral system. To test it, we propose to operationalize the concept of stake in terms of (a) possession by the voter of information about the contestants and the winner in the election; (b) the salience of election for him; and (c) treating of casting of vote as a duty. So operationalized, it is necessary for us to show that in each of these cases a voter belonging to higher status group manifests these attributes more than the one who stands at a lower scale of status hierarchy.

In regard to the information that a voter possesses about contestants and the winner, it is quite apparent that an interested voter must know who are the contestants so that he may arrive

---

15. Quoted in Giovanni Sartori, *Democratic Theory* (Calcutta : Oxford and IBH Publishing Co., 1965), p. 77.
16. *Loc. cit.*

at his own preference. Surely, if a voter knows neither who these contestants are nor who won the election from his constituency, he must be taken as a person who treats his vote with indifference. His inability to remember the name of the winning candidate immediately after the election is, therefore, a reflection of his lack of interest in the electoral process. As will be seen from Table 3:5, in all the states, the percentage of our respondents responding correctly to the question, "Who was elected to the Assembly in this (1969) election from this constituency?" is quite high. However, in each of the states the percentage of the respondents giving correct answers slowly falls off if one goes down the status scale. Note, for example, that the differences in the proportion giving correct answer from the high-status group and the low-status group amounts to 17 per cent in Bihar, 28 per cent in U.P. and 27 per cent in West Bengal. It is only in Punjab that one finds almost an equal proportion of respondents in all status groups giving correct answer. Further, note also that the lower the status, greater becomes the magnitude of incorrect answers.

It can be argued that to remember the name of the winning candidate does not constitute a true measure of the feeling of stake or of interest in the electoral system since the names of the candidates have been in the air for quite sometime. There may be some point in this argument. But, then, how do we explain the fact that more than one-fifth of our respondents in all the states barring Punjab manage to forget the name of the winning candidate just after the curtain is finally dropped on the electoral drama? Also, how is it that the largest incidence of this forgetfulness occurs in the case of low-statused respondents? Leaving aside these questions, we offer additional evidence to show that the relationship between socio-economic status and stake in the electoral system is not a matter of chance; there is some (as yet statistically unmeasured) correlation between status and stake. One of the additional evidence pertains to whether or not the voters care much about who wins from their constituency. As will be seen from Table 3:6, when it comes really to feeling concerned about who turns out to be the winning candidate, the percentage of those who care quite a lot slumps down quite considerably. Note, for example, that only 26.4 per cent of respondents in U.P., 38.8 per cent in Bihar,

TABLE 3 : 5

SES and Information of Voters by States (in per cent)

(Q: Who was elected to the assembly in this election, 1969, from this constituency ?)

| States | Bihar | | | Punjab | | | U.P. | | | W.B. | | |
|---|---|---|---|---|---|---|---|---|---|---|---|---|
| Information<br>SES Level | Correct | In-correct | Total | Correct | In-correct | Total | Correct | In-correct | Total | Correct | In-correct | Total |
| High | 86.8 | 13.2 | 76<br>100.0 | 93.4 | 6.6 | 61<br>100.0 | 89.5 | 10.5 | 76<br>100.0 | 90.2 | 9.8 | 61<br>100.0 |
| Medium | 78.2 | 21.8 | 142<br>100.0 | 93.9 | 6.1 | 148<br>100.0 | 81.6 | 18.4 | 189<br>100.0 | 81.6 | 18.4 | 125<br>100.0 |
| Low | 69.7 | 30.3 | 119<br>100.0 | 91.5 | 8.5 | 82<br>100.0 | 61.1 | 38.9 | 157<br>100.0 | 63.9 | 36.0 | 61<br>100.0 |
| N.A. | 66.7 | 33.3 | 3<br>100.0 | 100.0 | — | 1<br>100.0 | 83.3 | 16.7 | 6<br>100.0 | 100.0 | — | 2<br>100.0 |
| Total | 262<br>77.1 | 78<br>22.9 | 340 | 272<br>93.2 | 20<br>6.8 | 292 | 323<br>75.5 | 105<br>24.3 | 428 | 198<br>79.5 | 51<br>20.1 | 249 |

42.2 per cent in West Bengal and 43.5 per cent in Punjab cared quite a lot about who won in the election. Given the low interest in the candidate elected to represent the interests of the constituency in the state legislature, the impact of socio-economic status on the amount of interest in the electoral outcome is quite visible. The phenomenon of highest status inducing higher interest in the electoral outcome recurs with remarkable consistency. In Bihar, for example, 30.3 per cent of respondents in the high status group as compared to 51.3 per cent of their counterparts in the low status group say that they personally did not care at all about who was elected from their constituency. The corresponding figures for Punjab, U.P. and West Bengal respectively are: 14.8 per cent as against 46.3 per cent, 17.1 per cent as against 51.1 per cent and 24.6 per cent as against 44.3 per cent. Conversely, as the total makes quite clear, the percentage of those who care quite a lot about the electoral outcome steadily increases in each of the states as one goes up on the status scale. It is thus quite apparent that status differentiation does have a differential impact on the amount of interest a voter has in the electoral outcome.

One final evidence and we will be through with this aspect of our discussion. One hears a lot of talk about how contesting candidates provide transportation facilities to seemingly apathetic voters who without such inducement would rather stay back than take the trouble of making a trek to the polling booth. Observers and analysts of electoral processes emphasize the festive nature of the occasion and imply that it is curiosity rather than a sustained interest in the electoral process that draws the voters to the polling booth. It may possibly be true. However, this argument does not take into account the fact that the frequent recurrence of a particular phenomenon robs it of its novelty and, with novelty wearing thin, the thing becomes a part of one's life. With increasing habituation and exposure to political forces, one does in fact develop an interest in the electoral process. The crucial role of elections in permitting the electorate to punish recalcitrant politicians is another factor that should warn us against any facile generalization that elections are merely festive occasions for the voters to have fun and merriment.

Our data strongly indicate that the voters are quite wide

TABLE 3 : 6

Voters' Personal Involvement in Election by States (in per cent)

(Q: Generally speaking, would you say that you personally cared quite a lot, somewhat, or not at all about who won in the constituency in the elections just held ?)

| States | Bihar | | | | Punjab | | | | U.P. | | | | W.B. | | | |
|---|---|---|---|---|---|---|---|---|---|---|---|---|---|---|---|---|
| SES \ Responses | Not at all | Somewhat | Quite a lot | Total | Not at all | Somewhat | Quite a lot | Total | Not at all | Somewhat | Quite a lot | Total | Not at all | Somewhat | Quite a lot | Total |
| High | 30.3 | 21.1 | 48.7 | 76 100.0 | 14.8 | 24.6 | 60.7 | 61 100.0 | 17.1 | 40.8 | 42.1 | 76 100.0 | 24.6 | 23.0 | 52.2 | 61 100.0 |
| Medium | 34.5 | 24.6 | 40.8 | 142 100.0 | 24.3 | 27.7 | 48.0 | 148 100.0 | 36.0 | 37.6 | 26.5 | 189 100.0 | 27.2 | 27.2 | 45.6 | 125 100.0 |
| Low | 51.3 | 18.5 | 30.3 | 119 100.0 | 46.3 | 30.5 | 23.2 | 82 100.0 | 51.6 | 29.3 | 19.1 | 157 100.0 | 44.3 | 31.1 | 24.6 | 61 100.0 |
| N.A. | 33.3 | 33.3 | 33.3 | 3 100.0 | — | 100.0 | — | 1 100.0 | 50.0 | 33.3 | 16.7 | 6 100.0 | — | 50.0 | 50.0 | 2 100.0 |
| Total | 134 39.4 | 74 21.8 | 132 38.8 | 340 | 83 28.4 | 82 28.1 | 127 43.5 | 292 | 165 38.6 | 150 35.0 | 113 26.4 | 428 | 76 30.5 | 68 27.3 | 105 42.2 | 249 |

awake in regard to the importance of elections. And, what is more important, most of them do not need any inducement to go to the polling booth for exercising their franchise. To ascertain this we asked our respondents: Would you have gone to cast your vote had nobody come to you to ask for your vote? The responses to this question are presented in Table 3:7. A quick glance at the table reveals that more than 75 per cent of voters in each state claim that they would have gone to cast

TABLE 3 : 7

Voters' and Electoral Interest by States (in per cent)

(Q: Would you have gone to cast your vote had nobody come to you ask for your vote ?)

| Responses | Bihar | Punjab | U.P. | W.B. | Total |
|---|---|---|---|---|---|
| Yes | 77.35 | 87.67 | 83.18 | 83.94 | 81.81 |
|  | (263) | (256) | (356) | (209) | (1,084) |
| No | 20.59 | 12.33 | 16.36 | 13.25 | 15.97 |
|  | (70) | (36) | (70) | (33) | (209) |
| DK, NA | 2.06 | — | 0.46 | 2.81 | 1.22 |
|  | (7) |  | (2) | (7) | (16) |
| Total | 340 | 292 | 428 | 249 | 1,309 |
|  | 100.00 | 100.00 | 100.00 | 100.00 | 100.00 |

their votes even if no one went to them to ask for their votes. It is clear, then, that only about 12 to 20 per cent of voters can, if at all, be termed apathetic and indifferent to electoral outcomes. It is also interesting to note that the largest concentration of indifferent voters is in Bihar and the smallest in Punjab.

To summarize our discussion up to this point, it is quite clear that a vast majority of our respondents are fully aware of their responsibility to exercise their franchise and participate in the process of the selection of rulers. That only a small proportion of voters need to be induced to discharge their responsibility is clearly reflected in our data. In a broad sense, then, there is, in general, the acceptability of the election as a necessary political instrument in which the voters should participate. Given the generalized prevalence of the sense of obligation to vote, however, there is great variation in the amount of interest in and concern with matters electoral from one voter to another. As we have already seen, the interest in the electoral outcome as measured by the voters' knowledge of the winning candidate comes sharply down as compared to the sense of obligation to vote. Against this background, it is not surprising that there should be less concern with who wins the election. After all, to be concerned with the victory of a particular candidate is the symptom of a high degree of partisanship—a phenomenon that is observed in India at only a low pitch. That only about 40 per cent of the voters are so concerned with the electoral outcome is not at all unexpected. Moreover, as we suggested earlier, greater interest in electoral processes is a function of higher socio-economic status of voters.

In addition to the interest a voter has in the electoral process, two other broadly defined categories of influences enter into voting decision. In the first place, to be interested in something means the presence of a focal point at which the interest must be concentrated. To say that every citizen is moved by the overpowering sense of obligation to exercise his franchise in the light of his own judgment is to impute too much political awareness and rationality to an ordinary voter who by virtue of his own immediate concern is unable to take sustained and objective interest in political matters. In a large number of cases, the sparse politicized moments of the voter are usually concretized in some object, such as, party or candidate. To put it differently, for the generalized and, in many cases ambiguous interest in politics to become salient for electoral choice, some reference point in the shape of attachment either to a party or a candidate or ideological stance, etc. is needed. The strength and the nature of the voters' identification with a party and/or candidate are, therefore, one of the factors that impinge on voting decision.

In the second place, the forging of identification with a cause or a party or a candidate is never an autonomous process. It is mediated through, among others, the contextual factors that impinge on the individual. In addition to the fact that some transmission of political orientation from the parental generation is operative, much of the common man's interest in politics is moulded and shaped by diverse forces operating around him. It is entirely a different matter that an individual has acquired strong political preferences and is capable of resisting diverse pressures acting upon him to make him conform to a particular group norm which, left to himself, he will reject. However, this attribute can be found in only a small minority of voters. Most of the voters lack firm political convictions and, as a consequence, their electoral choice is most likely to be determined by cross-pressures emanating from their immediate environment pulling them in different directions. The pressures might originate from their family, peer groups, and village notables; or, they may just be swept away by the sleek campaigning of a particular candidate. Or, being in a quandary as to who to vote for, they may decide to consult those in whose opinion they have some confidence. The environmental pressures, therefore, constitute another set of factors that enter into the voters' voting decision.

It is, therefore, necessary to examine the extent to which these factors impinge on our respondents and incline them in one direction or the other. To begin with, we present in the next three tables some information on the degree to which our respondents manifest firmness in their electoral choice. This we do with the help of three measures. First, we enquire whether or not our respondents made a decision and later altered it. Second, we ask whether or not the voters, after having cast their vote, have had second thoughts about their decision and come to the opinion that it was incorrect. And, finally, with the help of a hypothetical question, we want to know if they would stay with the party of their choice even if it put up a candidate not to their liking.

In Table 3:8 is presented information on the firmness, or lack of it, of our respondents' voting decision. Responding to the question: "Before you voted (for this candidate/party) in this election, did you at any time think of voting for some other party/candidate?" 79.41 per cent of respondents in Bihar, 89.38 per cent in Punjab, 70.79 per cent in U.P. and 79.98 per cent in West Bengal replied in the negative. In other words, only some 8 to 12 per cent of voters had to change their minds. This

## TABLE 3 : 8

### Partisanship and Voters by States (in per cent)

(Q: Before you voted for [this candidate or party] in this election, did you at any time think of voting for some other party or candidate?)

| Responses | Bihar | Punjab | U.P. | W.B. | Total |
|---|---|---|---|---|---|
| Yes | 8.24 | 7.88 | 11.45 | 8.84 | 9.32 |
| No | 79.41 | 89.38 | 70.79 | 85.54 | 79.98 |
| Did Not Vote | 11.76 | 2.05 | 17.06 | 4.82 | 10.01 |
| D.K.; N.A. | 0.59 | 0.69 | 0.70 | 0.80 | 0.69 |
| Total | 340 100.00 | 292 100.00 | 428 100.00 | 249 100.00 | 1,309 100.00 |

indicates that a vast majority of our respondents tenaciously stick to the choice they finally make. It does not, however, point to the fact that the ultimate choice may have left a trail of vacillation and ambivalence. Nor does it bring to light either the appropriateness of a particular voting decision or the comparative salience of a particular stimulus to voting decision. It is, therefore, necessary to examine these additional dimensions of the parameters of voting decision.

In Table 3:9 we present information on the extent to which our respondents are convinced of the appropriateness of their voting decision. It is our assumption that a true partisan voter would neither take long to decide about who he should vote for, nor is he likely to revise his opinion once he has exercised his franchise. In other words, his voting decision is pre-empted by the strength of his partisanship if he can resist cross-pressures that are directed at him to deflect him from his partisan course. To put it differently, the phenomenon of delayed decision and doubts about the appropriateness of such a decision is most likely to occur in the case of those who have either a very weak sense of partisanship or have no definite political preference.

TABLE 3 : 9

**SES and Voters' Partisanship by States (in per cent)**

(Q: If you could vote again, would you still vote for the same party/candidate ?)

| States | Bihar | | | | Punjab | | | | U.P. | | | | W.B. | | | |
|---|---|---|---|---|---|---|---|---|---|---|---|---|---|---|---|---|
| SES Level | Yes | No | Others[1] | Total | Yes | No | Others | Total | Yes | No | Others | Total | Yes | No | Others | Total |
| High | 65.8 | 6.6 | 27.6 | 76<br>100.0 | 63.9 | 1.6 | 34.4 | 61<br>100.0 | 65.8 | 3.9 | 30.3 | 76<br>100.0 | 57.4 | 3.3 | 39.3 | 61<br>100.0 |
| Medium | 57.0 | 0.7 | 42.3 | 142<br>100.0 | 69.6 | 2.7 | 27.7 | 148<br>100.0 | 52.9 | 5.3 | 41.8 | 189<br>100.0 | 59.2 | 6.4 | 34.4 | 125<br>100.0 |
| Low | 58.8 | 2.5 | 38.7 | 119<br>100.0 | 59.8 | 2.4 | 37.8 | 82<br>100.0 | 59.9 | 1.9 | 38.2 | 157<br>100.0 | 52.5 | 3.3 | 44.3 | 61<br>100.0 |
| N.A. | 33.3 | — | 66.7 | 3<br>100.0 | 100.0 | — | — | 1<br>100.0 | 50.0 | — | 50.0 | 6<br>100.0 | 50.0 | 50.0 | | 2<br>100.0 |
| Total | 202<br>59.4 | 9<br>2.6 | 192<br>37.9 | 340 | 192<br>65.8 | 7<br>2.4 | 93<br>31.8 | 292 | 247<br>57.7 | 16<br>3.7 | 168<br>38.6 | 428 | 142<br>57.0 | 12<br>4.8 | 95<br>38.2 | 249 |

1. Others include D.K. and undecided cases.

While deferring the discussion of the former for a later occasion, we present in Table 3:9 some information on the latter.

When asked, "Would they still vote for the same party/candidate, if they were to vote again?" 59.4 per cent of our respondents in Bihar, 65.8 per cent in Punjab, 57.7 per cent in U.P. and 57.0 per cent in West Bengal affirm that they would do so. In other words, close to two-thirds of the voters in our sample seem to have no second thoughts on their voting decision. And yet it should not obscure the fact that about two-fifths of our respondents do not feel sure about the appropriateness of their choice. It is also clear that the highest incidence of doubts occurs in West Bengal. The socio-economic status does not seem to have any relationship with the voters' reappraisal of his own decision except for the fact that those who fall in the high status group are consistently higher in their partisanship in each state as against those in the low status group.

That a large proportion of our respondents are quite satisfied with the final decision about who to vote for is quite apparent. The question, however, remains: How would the voter react if the candidate put up by the party of his preference does not come up to his expectations? That this is an important measure of partisanship cannot be doubted since a strong identifier does not usually deviate from the path of his partisanship even if the candidate put up by his party does not fulfil his expectations. After all, it is the party that stands for certain policies and programmes and mobilizes voters for winning support for its cause. However, quite frequently a common man comes to be attached with a party through a candidate since the candidate may symbolize and articulate the motivating forces that impel the common man to participate in electoral processes. But if the individual does not grow out of his attachment to a candidate and succeeds in transferring his identification to the party, he remains vulnerable to the pulls of parochial loyalties. Viewed in this perspective, whether the object of a voter's allegiance is a party or a candidate becomes a crucial test of ascertaining the degree to which the voter imbibes the spirit of democratic politics.

To explore this, we asked our respondents: "Suppose there was an election when the party you support was running a candidate that you did not like. What would you do? Would you still vote for your party, or vote for another party, or not vote

TABLE 3 : 10

## SES and Partisanship of Voters by States (in per cent)

(Q: Suppose there was an election when the party you support was running a candidate that you did not like. What would you do? Would you still vote for your party or vote for another party or not vote at all in the election?)

| States | Bihar | | | | | Punjab | | | | | U.P. | | | | | W.B. | | | | |
|---|---|---|---|---|---|---|---|---|---|---|---|---|---|---|---|---|---|---|---|---|
| SES \ Partisanship | Will not vote | Vote another party | Vote same party | DK | Total | Will not vote | Vote another party | Vote same party | DK | Total | Will not vote | Vote another party | Vote same party | DK | Total | Will not vote | Vote another party | Vote same party | DK | Total |
| High | 5.3 | 28.9 | 51.3 | 14.5 | 76 | 9.8 | 27.9 | 49.2 | 13.1 | 61 | 1.3 | 34.2 | 55.3 | 9.2 | 76 | 14.8 | 34.4 | 44.2 | 6.6 | 61 |
| Medium | 7.7 | 30.3 | 48.6 | 13.4 | 142 | 3.4 | 31.8 | 54.0 | 10.8 | 148 | 5.8 | 46.6 | 34.9 | 12.7 | 189 | 5.6 | 24.0 | 58.4 | 12.0 | 125 |
| Low | 5.0 | 26.9 | 51.3 | 16.8 | 119 | 8.5 | 30.5 | 34.2 | 26.8 | 82 | 1.9 | 36.9 | 42.7 | 18.5 | 157 | 3.3 | 19.7 | 44.3 | 32.7 | 61 |
| Total | 22 | 99 | 169 | 50 | | 18 | 89 | 139 | 45 | | 15 | 176 | 176 | 60 | | 19 | 63 | 128 | 37 | |
|  | 6.5 | 29.1 | 49.7 | 14.7 | | 6.2 | 30.5 | 47.6 | 15.7 | | 3.5 | 41.1 | 40.9 | 14.5 | | 7.6 | 25.3 | 41.4 | 15.7 | |

at all?" The result is presented in Table 3:10. It is obvious from the table that 3 to 7 per cent of voters can be treated as disgruntled voters inasmuch as they would rather stay back than vote. It is of interest to note that the percentage of those who are dissatisfied with the candidate of their party is highest in U.P. (41.1 per cent) and lowest in West Bengal (25.3 per cent). And yet, as we shall argue later, the inference that voters in West Bengal are highly partisan and that the object of their partisanship is the party rather than the candidate does not seem tenable. We shall return to this point later. For the moment, we should also consider the fact that near about 15 per cent of respondents in each state express their inability to decide about the possible course of action they may take. All in all, then, only 40 to 50 per cent of our respondents seem to constitute the hard core of partisans; the rest would have no hesitation in defecting from the party they usually support, in case its candidate choice is wrong. And if our data is any guide, a large-scale defection is likely to occur in U.P., if voters do not approve of the choice of the candidate put up by the party they support.

In addition to the question of the degree of voters' partisanship, there is also the question of the salience of different kinds of group pressures that impinge on voting decision. The individual is not an atom; his political dispositions and interest are shaped by diverse forces. One crucial factor is his location in his immediate environment. Given the differences in individuals due to psychological make-up and differential exposure to the outer world, the norms prevailing in their immediate neighbourhood have a greater salience for their voting decision. All around, the individual voter is surrounded by a network of expectations and he must choose which expectations he should fulfil and which ones he should ignore. To put it differently, the parameters of the individual's action are defined by his realm of relevance which is usually ordered on the basis of the varying intensity and importance of multifarious ties with different components of the environment. Recognizing that elections are political and their outcomes have political consequences, it should also be recognized that they are also social and on such occasions various social obligations come into play and have to be exchanged or paid off.

The operating group pressures on individual voting decision

are as real as individualized political orientations. We should, in this context, also consider the crucial importance of the process of individuation for the robustness of democratic institutions. The group pressures emanate mostly from diverse primordial identities. This is particularly true in the developing countries which, in their drive for modernity, are impelled to initiate and strengthen the process "in which major clusters of old social, economic and psychological commitments are eroded or broken down and people become available for new patterns of socialization and behaviour."[17] The success of this process depends on the extent to which people placed in diverse life situations rise above the divisive primordial bonds and relate in several crucial ways their existence to a larger entity that overarchs numerous divisions. In other words, the basic problem in the developing countries is to integrate diverse elements in one overpowering sense of nationality and, through this, promote in the people a sense of citizenship which takes its inspiration from an urge for preserving and sustaining the political system.

One of the requirements for such a development to take place is the subordination of the parochial to the universal. In practice, however, this ideal is never realized; all political systems, whether developed or not, remain a queer admixture of these two elements. The determination of the composition of this admixture and its implications for the functioning of the political system are theoretically very important questions but not relevant to our purposes. What interests us is the extent to which the process of individuation, as it relates to autonomous decision-making in regard to voting, is gaining strength. Closely related with this is our second objective which is concerned with exploring the relative importance that voters attribute to parochial and universal factors in the process of decision-making regarding how to exercise their franchise.

We asked our respondents a battery of questions (see Table 3:11). As will be seen from the table, items 2, 4, 5, 6 and 8 are intended to tap the relative salience of various kinds of pressures

---

17. Karl W. Deutsch, "Social Mobilization and Political Development," *American Political Science Review*, LV : 3 (September 1961), p. 494.

that emanate from the voters' immediate environment. That is, these items pertain to such sources of influence that the voter encounters in the daily rounds of his life, regularly interacts with them and establishes a meaningful relationship with these sources of influence. Most of the time, however, the voter is born into a web of relationships that carry various obligations. The rest of the items relate to themes that are antithetical to and broader than the previously mentioned themes. These stimuli are quite different in nature and call for considerations that have nothing to do with conditions that relate to the individual's locally meaningful concerns. The various items are ordered such that a continuum formed of least salient factors to most salient factors is discernible.

A quick glance at the table suggests that as far as voting decision is concerned, there is strong indication that an individual voter does depend much more on his own judgement than on advice received from others whether they be his immediate kith and kin or village notables. In other words, the process of individuation, that is, making of decisions in one's own light, is quite marked. But we must not hasten to infer that voters in India have completely freed themselves from the shackles of traditional and primordial ties. Given the centrality of the individual's own judgement for voting decisions, we cannot, however, brush aside the importance of other forces. Recognizing the central importance of individual judgement in regard to voting decision, the relevance of seeking assurance from those who count in the influence structure of the environment is also of great importance. Although we do not have any direct statistical measure to indicate the relative strength of other salient forces, certain inferences, based on the data presented in the tables and other relevant factors, can certainly be hazarded. Note, for example, that even if we accept the crucial role of individual judgement for voting decision, it does not mean that secularizing tendencies are at work. Mention can be made of the fact that out of three items relating to non-traditional forces as determinants of voting decision, only one, namely, the necessity to evaluate the performance of different parties, receives any substantial support from our respondents. The other two items—policies and programmes of different parties and views of different parties and candidates—receive respectively 43.7 per cent and

## TABLE 3 : 11

**Environmental Pressures and Voting Decision—States Combined (in per cent)**

(Q: In deciding whom to vote for, people often mention the following things as useful......Please tell me whether you consider each of the following helpful or not helpful in making your decision about whom to vote)

| | Useful | Not Useful | D.K. N.A. | N (1309) |
|---|---|---|---|---|
| 1. To follow one's own judgement | 90.0 | 8.9 | 1.1 | 100.0 |
| 2. To consult/follow the advice of family members | 65.1 | 33.5 | 0.4 | 100.0 |
| 3. To make decision after evaluating the performance of different parties | 57.8 | 39.2 | 4.4 | 100.0 |
| 4. To consult/follow the advice of respectable men in the village | 56.4 | 41.6 | 1.6 | 100.0 |
| 5. To consult/follow the advice of caste or religious leaders | 49.7 | 45.2 | 5.1 | 100.0 |
| 6. To follow the majority of castemen | 47.0 | 50.8 | 2.2 | 100.0 |
| 7. To make a decision after considering policies and programmes of different parties | 43.7 | 52.0 | 4.3 | 100.0 |
| 8. To follow the majority of village/town/city folks | 39.3 | 58.4 | 2.3 | 100.0 |
| 9. To make a decision after hearing what different candidates or parties say | 37.8 | 57.8 | 4.4 | 100.0 |

37.8 per cent of voters' preference. In contrast, such social environmental factors as the advice of family members, that of village notables, caste and religious leaders, etc., seem to be more salient for individual decision-making. The picture would have been consistent and the conclusion inescapable that only social environmental factors affect voting decision had the necessity of evaluating the performance of different parties not received third highest vote. However, the question remains, is this process of evaluating the performance of various parties so individualized as to neutralize the impact of social environmental factors? The salience of context for individual action would suggest that it is not so. Even the standards of evaluation are permeated with group thinking and belief.

In view of these considerations, we are led to the conclusion that the process of individuation is conditioned by the forces operating in the immediate milieu of the individual. In fact, formation of individual judgement itself is a compound of these forces. As our data suggest, the individual must make his own decision; but, while doing so he must range various forces acting upon him in a hierarchy of valuation and weigh the relative importance of each on the basis of his own realm of relevance for arriving at a decision. Even if the manifest reality surrounding different voters may be the same, the ordering of various objects on a scale of valuation will differ from individual to individual depending upon the precise nature of the realm of relevance.

We have so far been concerned with some of the factors that become salient while making a voting decision. We now turn to the decision itself and look at three of its interrelated aspects: main considerations entering into the voting decision, the timing of decision and the nature of decision. In Table 3:12 is presented information on the main considerations that impelled the voters to vote one way or the other. We asked an open-ended question of all our respondents: "What were the main considerations that made you vote the way you did in 1969 elections?" The results are summarized in the table below. It can be readily seen that the necessity to conform to group norms is highest in U.P. followed by Bihar. What is most important is the fact that 31.7 per cent of respondents in West Bengal say that the main consideration for them was the candidate. Punjab too scores high on this count (24.7 per cent). Attachment of Congress seems highest in Punjab and lowest in West Bengal. Similarly, anti-Congress feelings are more widespread in Punjab and West Bengal. If we merged categories 3 and 4, the greater salience of parties as a referent point for voting decision is observed once again in Punjab (56.9 per cent) and very low in U.P. (26.4 per cent). By the same token, merging categories

TABLE 3 : 12

Considerations Influencing Voting Decision by States (in per cent)

| S. No. | Considerations | States | | | | |
|---|---|---|---|---|---|---|
| | | Bihar | Punjab | U. P. | W.B. | Total |
| 1. | Group pressures | 10.6 | 6.8 | 24.7 | 9.2 | 14.13 |
| 2. | Candidate | 15.9 | 24.7 | 22.2 | 31.7 | 22.92 |
| 3. | Attachment with Congress | 26.4 | 31.9 | 19.6 | 10.8 | 22.46 |
| 4. | Salience of non-Congress Parties | 17.4 | 25.0 | 6.8 | 21.4 | 16.35 |
| 5. | Miscellaneous | 10.9 | 6.8 | 4.7 | 18.9 | 9.47 |
| 6. | D.K., Inap. etc. | 18.8 | 4.8 | 22.0 | 8.0 | 14.67 |
| | Total | 340 | 292 | 428 | 249 | 1,309 |
| | | 100.0 | 100.0 | 100.0 | 100.0 | 100.00 |

1 and 2, voters in U.P. seem to be highly vulnerable to parochial considerations in making voting decision.

Our data, then, suggest that for a large majority of voters, party as a referent for making voting decision is very weak. It is only in Punjab that the highest incidence of articulation of partisanship is discernible. Since the salience of party in voting decision-making is so low, it follows that only a small proportion of voters would make their voting decision without waiting for the campaign to unfold. They are dedicated partisans and need neither the stimuli provided by the campaign as well as local pressures nor do they need any breathing spell for taking the final leap of deciding to vote for a candidate. As we have already seen, only a small proportion of our respondents revise their decision. This reinforces the inference that voters with a weak sense of partisanship must take time to decide and, for doing so, grapple with often conflicting stimuli emanating from various sources.

TABLE 3 : 13

SES and Timing of Voting Decision: All States (in per cent)

| SES | Bihar | | | | | Punjab | | | | | U.P. | | | | | W.B. | | | | |
|---|---|---|---|---|---|---|---|---|---|---|---|---|---|---|---|---|---|---|---|---|
| When decided to vote? | High | Medium | Low | NA | Total | High | Medium | Low | NA | Total | High | Medium | Low | NA | Total | High | Medium | Low | NA | Total |
| On polling day | 17.1 | 25.4 | 23.5 | — | 77 / 22.6 | — | 8.1 | 6.1 | — | 17 / 5.8 | 11.8 | 15.3 | 17.2 | — | 65 / 15.2 | — | 17.6 | 36.1 | — | 44 / 17.8 |
| A few days before the poll | 38.2 | 35.9 | 35.3 | 33.3 | 123 / 36.2 | 18.0 | 21.6 | 30.5 | — | 68 / 23.3 | 15.8 | 24.3 | 22.3 | 16.7 | 94 / 22.0 | 16.4 | 32.0 | 37.7 | — | 73 / 29.3 |
| Just after the campaign started | 9.2 | 14.8 | 21.8 | 33.3 | 55 / 16.2 | 8.2 | 10.1 | 15.9 | — | 33 / 11.3 | 18.4 | 20.1 | 14.0 | 16.7 | 75 / 17.5 | 18.0 | 17.6 | 16.4 | — | 43 / 17.3 |
| Before the campaign started | 32.9 | 19.0 | 12.6 | 33.3 | 68 / 20.0 | 73.8 | 59.5 | 46.3 | 10.0 | 172 / 58.9 | 52.6 | 36.5 | 34.4 | 66.7 | 167 / 39.0 | 63.9 | 27.2 | 9.8 | 10.0 | 81 / 32.5 |
| Did not vote | 2.6 | 4.9 | 6.7 | — | 17 / 5.0 | — | 0.7 | 1.2 | — | 2 / 0.7 | 1.3 | 3.2 | 11.5 | — | 25 / 5.5 | 1.6 | 5.6 | — | — | 8 / 3.2 |
| Total | 76 / 22.4 | 142 / 41.8 | 119 / 35.6 | 3 / 0.9 | 340 / 100.0 | 61 / 20.9 | 148 / 50.7 | 82 / 28.1 | 1 / 0.3 | 292 / 100.0 | 76 / 17.8 | 189 / 44.2 | 157 / 36.7 | 6 / 1.14 | 340 / 100.0 | 61 / 24.5 | 125 / 50.2 | 61 / 24.5 | 2 / 0.8 | 249 / 100.0 |

As will be seen from Table 3:13, the largest number of our respondents making voting decision much before the start of the campaign is located in Punjab (58.9 per cent), followed by U.P. (39.0 per cent), West Bengal (32.5 per cent), and Bihar (20.0 per cent). Further, it is in Bihar followed by West Bengal that about one-fifth of our respondents say that they finally decided whom to vote for on the polling day itself. If we add two middle categories in the table, i.e., "a few days before the poll" and "just after the campaign started," we get yet another picture. Note, for example, that as much as 52.4 per cent of respondents in Bihar and 46.6 per cent in West Bengal make up their mind only during the campaign. The corresponding figures for U.P. and Punjab respectively are 42.27 per cent and 34.6 per cent.

Leaving aside state variations what is also noteworthy is the fact that socio-economic status of the respondents seems to have some impact on when the voters actually make up their mind. Generally speaking, the tendency that a large proportion of persons in high social status make up their mind very early—even before the campaign starts—is noticeable. Note, for example, that 32.9 per cent of respondents in the high status category in Bihar, 73.8 per cent in Punjab, 52.6 per cent in U.P. and 63.9 per cent in West Bengal arrive at their voting decision even before the campaign starts.

We now turn to discussing how our respondents vote in different states. In Table 3:14, we present votes cast for each party holding constant the socio-economic status of our respondents. Some interesting patterns emerge from our data. In Bihar, for example, support for Congress is quite diffuse inasmuch as respondents voting for Congress are equally distributed in all status categories. In regard to left parties, such as the Communists and the Socialists, there is a discernible tendency, although weak but nonetheless clear, towards people in lower status groups preferring left parties. This trend is, however, reversed in the case of right parties, such as the Jana Sangh. If one goes down the status scale, one finds lesser and lesser number of people voting for right parties. In U.P. again similar tendencies relating to Congress and Right parties can be observed to be operating. What is surprising is the fact that even in the case of Socialist parties, a trend similar to that of the Right parties is discernible. In West Bengal, support for Congress

## TABLE 3 : 14

### SES Level and Party Preference by States (in per cent)

| SES | State | Congress | Communists | Right | Socialists | Others (including Independents) | Ref. | Inap. | Total |
|---|---|---|---|---|---|---|---|---|---|
| 1 | 2 | 3 | 4 | 5 | 6 | 7 | 8 | 9 | 10 |
| High | Bihar | 31.6 | 13.2 | 19.7 | 13.2 | 11.8 | 3.9 | 6.6 | 76 100.0 |
|  | Punjab | 54.1 | 23.0 | — | — | 21.3 | — | 1.6 | 61 100.0 |
|  | U.P. | 36.9 | — | 15.8 | 14.5 | 19.7 | 1.3 | 11.8 | 76 100.0 |
|  | W.B. | 21.3 | 16.4 | 1.6 | 26.3 | 29.5 | 1.6 | 3.3 | 61 100.0 |
| Medium | Bihar | 31.0 | 14.1 | 5.6 | 26.8 | 5.6 | 2.1 | 14.8 | 142 100.0 |

| 1 | 2 | 3 | 4 | 5 | 6 | 7 | 8 | 9 | 10 |
|---|---|---|---|---|---|---|---|---|---|
| Medium | Punjab | 44.6 | 37.8 | — | — | 14.2 | 0.7 | 2.7 | 148<br>100.0 |
| | U.P. | 31.7 | — | 7.9 | 12.2 | 31.7 | 1.6 | 14.9 | 189<br>100.0 |
| | W.B. | 27.2 | 24.8 | — | 26.4 | 14.4 | 0.8 | 6.4 | 125<br>100.0 |
| Low | Bihar | 31.1 | 19.3 | 3.4 | 25.2 | 8.4 | 0.8 | 11.8 | 119<br>100.0 |
| | Punjab | 57.4 | 26.8 | — | — | 13.4 | 1.2 | 1.2 | 82<br>100.0 |
| | U.P. | 41.3 | — | 6.4 | 7.0 | 18.5 | 4.5 | 22.3 | 157<br>100.0 |
| | W.B. | 23.0 | 47.5 | — | 16.4 | 9.8 | — | 3.3 | 61<br>100.0 |

is low in every status category. That a larger proportion of voters in lower status groups should vote for the left parties, such as, the CPI and the CPI (M), is not surprising. Also interesting is the fact that the Socialist parties, especially the SSP, should draw heavy support from the high- and medium-statused groups. It is quite possible that the voters belonging to high status, after being disillusioned with Congress, are turning to the Socialist and local parties. It is in Punjab that Congress draws heaviest support from almost all sections. As expected, the Communist Party, again seems more popular in lower status groups. In contrast, the support for the Akali Dal goes on diminishing when one goes down the status scale.

We focussed our attention in this chapter on the socio-economic profiles of our respondents in the four states and delineated some of the factors that impinge on their voting decision. As our data indicate, state differentials in the voters' socio-economic profiles are quite significant. For example, near about 32 per cent of the respondents from West Bengal come from urban areas, while the proportions of urban voters in our sample in other states veer round 17 to 20 per cent. Similarly, it is in West Bengal again that the proportions of both highly educated voters and economically very poor voters (as reflected in the distribution of land holdings) are the highest.

Given these differences in the socio-economic attributes of our respondents, there are some other differences that set apart voters in one state from those in another. Note, for example, that the direction of political preferences as reflected in the way they voted in the 1969 elections differs from state to state. What is even more interesting, there is also discernible a differential configuration of predispositions entering into the voters' voting decision. Partisanship is, as we have argued, one of the crucial factors that condition voting preference. Our data show that in respect of this attribute, our respondents from West Bengal manifest quite a different pattern than those in other states. Note, for example, that the lowest proportion of respondents expressing their willingness to vote again for the same party is in West Bengal. Again, as much as half of our respondents in West Bengal indicate that they would not vote for the party of their choice if its choice of candidate were not acceptable to them. Comparable figures elsewhere are:

Bihar 34.2 per cent; Punjab 37.7 per cent; and U.P. 35.5 per cent. This is also reflected in the fact that as much as 31.7 per cent of respondents in West Bengal say that the main consideration inclining them to vote the way they did was the candidate. While politicization has increased, a large number of voters in West Bengal do not seem to have settled down politically to lend stability to political processes.

# CHAPTER FOUR
# Voters and Partisanship Variability

In the last Chapter we discussed the salience of certain factors for voting decision. We left off by indicating, in a very general way, how voters in different states expressed their partisan preference. Earlier we referred to the fact that the 1967 general election was in a very real sense a watershed in Indian politics. The consequences of the disintegration of a dominant one-party system have been the emergence, at the state level, of a multi-party system and the instability of coalition governments. The midterm election in 1969 failed both in restoring Congress to a position of dominance and producing a stable majority. As we also pointed out earlier, except in U.P., Congress lost further ground to other parties both on the left and the right. The increasing magnitude of desertions from the Congress raises several questions. In the first place, apart from the question of what is in store for Congress in the successive elections—a question that concerns us only marginally—there is also the question of possible developments in the party system in different states. One can, for example, fruitfully explore the chance of any one or two parties emerging to provide stable government. In the second place, since the electorate itself has a very crucial role to play in the emerging patterns of party system in different states, it is of interest to examine two inter-related questions. First, we have to ascertain who are the shifters and, second, what are some of the political attributes that distinguish regular voters, i.e., those who vote consistently for one party at the elections from those who shift their party allegiance from one election to the next.

To rephrase these questions: studies of American voting behaviour emphasize the fact that, in the first place, socio-economic background is not a meaningful way to examine the composition of the electorate in terms of regulars and shifters. The argument is based on the fact that the crucial factors accounting for firm partisanship, or lack of it, are the extent of individual voters' concern with political matters and the intensity of their attachment to one of the competing parties. As Campbell argues, "the level of interest is an enduring personal characteristic...(and) it typically develops during the process of early socialization and, having reached its ultimate level, persists as a relatively stable attribute of the adult interest pattern. It is not simply a function of social or economic background; people of high and low political interest are found at all levels of the electorate."[1]

Similarly, in regard to the intensity of partisanship, it is argued that "identifications perform for the citizen an exceedingly useful evaluative function." Since affairs of government are very remote from an average voter, he tends to view and judge public issues through the blinkers provided by his party identification. As Stokes argues, "...the capacity of party identification to color perceptions holds the key to understanding why the unfolding of new events, the emergence of new issues, the appearance of new political figures, fail to produce wider swings of party fortunes. To a remarkable extent these swings are dampened by processes of selective perception."[2] In other words, identification colours an individual's political perspective becoming a sort of funnel through which political stimuli are sifted, differentiated and selectively assimilated. Identification, thus, becomes a crucial factor in determining the way individual voters articulate their political preferences. As a corollary, the stronger the sense of identification, less likely it is that a voter would in normal times defect from the party of his choice. Converse points to this same phenomenon when he talks of the crucial role of habituation in crystallizing party loyalties. "When these loyalties have not yet had time to develop, it seems likely that electoral support will have numerous capricious overtones, and that in times of severe distress, non-traditional and anti-democratic parties may find ready support."[3]

---

1. Angus Campbell, "Surge and Decline: A Study of Electoral Change," in Campbell, et al., *Elections and the Political Order* (New York: John Wiley and Sons, Inc., 1966), p. 42.
2. Donald E. Stokes, *ibid.*, p. 127.
3. Philip E. Converse, "On Time and Partisan Stability," *op. cit.*, p. 141. See also his contribution in *Election and Political Order*, pp. 136-57.

It would seem, then, that a meaningful analysis of shift in party allegiance as reflected in electoral outcome must be based not on identifying any demographic or socio-economic explanations for such a phenomenon, but on the exploration of the level of voters' concern with political matters, on their responsiveness to political stimulation, and on the salience of politics in their psychological environment.[4] To put it simply, social and economic background as a potent explanatory variable, relevant for illuminating voting shift at the individual level, must be devalued in comparison to political variables, particularly interest and identification. To contest this view is to challenge the carefully planned and competently analyzed studies of voting behaviour that strongly support this conclusion. However, we must recognize that such a view reduces the individual to an abstract category easily detachable from the context that gives some shape to his individuality and reducible to basic psychological urges. While it is recognized that such a procedure simplifies analytical problems, it should also be emphasized that this puts the complexity of a dynamic situation into a straightjacket and is, therefore, liable to distort the perspective that should inform the analysis of social reality.

It should also be made clear at this point that we do not doubt the relevance of political variables *per se* as explanatory tools. What we consider as distortion is the fact that by denigrating the value of social and economic background as against political variables, an unbalanced perspective is presented. We must recognize that a syndrome of certain political attributes is usually the outcome of certain contextual factors including those related with social and economic background, certain sociological factors, such as, choice of friendship and group association and, finally, the differential access to source of information.[5] Given the salience of the context and different life

---

4. Campbell, *op. cit.*
5. It should, however, be pointed out that a phenomenon of what Himmelstrand calls "homopolitical selectivity" operates here. In Himmelstrand's term, this refers to a tendency for like individuals consciously to seek each other out for formal and informal interaction. This results also in the differential salience of information with same content for individuals located in different milieus. See Ulf Himmelstrand, *Social Pressures, Attitudes and Democratic Process* (Stockholm : Almquest and Wicksell, 1960), pp. 399-408.

situations of individuals, the insistence on treating political variables as primary is tantamount to concentrating on what can be termed as outcome rather than on the process that brings about a particular outcome.[6] To put it differently, why an individual acquires a particular syndrome of political attributes is dependent not only upon his psychological make-up but also upon the type of milieu he is born and raised in, the type of experience he goes through and the type of bonds he develops. Clearly, then, the social and economic background of the individual must be given a due place in any explanatory scheme as a conditioning, if not as the prime explanatory factor. For, it must be accepted that social and economic background provides the individual with certain resources which can be used to establish certain kinds of relationship with the environment. The lack of these resources may seriously handicap certain individuals in establishing a meaningful relationship with their environment.

Even more important in this regard is the fact that in a country where after a long period of economic stagnation, economic growth has gained some momentum, distribution of economic and other resources is characterized by a great amount of disparity not only between regions but also within regions. This has certain implications for the way political orientations take on differential patterns. Although the full implications of such a differential and unequal distribution of basic resources for political predispositions and attitudes still await fuller exploration, some contours of the differential configurations of politically relevant attitudes are visible.[7] Mention may in this regard be made of the fact that the developmental level of a particular areal unit is clearly reflected in the distribution of social and economic resources and, through this, in the acquisition of political attitudes. To put it in another way and as we

---

6. For a discussion of the relevance of contextual factors for voting behaviour see, among others, David R. Segal and Marshall Meyr, *op. cit.*, Robert D. Putnam, "Political Attitudes and the Local Community," *American Political Science Review,* 60 (1966), pp. 640-54; and Kevin R. Cox, "The Spatial Structuring of Information Flow and Partisan Attitudes," in Dogan & Rokkan, *op. cit.*, pp. 157-85.

7. See my "Social Diversity, Economic Development, and Political Integration," *op. cit.*

shall demonstrate in greater detail later on, the higher the socio-economic status of an individual, the higher the levels of his political information and other concomitant factors are likely to be.

In view of these considerations, it is necessary to reformulate the hypotheses presented above in order to bring them closer to reality and endow them with greater relevance as explanatory variables. Recognizing the importance of socio-economic status, we propose to reinstate it as a major conditioning factor. Because of the unequal distribution of social resources, individual voters manifest unequal degrees of interest in external objects depending on their location—on the scale of closeness-remoteness. Given the priority of socio-economic status, political factors must, then, be treated as intervening variables whose strength or weakness will, to a considerable extent, determine the nature of partisanship. This should not, however, give the impression that partisanship is an enduring quality. The strength of partisanship varies from individual to individual and, if the assumption of normal distribution of partisan orientation is not improper, only a small proportion of the electorate can be characterized either intensely partisan or highly politically indifferent. Taking into consideration the fact that the phenomenon of homopolitical selectivity is most likely to operate at the intensely partisan end of the curve, the deflection of the truly partisans from the preferred political choice is highly unlikely. Similarly, the highly indifferent voters are also unlikely to be influenced by the political mood either prevailing in their own milieu or transmitted from outside. It is, therefore, quite likely that the element of partisan conversion will be considerably heightened in persons characterized by only a moderate degree of partisanship.

In short, then, we propose to examine in this chapter the extent of shift in party allegiance of the voters as reflected in our data, ascertain demographic characteristics of different types of voters, and tap certain—primarily the political—variables that seem to be associated with the phenomenon of partisan conversion. Since Congress has been the centre-piece of the party system in India and, since no stable party alignment in any of the states under study is in sight, following the demise of the one-party dominance system, it will be more fruitful to show the extent to which voters have moved away from Congress. A word about our voter classification is also in order. We classify our voters into five categories: regular, shifter, indifferent, new and non-voters. We should also warn that our classification is based on recall data.[8] We use this classification in conjunction with other demographic and political variables in order to determine the nature of shift in voting. Our procedures for such a demonstration are simple and crude but they have one quality. They highlight relationships among different variables in a straightforward manner and are, therefore, easily comprehensible.

We begin, first, with providing some idea about shift in Congress support. As we indicated in Chapter Two, there has been extensive movement in all states from one party to another between the 1967 and 1969 elections. According to our survey data, only 30.9 per cent of our respondents in Bihar voted for Congress in 1969 as against 46.2 per cent in 1967. 36.0 per cent as against 45.6 per cent in U.P. and 24.9 per cent as against 35.3 per cent in West Bengal.[9] It is only in Punjab that we find a larger proportion of voters in our sample report to have voted Congress than is true when compared with aggregate electoral data. Whatever the case, a considerable shift in the support structure of Congress is discernible. Relating this shift to age cohorts, we get distinct patterns in different states.

---

8. We are well aware of the shortcomings of any classification based on recall data. Converse's warning that "if we try to establish the fact of a vote shift from the individual's recall of his next prior vote, we are at the mercy of the accuracy of his report" has to be ignored in our case simply because we could do no better. Our "regular" voters are those who claimed to have voted for the same party both in 1967 and 1969. "Shifters", on the other hand, are those who voted one way in 1967 and differently in 1969. In contrast, the "indifferent" voters could not remember how they voted in any of the two elections. "New" and "non-voters" need no comments.

9. The corresponding figures for other parties are:

|  | Left | | Right | | Socialists | | Others | |
|---|---|---|---|---|---|---|---|---|
|  | 1967 | 1969 | 1967 | 1969 | 1967 | 1969 | 1967 | 1969 |
| Bihar | 10.6 | 15.9 | 2.1 | 8.2 | 15.3 | 23.2 | 0.3 | 7.9 |
| Punjab | 23.6 | 31.5 | 1.0 | — | — | — | 9.2 | 15.4 |
| U.P. | — | — | 6.5 | 8.9 | 7.0 | 10.5 | 7.9 | 25.0 |
| W.B. | 20.9 | 28.5 | 0.4 | 0.4 | 15.5 | 23.7 | 11.6 | 16.9 |

But before we examine this aspect, we shall dwell momentarily on the pattern revealed by the 1967 votes of our respondents. As will be seen from Figure 4:1, a more or less similar pattern of relationship between age and vote is noticeable in all the states except West Bengal. Note, for example, that starting from different baselines, percentage of Congress vote in each of the three states steadily increases as habituation increases with more and more participation in electoral politics till it reaches its apogee at around the age of 37. After that, a decline is clearly visible with an upswing in old age, that is after 52. In the case of West Bengal, however, while the over-all pattern is similar, there are certain crucial deviations from the patterns that obtain in other states. In the first place, a sharp dip in the Congress vote is noticeable just after the young voters have most probably been exposed to electoral politics once. In the second place, persons belonging to the age group 50–55 who vote for Congress form the largest proportion as compared to other states. And, finally, barring the age groups 20–25 and 50–55, the preference of all other age groups for Congress is substantially lower than the comparable age groups elsewhere.

And yet, the distribution of Congress votes among age cohorts in these states presents a symmetric look. This is no longer the case when we compare 1967 data with that of 1969 (see Fig. 4:2). Widespread defections in almost all age groups are discernible. However, patterns differ from one state to the next. In Bihar, for example, no shift seems to have occurred in the case of very young voters. But as the age increases, so does the magnitude of shift. The growing gap narrows somewhat in the case of those falling in the age group 40–45; it again widens and becomes quite large in oldest voters. In contrast, Punjab presents a different pattern. Younger voters have, as a matter of fact, voted for Congress in larger numbers than in 1967. It is only in age group 35–45 that a sizeable shift is noticeable. Congress picks up strength again in the 45–50 age group but loses support in the last two age groups.

In U.P., Congress increased its support in the youngest age cohorts but then suffered increasing losses in other young age cohorts registering heaviest losses in the 35–40 age group.

From then on, the margin of its losses grows lesser and lesser. West Bengal offers yet another picture. With growing age,

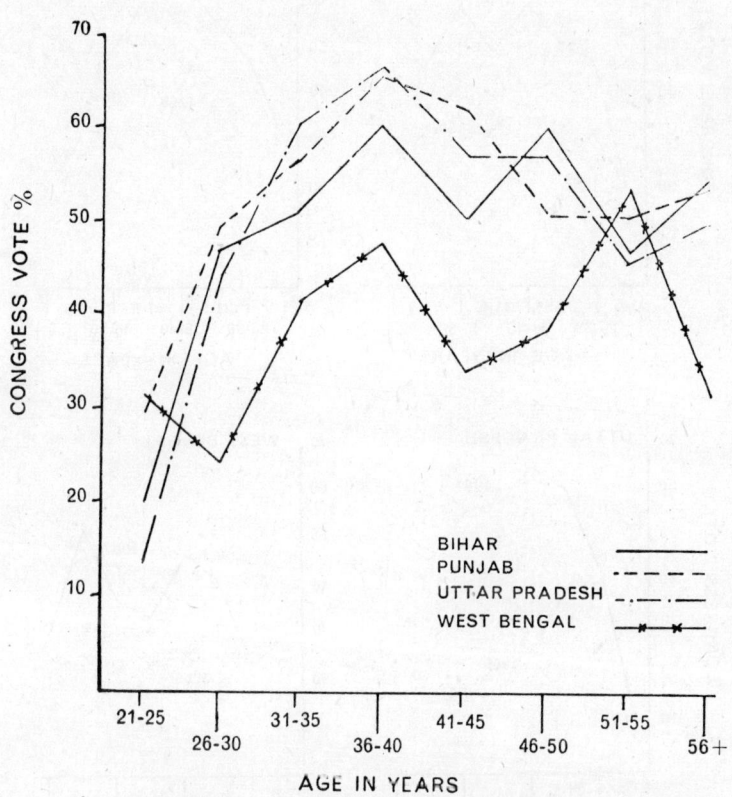

FIG. 4.1. Age and Congress vote in the four states : 1967

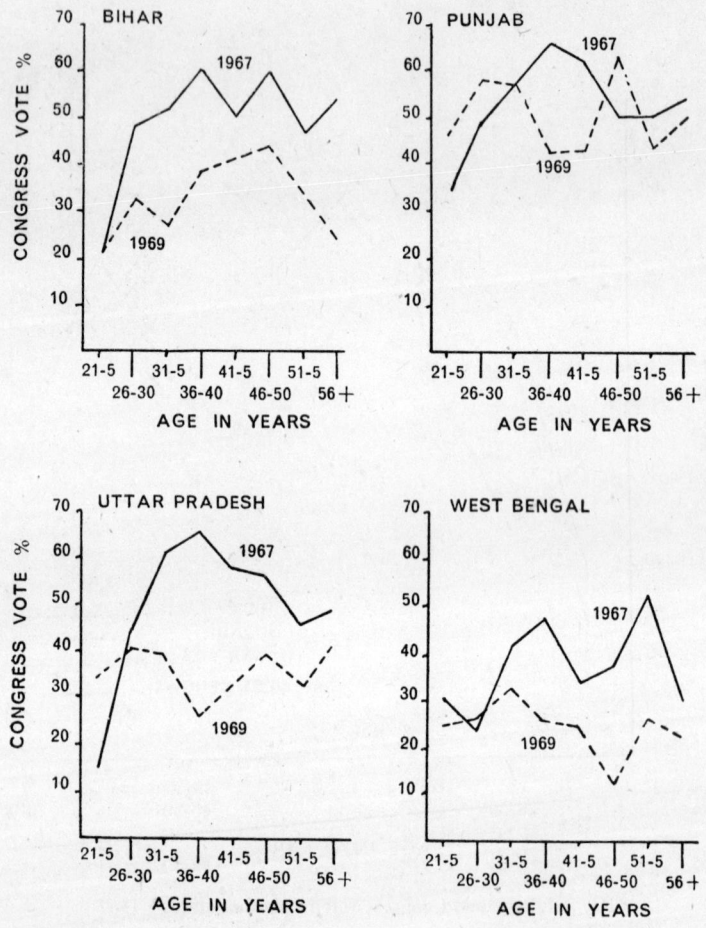

FIG. 4.2. Age and Congress vote in the four states : 1967-69

support for Congress declines. At only one point, vote for Congress in 1969 is somewhat larger than that of 1967 (i.e., in the case of the 25-40 age cohort). Otherwise, with increasing exposure to electoral politics, voters of all age groups seem to be getting more and more dissatisfied with Congress. It is only in the oldest age category that large shift away from Congress does not seem to have occurred.

Our data, then, show that the magnitude of disatisfaction with and, therefore, defection of voters from Congress in different age groups varies from one state to another. In Bihar, the youngest and the middle-aged voters seem to be less disatisfied with Congress than voters in other age groups. In Punjab, it is only in the case of middle-aged voters that disatisfaction with the Congress seems to be quite considerable. In U.P. the younger voters may be attracted to Congress but after a couple of elections dissatisfaction grows and defection increases. With increasing age, however, the extent of defection decreases. In West Bengal, the increasing participation in electoral politics seems to induce greater dissatisfaction with the ruling party and, as a consequence, defection increases.

What we discussed above is enough to show the magnitude of defection from Congress in the course of two years. A crude indication of this is the fact that in each state above 15 to 20 per cent of our respondents have changed their party preferences between 1967 and 1969. This is undoubtedly a sizeable proportion and raises the questions as to who are these defectors and what impels them to change their partisanship lable? We begin, first, with certain demographic characteristics of our respondents in terms of their voting record and then proceed to discuss certain factors associated with the phenomenon of partisan conversion.

A quick glance at Table 4:1 will indicate the general confirmation of the proposition that as the electorate becomes habituated through greater experience of electoral politics, its party loyalty becomes firmer. In other words, as individual voters advance in age and participate several times in producing an electoral verdict, they come to stick to the party of their choice. This is indicated by the fact that as we move up into higher age brackets, the proportion of regular voters, i.e, those who voted for the same party both in 1967 and 1969, increases.

TABLE 4 : 1

Age and Voter Types (in per cent)

| States | Types Age in years | Regular | Shifter | Indifferent | New | Non-Voter | Total |
|---|---|---|---|---|---|---|---|
| 1 | 2 | 3 | 4 | 5 | 6 | 7 | 8 |
| BIHAR | 21—25 | 27.5 | 21.6 | 5.9 | 33.3 | 11.7 | 100.0 ( 51) |
| | 26—35 | 41.9 | 30.8 | 18.0 | 6.8 | 2.5 | 100.0 (117) |
| | 36—45 | 54.9 | 22.5 | 15.5 | 2.8 | 4.2 | 100.0 ( 71) |
| | 46—55 | 55.0 | 15.0 | 25.0 | 5.0 | — | 100.0 ( 40) |
| | 56+ | 47.8 | 26.1 | 23.9 | 2.2 | — | 100.0 ( 46) |
| | NA | 6.7 | 3.3 | — | 66.7 | 13.3 | 100.0 ( 15) |
| | Total | 45.0 (147) | 24.9 (83) | 17.2 (56) | 9.2 (40) | 3.7 (14) | 100.0 (340) |

(*Contd.*)

| 1 | 2 | 3 | 3 | 5 | 6 | 7 | 8 |
|---|---|---|---|---|---|---|---|
| PUNJAB | 21—25 | 47.0 | 9.1 | 1.5 | 40.9 | 1.5 | 100.0 ( 66) |
| | 26—35 | 66.7 | 24.4 | 1.3 | 6.4 | 1.2 | 100.0 ( 78) |
| | 36—45 | 57.5 | 31.9 | 6.4 | 2.1 | 2.1 | 100.0 ( 47) |
| | 46—55 | 68.2 | 22.7 | 6.8 | 2.3 | — | 100.0 ( 44) |
| | 56+ | 67.3 | 21.1 | 7.7 | 3.9 | — | 100.0 ( 52) |
| | NA | 20.0 | 20.0 | — | 60.0 | — | 100.0 ( 5) |
| | Total | 61.0 (176) | 21.2 (62) | 4.2 (12) | 12.5 (36) | 1.1 (3) | 100.0 (292) |
| UTTAR PRADESH | 21—25 | 14.3 | 9.5 | 8.3 | 51.2 | 16.7 | 100.0 ( 84) |
| | 26—35 | 39.5 | 31.7 | 12.5 | 9.6 | 6.7 | 100.0 (104) |
| | 36—45 | 36.9 | 29.8 | 25.0 | 4.8 | 3.5 | 100.0 ( 84) |
| | 46—55 | 39.2 | 24.3 | 24.4 | 5.4 | 6.8 | 100.0 ( 74) |

(*Contd.*)

| 1 | 2 | 3 | 4 | 5 | 6 | 7 | 8 |
|---|---|---|---|---|---|---|---|
|  | 56+ | 44.9 | 24.4 | 23.1 | 2.5 | 5.1 | 100.0 ( 78) |
|  | NA | — | — | — | 75.0 | 25.0 | 100.0 ( 4) |
|  | Total | 34.9 (148) | 24.3 (103) | 18.2 (77) | 14.9 (66) | 7.7 (34) | 100.0 (428) |
| WEST BENGAL | 21—25 | 28.9 | 26.6 | 8.9 | 35.6 | — | 100.0 ( 45) |
|  | 26—35 | 62.3 | 24.7 | 4.7 | 5.9 | 2.4 | 100.0 ( 85) |
|  | 36—45 | 42.1 | 40.3 | 7.1 | 10.5 | — | 100.0 ( 57) |
|  | 46—55 | 48.6 | 37.1 | 11.4 | — | 2.9 | 100.0 ( 35) |
|  | 56+ | 63.0 | 14.8 | 11.1 | 11.1 | — | 100.0 ( 27) |
|  | Total | 49.8 (128) | 29.3 (73) | 7.6 (19) | 12.1 (30) | 1.2 | 100.0 (249) |

Given this general picture, however, there is some slight variation from one state to another. In Bihar, for example, it is in the oldest age bracket that the slope for regular voting curls down. In Punjab and West Bengal, it is in the 36–55 age group that the proportion of partisans has recorded a decline. Another interesting feature pertains to state differences in partisanship strength. Note, for example, that the greatest degree of partisanship strength is noticeable in Punjab and West Bengal, although in the latter case it varies quite sharply from one age group to another. In Bihar and U.P., on the other hand, the proportions of regular voters vary respectively between 41 to 55 per cent and 36 to 44 per cent.

Coming to new voters, U.P. has the largest concentration (14.9 per cent) followed by Punjab (12.5 per cent), West Bengal (12.1 per cent) and Bihar (only 9.2 per cent). It is also interesting to note that new voters, that is, those voting for the first time, can be located in all age groups. This is indicative of the mobilization of non-voters because of some new stimulus provided by the 1969 election. Interesting also in this regard is the fact that, generally speaking, as age advances the proportion of new voters declines. There are, however, exceptions to this. Note, for example, that in Bihar and U.P. about 5.0 per cent of the respondents falling in the 46–55 age group are new voters. In contrast, the proportions of new voters falling in age groups 36–45 and above gradually increase. We may also note that the highest incidence of non-voting occurs in U.P. (7.7 per cent) followed by Bihar (3.7 per cent).

In regard to our respondents who have switched from one party to another, it should be pointed out that the range of shift varies not only from one age group to another but also from one state to the next. Taking an overview and combining the two categories of shifters and indifferent voters as a measure of unstable element in the electorate, it can be seen that voters in Punjab seem to have acquired the greatest awareness of the necessity to participate in the electoral process. This is indicated by the fact that only about 25 per cent as compared to West Bengal's 37 per cent, U.P.'s 42.5 per cent and Bihar's 42 per cent of the electorate have either changed parties or shown indifference to elections. Also worth mentioning is the fact that it is again in Punjab that the proportions of both shifters and indifferent voters are smallest as compared to other states. It is in U.P. and Bihar that we observe the highest proportion of indifferent voters (18.2 and 17.2 per cent in U.P. and Bihar, respectively). In contrast, in West Bengal and Punjab, the corresponding figures are 7.6 and 4.2 per cent, respectively, suggesting the inference that as level of development rises, indifference to electoral processes due to backward economy and its consequences decreases.

If indifference seems in a very general sense to be associated with backwardness, what kind of relationship does it have with age? A quick glance at the appropriate column in Table 4:1 will certainly bring home the fact that as age increases, the size of indifferent voters in each state also increases. A probable explanation of this phenomenon may lie in the fact that this may be a function of the lower level, or the complete lack, of educational attainments, on the one hand, and very low or no interest in public affairs, on the other, of the electorate of the older generations. Whether this is true or not, we cannot assert at this moment. However, the consistency of the pattern in all the four states strongly suggests this hypothesis.

Coming now to the shifters, West Bengal can be seen to have the largest concentration of them. Bihar, U.P. and Punjab follow West Bengal in that order. Taking each state separately, most of the shifters in Bihar are located in the 26–35 age group. In Punjab, the largest proportion of shifters is located in the 36–45 age group followed by the 26–35 age group. In U.P., the 26–35 age group followed by the 36–45 age cohorts contain the two highest proportions of shifters. In West Bengal, the 36–45 and the 46–55 age groups contain the two largest proportions of shifters. In sum, then, in Bihar and U.P. dissatisfaction with the chosen party starts earlier in comparison to Punjab and West Bengal where it usually becomes manifest after two elections and then gradually subsides.

Our data, then, suggest that there is some association between age and the strength of partisanship. Although the pattern varies from one state to the next, the salience of age as a conditioning factor of partisanship strength cannot be denied. What about other social and economic background variables?

In Table 4:2 we present rural-urban background of different types of voters. A close look at the table reveals some interesting patterns. In the first place, in each of the states the proportion of regular voters in urban areas is small when compared to their counterparts in rural areas. Note, for example, that as against 46.7 per cent of regular rural voters in Bihar, only 30.0 per cent of urban voters have consistently voted in the 1967 and the 1969 elections. This pattern can be seen to be operating in other states too. In the second place, the greatest magnitude of consistency in vote can be observed in Punjab and lowest in U.P. This is true of voters in both rural and urban areas. In the third place, it is true that the second largest incidence of regularity in voting pattern is noticeable in West Bengal. It is also in this state that the largest proportions of shifters in both rural and urban areas can be located. Note, for example, that while the proportion of shifters in rural areas is 30 per cent, it is about 28 per cent in urban West Bengal. The phenomenon of partisan conversion seems to affect one out of every four rural voters in Bihar and U.P. It is also of interest to note that the magnitude of shift in voting is larger in rural areas as compared to urban areas. It is only in Punjab that shifters are located in equal proportions in both rural and urban areas.

In the fourth place, the phenomena of indifference to voting and non-voting occur largely in economically backward states. And, quite interestingly, urban voters in these states are more likely to be indifferent than those in the rural areas. Note, for example, that 25.8 per cent of urban voters as against 14.1 per cent of rural voters in Bihar can be characterized as indifferent voters. Similarly, the proportion of indifferent urban voters is twice as large as that of indifferent rural voters in U.P. If we combine the categories of "shifters" and "indifferent" voters in rural areas, U.P. has the largest proportion (40.7 per cent) of those voters who are either unstable in their partisan preference or quite indifferent to the importance of their votes. Bihar comes second (39.7 per cent) followed by West Bengal (37.1 per cent) and Punjab (25.9 per cent). The same pattern obtains in the case of urban voters in these states.

Our data, then, clearly demonstrate that stable partisanship is characteristic of largely the rural voters. While this is true, it is also true that the level of economic development has some impact on regularity of voting. Our data indicate that the proportion of regular voters is larger in two economically

TABLE 4:2

Place of Residence and Voter Types (in per cent)

| Voter Types | Rural | | | | | | Urban | | | | | |
|---|---|---|---|---|---|---|---|---|---|---|---|---|
| States | Regular | Shifter | Indi-fferent | New | Non-Voters | Total | Regular | Shifter | Indi-fferent | New | Non-Voters | Total |
| Bihar | 46.7 | 25.6 | 14.1 | 10.3 | 3.3 | 270<br>100.0 | 30.0 | 20.0 | 25.8 | 17.1 | 7.1 | 70<br>100.0 |
| Punjab | 60.8 | 21.3 | 4.6 | 12.5 | 0.8 | 240<br>100.0 | 57.7 | 21.2 | 1.9 | 17.3 | 1.9 | 52<br>100.0 |
| Uttar Pradesh | 36.7 | 25.5 | 15.2 | 14.6 | 8.0 | 349<br>100.0 | 25.3 | 17.7 | 30.4 | 19.0 | 7.6 | 79<br>100.0 |
| West Bengal | 54.1 | 30.0 | 7.1 | 8.2 | 0.6 | 170<br>100.0 | 40.5 | 27.9 | 8.9 | 20.2 | 2.5 | 79<br>100.0 |

advanced states like Punjab and West Bengal. If voters in rural areas are more consistent in their voting preference, they are also less likely to be indifferent to their right of franchise. This is true of all states except Punjab.

If place of residence seems to have some impact on the stability of partisan choice, what about the caste of our respondents?

In Table 4:3 we present the caste background of different types of voters. We indicated earlier that old voters seem to be indifferent to electoral processes and we argued that this may be due to their illiteracy or low educational attainment. This hypothesis is, to a considerable extent, supported by Table 4:3. Note, for example, that as we move down in the caste hierarchy, the proportion of indifferent voters increases. There are, however, some variations. In Bihar, for example, the proportion of indifferent voters in the upper castes is larger than that in the middle castes. Similarly, in Punjab, there are less indifferent voters in the middle castes than in the upper castes. Again, scheduled castes and tribes in U.P. seem less indifferent than voters in other caste groups.

It can, however, be asked: granted that the lower the caste of a voter, more likely it is that he will manifest lower interest in elections, how does it relate to the earlier hypothesis that seeks to establish a relationship between lack of education and indifference? The answer is very simple. Since social resources are unevenly distributed, developments induced by the modernization process have given rise to the phenomenon of what Robert Dahl calls "cumulative inequality" by which is meant the accrual of benefits to the privileged as against underprivileged social groups. In India, the upper castes have usually been enjoying higher social status, controlling economic resources and through these, taking advantage of non-traditional channels, such as education, of social mobility. As a result, persons placed at the lower rungs of social hierarchy have been unable, due mainly to the lack of resources, to equip themselves with modern education. It is only now that they are taking to modern education. It is, therefore, not surprising that the older voters from lower castes manifest lower degree of interest in electoral processes.

When we come to shifters, the picture is somewhat different.

Note, for example, that while in Bihar the voters of the upper castes seem to have a very fragile sense of partisanship, in Punjab it is those of the middle castes, in U.P. those of both upper and middle castes and in West Bengal those of almost all caste groups. How can it be explained? While a firm conclusion cannot be drawn for want of relevant data, it can, in very general terms, be indicated that the particular pattern of political development in each of the states has much to do with the differential caste-based orientations. It should at this point be emphasized that the shifters differ from indifferent voters in one very crucial respect. If due to insufficient interest in politics, the indifferent voters are unconcerned not only with what is politically significant but also with the importance of their own role in affecting the course of politics, the shifters, on the contrary, must be credited with a high amount of political interest but not necessarily identification. Like weathercocks, they are affected by any change in the political wind and, by changing their position, indicate the changing criterion of evaluation of personally relevant political events. In short, then, partisan shift can be taken to mean a change in the relevance of particular political stimuli.

Keeping this in view, the recent political happenings in different states shed some light on the phenomenon of caste basis of partisan conversion. The Congress Party, as we indicated earlier, has been the king-pin of the Indian party system. Although endowed with a support structure spanning over various social divisions, it had come to be clearly identified with certain socio-economic vested interests. With the gradual decline of the Congress and with differential patterns of development in party system in each state, voters from different caste groups in different states react and respond to political stimuli. In Bihar, for example, men from upper castes have been the major beneficiaries of Congress rule and as its importance declined, they have had to find other protective umbrellas. In Punjab, the large size of the middle castes and the entanglement of communalism with politics impel in certain circumstances the voters of the middle castes to change sides. In U.P., there is noticeable a pattern similar to that of Bihar but here the voters in the middle caste constitute the largest proportion of shifters. This is explained by the fact of the coming into

TABLE 4:3

Caste and Voter Types (in per cent)

| States | Caste | Types Regular | Shifter | Indifferent | New | Non-Voter | Total |
|---|---|---|---|---|---|---|---|
| 1 | 2 | 3 | 4 | 5 | 6 | 7 | 8 |
| BIHAR | Upper | 36.0 | 35.0 | 14.0 | 11.0 | 4.0 | 100.0 (100) |
| | Middle | 54.1 | 18.8 | 11.8 | 9.4 | 5.9 | 100.0 ( 85) |
| | Low | 35.3 | 21.6 | 23.5 | 15.7 | 3.9 | 100.0 ( 67) |
| | Sch. Castes & Tribes | 35.3 | 21.6 | 23.5 | 15.7 | 3.9 | 100.0 ( 51) |
| | Non-Hindu | 50.0 | 22.2 | 11.1 | 13.9 | 2.8 | 100.0 ( 36) |
| | NA | — | 100.0 | — | — | — | 100.0 ( 1) |
| | Total | 43.4 (147) | 24.2 (83) | 16.5 (56) | 11.8 (40) | 4.1 (14) | 100.0 (340) |

(Contd.)

| 1 | 2 | 3 | 4 | 5 | 6 | 7 | 8 |
|---|---|---|---|---|---|---|---|
| PUNJAB | Upper | 70.0 | 20.0 | 6.7 | 3.3 | — | 100.0 (30) |
|  | Middle | 61.5 | 23.3 | 1.9 | 12.0 | 1.3 | 100.0 (159) |
|  | Low | 57.4 | 16.4 | 6.6 | 18.0 | 1.6 | 100.0 (61) |
|  | Sch. Castes & Tribes | 53.8 | 20.5 | 7.7 | 18.0 | — | 100.0 (39) |
|  | Non-Hindi | 33.3 | 33.3 | — | 33.3 | — | 100.0 (3) |
|  | Total | 60.3 (176) | 21.2 (62) | 4.1 (12) | 13.4 (39) | 1.0 (3) | 100.0 (292) |
| UTTAR PRADESH | Upper | 41.7 | 29.1 | 16.5 | 11.4 | 1.3 | 100.0 (79) |
|  | Middle | 28.2 | 34.7 | 16.1 | 15.3 | 5.7 | 100.0 (124) |
|  | Low | 40.0 | 17.7 | 20.0 | 15.6 | 6.7 | 100.0 (45) |
|  | Sch. Castes & Tribes | 35.0 | 18.5 | 15.5 | 16.5 | 14.5 | 100.0 (103) |
|  | Non-Hindu | 34.7 | 13.3 | 25.3 | 17.3 | 9.3 | 100.0 (75) |
|  | NA | — | — | — | 50.0 | 50.0 | 100.0 (2) |
|  | Total | 34.7 (148) | 24.2 (103) | 18.1 (77) | 15.3 (66) | 7.7 (34) | 100.0 (428) |

(Contd.)

| 1 | 2 | 3 | 4 | 5 | 6 | 7 | 8 |
|---|---|---|---|---|---|---|---|
| WEST BENGAL | Upper | 56.1 | 24.2 | 4.6 | 15.1 | — | 100.0 ( 66) |
| | Middle | 42.1 | 29.8 | 8.8 | 17.5 | 1.8 | 100.0 ( 57) |
| | Low | 47.2 | 27.8 | 13.9 | 9.7 | 1.4 | 100.0 ( 72) |
| | Sch. Castes & Tribes | 54.6 | 45.4 | — | — | — | 100.0 ( 22) |
| | Non-Hindu | 53.1 | 31.3 | 3.1 | 9.4 | 3.1 | 100.0 ( 32) |
| | Total | 49.8 (124) | 29.3 (73) | 7.6 (19) | 12.1 (30) | 1.2 (3) | 100.0 (249) |

prominance of the BKD and the Jana Sangh—largely a middle caste phenomenon—these parties become the focal points of partisan conversion. In West Bengal, the middle and the lower caste voters are probably attracted to left parties because of their prominent role in the coalition governments and their decided antagonism to vested interests.

If different caste groups perceive political stimuli in different ways and if such a perception influences—even though slightly—their political behaviour, it can, then, be argued that differential distribution of economic resources should also act as a catalyst for the formation of different kinds of political orientations leading to varying degrees of partisanship depending upon the nature and relevance of particular political stimulus. We take land ownership as a measure of differential distribution of economic resources and present in Table 4:4 information on voter types against land distribution. Given the state differences, three broad patterns are revealed by the table. In the first place, the proportion of indifferent voters decreases as the size of land owned increases. The only exception to this general pattern is discernible in Bihar where voters in the 5.1 and more acres of land ownership category seem to have greater amount of indifference than those in the medium category. Even here, however, they seem to be less indifferent when compared to those in the smallest land-size category. In the second place, in contradistinction to indifferent voters, the proportion of shifters increases as we move up from small land-holding size to bigger ones. It is only in the case of Punjab and West Bengal that we find medium land-holders less vulnerable to the phenomenon of partisan conversion than either the small or the big farmers.

A mixture of these two elements, that is caste and land-ownership, has inevitably some consequences for firm partisanship. We could have asserted that voters possessing bigger land-holdings are most likely to be firm in their partisanship as compared to those with smaller land-holdings. However, this pattern does not hold true in Bihar, Punjab and West Bengal. In Bihar, the big farmers are less partisan than the small and the medium farmers. In Punjab and West Bengal, the medium farmers happen to evince the highest degree of partisanship. This is indicative of the fact that the big farmers react and respond to political stimuli in different ways in these states. Given this, however, the fact remains that the differential pattern of the distribution of economic resources does have salience for evaluating political events and the consequent action.

Till now our discussion was restricted to some of the socio-economic background variables that are, to state the obvious, related with traditional social organization with its built-in inequalities and glaring disparities. Many of the consequences of such a social order can, however, be neutralized if the traditionally inert social sectors make a determined bid through the existing facilities of modern education to break the barriers to social mobility. Also, it is through education that the curtain of isolation can be lifted and a meaningful relationship with the larger environment established. Conversely, capabilities developed through access to modern education can be utilized on the privileged groups to protect their interests. In view of these considerations, the question as to how our respondents with different amount of educational attainments compare on the dimension of partisanship becomes important.

In Table 4:5 we compare voter types against their educational background. It is generally true that the higher the level of education, the lower is the magnitude of indifference. However, differences are too small to permit any firm conclusion. What is quite revealing is that 15.4 per cent of better-educated respondents in Bihar as compared to 16.7 per cent of illiterate voters in Bihar can be characterized as indifferent voters. Similarly, indifferent voters constitute equal proportions both among illiterate and well-educated voters in West Bengal. It is only in Punjab and U.P. that a pattern of higher education leading to lesser indifference can be observed. Also, in the case of shifters, the level of education does not seem to play any differential role in inducing shift in partisan choice. If anything, there are two contradictory trends revealed by the data presented in Table 4:5. Note, for example, that the proportions of shifters among educated voters in Punjab and U.P. are less than those of their counterparts among illiterate voters. In contrast, 29.5 per cent of better-educated voters as against 23.5 per cent of illiterate voters in Bihar and 30.7 per cent of better-educated voters as against 31.5 per cent of illiterate voters in West Bengal constitute shifters. Also interesting is the fact that the proportion

TABLE 4 : 4

Landownership and Voter Types (in per cent)

| States | Bihar | | | | | Punjab | | | | U.P. | | | | | W.B. | | | | |
|---|---|---|---|---|---|---|---|---|---|---|---|---|---|---|---|---|---|---|---|
| Land (in acres) | 0–1 | 1.1–5 | 5.1+ | NA | TOTAL | 0–1 | 1.1–5 | 5.1+ | TOTAL | 0–1 | 1.1–5 | 5.1+ | NA | TOTAL | 0–1 | 1.1–5 | 5.1+ | NA | TOTAL |
| Voter Types | | | | | | | | | | | | | | | | | | | |
| Regular | 43.6 | 46.1 | 39.8 | — | 147 / 43.3 | 59.1 | 66.0 | 58.9 | 176 / 60.3 | 30.0 | 36.4 | 40.0 | 33.3 | 147 / 34.6 | 40.7 | 57.3 | 43.5 | — | 124 / 50.0 |
| Shifter | 22.2 | 25.5 | 28.7 | — | 83 / 24.4 | 19.7 | 15.1 | 26.1 | 62 / 21.2 | 18.9 | 22.9 | 34.3 | 33.3 | 103 / 24.0 | 29.9 | 22.7 | 47.9 | 100.0 | 73 / 29.0 |
| Indifferent | 20.2 | 9.8 | 17.9 | — | 56 / 16.5 | 6.9 | — | 2.9 | 12 / 4.1 | 23.3 | 15.7 | 12.4 | — | 77 / 18.1 | 8.8 | 6.7 | 4.3 | — | 19 / 7.7 |
| New | 10.4 | 17.7 | 10.9 | 66.7 | 40 / 11.4 | 12.9 | 17.0 | 12.1 | 39 / 13.4 | 15.0 | 19.3 | 10.4 | 33.3 | 66 / 15.3 | 13.3 | 12.0 | 4.3 | — | 30 / 12.1 |
| Non-Voter | 3.6 | 4.9 | 2.7 | 33.3 | 14 / 4.4 | 1.4 | 1.9 | — | 3 / 1.0 | 12.8 | 5.7 | 2.9 | — | 34 / 8.0 | 1.3 | 1.3 | — | — | 3 / 1.2 |
| Total | 163 / 100.0 | 102 / 100.0 | 73 / 100.0 | 2 / 100.0 | 340 / 100.0 | 132 / 100.0 | 53 / 100.0 | 107 / 100.0 | 292 / 100.0 | 180 / 100.0 | 140 / 100.0 | 105 / 100.0 | 3 / 100.0 | 428 / 100.0 | 150 / 100.0 | 75 / 100.0 | 23 / 100.0 | 1 / 100.0 | 249 / 100.0 |

TABLE 4 : 5

Education and Voter Types (in per cent)

| State | Bihar | | | | | Punjab | | | | U.P. | | | | | W.B. | | | | |
|---|---|---|---|---|---|---|---|---|---|---|---|---|---|---|---|---|---|---|---|
| Education → | None | Upto Primary | Middle & above | NA | Total | None | Upto Primary | Middle & above | TOTAL | None | Upto Primary | Middle & above | NA | Total | None | Upto Primary | Middle & above | NA | Total |
| Voter Types ↓ | | | | | | | | | | | | | | | | | | | |
| Regular | 46.2 | 46.5 | 33.3 | — | 147 / 43.4 | 61.1 | 61.2 | 57.1 | 176 / 60.3 | 33.9 | 33.3 | 38.2 | 50.0 | 148 / 34.5 | 53.9 | 57.9 | 43.9 | — | 124 / 50.2 |
| Shifter | 23.5 | 21.2 | 29.5 | 100.0 | 83 / 24.2 | 21.5 | 23.5 | 18.9 | 62 / 21.2 | 24.8 | 25.9 | 18.4 | 50.0 | 103 / 23.9 | 31.5 | 22.8 | 30.7 | 50.0 | 73 / 29.2 |
| Indifferent | 16.7 | 17.2 | 15.4 | — | 56 / 16.5 | 4.2 | 4.7 | 2.5 | 12 / 4.1 | 21.1 | 14.8 | 13.1 | — | 77 / 18.1 | 7.9 | 8.8 | 7.0 | — | 19 / 7.7 |
| New | 9.3 | 11.1 | 18.2 | — | 40 / 11.8 | 13.2 | 9.4 | 19.0 | 39 / 13.4 | 12.8 | 15.7 | 23.7 | — | 66 / 15.5 | 6.7 | 8.8 | 16.7 | 50.0 | 30 / 11.7 |
| Non-Voter | 4.3 | 4.0 | 3.6 | — | 14 / 4.1 | — | 1.2 | 2.5 | 3 / 1.0 | 7.4 | 10.2 | 6.6 | — | 34 / 8.0 | — | 1.7 | 1.7 | — | 3 / 1.2 |
| Total | 162 / 100.0 | 99 / 100.0 | 78 / 100.0 | 1 / 100.0 | 340 / 100.0 | 144 / 100.0 | 85 / 100.0 | 63 / 100.0 | 292 / 100.0 | 242 / 100.0 | 108 / 100.0 | 76 / 100.0 | 2 / 100.0 | 428 / 100.0 | 76 / 100.0 | 57 / 100.0 | 114 / 100.0 | 2 / 100.0 | 249 / 100.0 |

of regular voters among better-educated respondents is lowest in Bihar (33.3 per cent) and highest in Punjab (57.1 per cent). Given these differences, however, the level of education does not seem to be as crucial a variable as other socio-economic background variables in conditioning firm partisan choice.

Our discussion of the relationship between socio-economic background variables and firmness of partisanship highlights the way the former intervenes to shape the strength of partisanship. Variables such as age, caste and landownership have, as we saw earlier, affected to a considerable extent, the way our respondents in each of the states under study have developed firm or shifting partisanship. Although we have not offered any statistical demonstration of the strength of association between socio-economic background variables and the strength of partisanship, the very distribution of frequencies brings home the relevance of socio-economic background variables for formation of certain political orientations. In other words, these variables cannot be ignored; they have to be reinstated as important conditioning factors that determine not only the access of an individual to certain resources necessary for the acquisition of capacity to meaningfully interact with his environment. They also determine certain politically relevant attitudes that usually go with his location in a particular social status category. Thus the socio-economic background variables act both directly and indirectly through opportunities made available to shape the individual's political orientations. The importance of structural factors in moulding politically relevant attitudes and orientations cannot, therefore, be over-emphasized.

We recognize that, given a similar social and economic background, individuals do, however, behave differently. But before we discuss the impact of non-structural factors on voter's partisanship, we offer two pieces of evidence in order to emphasize that the so much talked-about salience of political interest for influencing the strength of partisanship is in fact a function of certain capabilities dependent, in turn, on certain structural factors. In the following two graphs we present some idea as to how socio-economic factors enter *into the shaping of political interest*.[13]

---

13. Our index of political interest is derived from a set of three questions :
   1. Leaving aside the period of elections, how much interest do you take

In Fig. 4.3 is depicted the relationship between the level of income and that of political interest while in Fig. 4.4 we examine the level of political interest against educational background of our respondents. As will be seen, we have included the entire sample in these figures without giving any statewise breakdown. We have satisfied ourselves that the relationship depicted in these figures holds true also in the case of each state. Therefore, instead of cluttering up the next pages with a plethora of graphs, one composite picture will be sufficient to demonstrate the relationship between the two variables.

Now, coming to Fig. 4.3, we find that there is certainly some measure of association between the levels of income and political interest. Note, for example, that in the lowest income group, those very low on political interest constitute about 51 per cent, those with medium political interest about 33 per cent and those with high interest only about 16 per cent. As we move up into higher income brackets the proportion of those with low political interest steadily decreases till it reaches a low of 30 per cent in the highest income bracket. Also along with this, the proportion of those manifesting medium political interest rises steadily with the rising income till it reaches the highest point (about 46 per cent) in the 151–450 income group. However, in the highest income group, it slides down to 39 per cent. In contrast, the curve for those who are high on political interest starts at a higher point in the lowest income group, dips down in the second lowest income group and then rises again in the next two income brackets. However, the difference between those low on interest and those with high interest in the highest income group is barely one percentage point.

This should make it clear that although there is obviously some association between the levels of income and political

---

in politics and public affairs? Do you take a great deal of interest, some interest, or no interest at all? 2. In general, how often do you discuss politics and the affairs of the nation? 3. How interested are you in politics and affairs of the nation? After assigning integer weights to responses depending upon their positive and negative contents, total scores of individual respondents on all items were counted. Deciding, then, the cut-off points, respondents were ranked on low to high political interest. This procedure of index construction has been followed throughout and needs, therefore, no mention elsewhere.

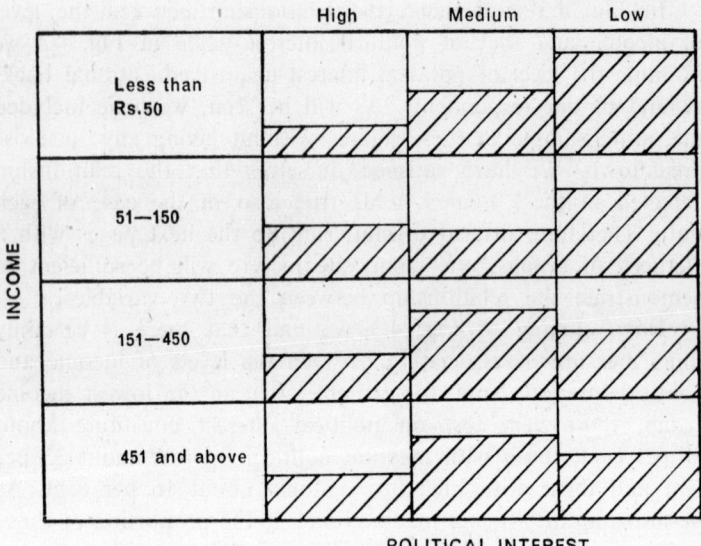

FIG. 4.3 Income and political interest

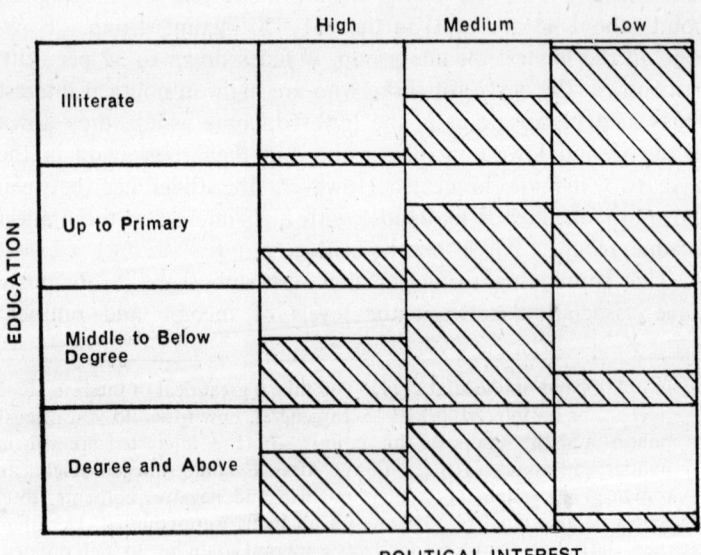

FIG. 4.4 Education and political interest

interest, we cannot, however, assume that such a relationship is either linear or very sharp. We cannot, for example, assume that rising income will necessarily induce a rise in the level of political interest also. We can only say that in all likelihood political interest will be greater in those who enjoy higher income. However, there comes a point at which the level of political interest levels off even though the income one enjoys is higher. At best, then the relationship between income and level of political interest is curvilinear.

In contrast, the relationship between level of education and that of political interest seems to be more direct. Note, for example, that as the level of education rises, the percentage of those low on the index of political interest steadily declines and the corresponding percentage of voters with high interest steadily rises. Also the highest proportion of voters with low interest is composed of illiterate voters. Similarly, in the highest educational category only a little over 7 per cent of our respondents are low on political interest as compared to 48.7 per cent high on it. Without belabouring the point, it can be asserted that there is very close association between the levels of education and political interest. When viewed in conjunction with the data on income and political interest, the implication of higher political interest associated with higher education for political dispositions is clear. It does not need to be demonstrated that the access to modern higher education is dependent upon the availability of higher income. In a country where per capita income is very low and its distribution very unequal, it is difficult to imagine how a large number of the electorate with low income and education can be expected to acquire a sustained and deeper interest in politics and public affairs. They can at best be expected to have only a fleeting interest shaped mostly by the heightened political competition induced by electoral battles.

Our data, then, offer enough evidence to suggest that structural factors are crucial agents for conditioning certain political dispositions which then become activated at the time of elections. Analysts of voting behaviour emphasize the central importance of the level of general interests in politics and public affairs and strength of identification for predicting the firmness of partisanship. Although we recognize the importance of these variables for ascertaining the degree to which voters manifest firmness of partisan choice, we are not sure about any direct linkage between the two. Contextual studies in political behaviour in particular, and socially rooted behaviour in general, have underscored the fact that several processes mediate between an individual's predisposition and his behaviour.[14] Although this study was not designed to investigate specifically the way certain structural variables intervene between predisposition and action, our data do suggest that certain contextual factors enter into converting or obstructing the conversion of predispositions into action.

It will be readily recognized that certain political attributes of the voter act as potent factors inducing him to behave in a particular way. We have already referred to the fact that strong identification with a political party is one of the political attributes that is conducive to partisan stability. What other attributes can we identify that have salience for the phenomenon of partisan stability or conversion?

To pose this question differently, what are the political attributes that differentiate a consistent voter from, say, a shifter? It may be argued that by rephrasing the question, emphasis has been shifted from identifying political traits that help or hinder partisan stability to enumerating the distinguishing political attributes of regular and other voters. This is, however, not the case. To vote consistently or otherwise is the behavioural reflection of certain social and political predispositional factors. It is not the manifest behaviour that determines the nature of these factors; it is these dispositional factors that are reflected in the voters' behaviour. Given this, it is legitimate to explore the syndrome of these attributes that may be associated with partisan stability or lack of it. If association between two variables

---

14. Among such studies, Emile Durkheim's *Suicide* (Glencoe, III., Free Press 1951) must receive a place of honour in that it pointed to the role of norms concerning divorce mediating in the relationship between marital status and suicide. Recently, Stephen Cole has shown how the presence or absence of social support cross-pressures and structurally determined fear of sanctions mediate between New York teachers' predisposition to strike and their actual behaviour. See his "Teacher's Strike : A Study of the Conversion of Predisposition into Action," *American Journal of Sociology*, LXXIV:5 (March 1969), pp. 506-520.

offers a strong presumption of causal relationship, the factors associated with the phenomenon of partisan stability must also be presumed to be predisposing ones if they are the underlying forces from which action springs. In other words, the concern remains the same even if the way of looking at it is changed.

To return to our question, if consistency in voting over more than one election is a reflection of strong partisan indentification, it follows that shifters, indifferent and non-voters must be characterized by a weak sense of party indentification. In other words, a regular voter is so much attached to his party that even if it seems to be deficient in certain respects, he will most probably ignore them and stick to it through thick and thin. His perception of politically relevant factors is generally coloured by his attachment to his party. The party provides to him a yard-stick for measuring the relevance of different political factors. In contrast, a shifter represents a different kind of political animal. The very act of his transference of allegiance from one party to another indicates his dissatisfaction from one and a hopeful expectation from the other. Why does he shift his allegiance? It is very difficult to answer this question because there is no set pattern behind this phenomenon. However, we can hypothesize basic conditions which may lead a voter to partisanship conversion. In the first place, the reason may lie in purely personal factors; he may be persuaded to believe that the party he has voted for is incapable of protecting or serving his interests. He, therefore, must transfer his allegiance to a party that seems to do better in this regard. In the second place, the voter may not be motivated by self-interest; he may evaluate and judge the performance of the party he voted for previously and may find it lacking. What is important in this regard is his conception of what the party stands for and how useful it is for the political system. And, lastly, the voter may be influenced neither by the sense of self-interest nor by the secular evaluation of the party. He may, on the other hand, be swept away from his partisan course by group pressures emanating from his immediate environment.

It is our belief that the syndrome of political orientations characterizing a shifter would vary depending on what prompts the voter to shift his vote from one party to another. If the reasons for such a shift pertains either to self-interest or to evaluation of party performance in a secular sense, it is our contention that the shifter would manifest a high degree of political interest. If, on the other hand, his partisan preference is susceptible to community environment, he is likely to evince a lower degree of political interest. Apart from this, inasmuch as the phenomenon of partisan shift is dependent upon the knowledge and understanding of political forces and the particular location of various parties among these forces, a shifter more than a regular voter, is likely to take greater interest in politics and public affairs. This leads us also to expect that a shifter will be much more critical of and dissatisfied with the performance of the representative than a regular voter. Given this, however, a regular voter would be much more attached to his party than the shifter. In the case of indifferent voters and non-voters, we can legitimately expect them to be very low on political interest.

In the remainder of this chapter we discuss some of the political attributes that characterize different types of voters. Needless to say that our discussion is informed by the concerns delineated above. As we shall shortly see, our data reveal a great amount of variation in the differential syndrome of these characteristics suggesting the inference that in each of the states certain structural factors intervene to influence the distribution of these attributes from one state to the next. We do not at this stage offer any proof to demonstrate their intervention. However, our data strongly suggest their presence.

In Table 4:6[15] we present information on the level of political interest of different types of voters. It will be immediately noted that only a very small proportion of our respondents in each state shows great interest in politics and public affairs. Punjab is high with 27.6 per cent followed by West Bengal (20.5 per cent), U.P. (15.3 per cent), and Bihar (only 12.0 per cent). About one-third to one-half of our respondents show no interest in politics. Given this low political interest, two patterns seem to emerge from the table. Our hypothesis that more shifters than regular voters will have greater interest in politics is only

---

15. Information presented in this table is based on the question, "Leaving aside the period of election, how much interest do you take in politics and public affairs?"

partly validated. Note, for example, that it is only in Punjab and West Bengal that a larger proportion of shifters as compared to regular voters show a great deal of interest in politics; 33.8 per cent of shifters as compared to 26.3 per cent of regulars in Punjab and 23.2 per cent as against 19.3 per cent in West Bengal. In contrast, in Bihar and U.P., regulars more than shifters are greatly interested in politics: 17.1 per cent of regulars as against 9.7 per cent of shifters in Bihar and 21.6 per cent as against 13.7 per cent in U.P.

Our data, then, amply indicate that it is not necessary that the voters who are unstable in their partisan preference need be greatly interested in politics and public affairs. Our data also suggest that in economically backward states, such as Bihar and U.P., shifters are less interested in politics than their counterparts in economically advanced states like Punjab and West Bengal. This is indicative of the salience of context for interest in politics. It is a well recognized fact that with industrialization taking rapid strides, a qualitative change in the life style of the common man takes place. While greater social mobility liberates the individual from the traditional hold of his milieu, greater physical mobility, exposure to mass media, the need to establish a meaningful relationship with his new environment, etc., induce a greater interest in civic and community affairs."[16] As a result, the voter located in an economically advanced state is much more likely to show greater interest in politics than his counterpart in an economically backward state. Also, his interest in politics will relatively be freer of group influence than that of the voter living in an economically backward state. This is indicated not only by the fact that a larger proportion of voters in Punjab and West Bengal shows greater interest in politics but also by the fact that a larger proportion of shifters than regular voters shows greater interest in politics.

If regular voters and shifters manifest a differential pattern of political interest depending upon the context they are placed in, what about party identification? If partisan stability is a function of strong party identification, it can be expected that

---

16. On this point, see Alex Inkeles, "Making Men Modern : On the Causes and Consequences of Individual Change in Six Developing Countries," *American Journal of Sociology*, LXXV: 2 (September 1969), pp. 208-225.

## TABLE 4 : 6

### Voter Types and Interest in Politics (in per cent)

| States | Voter Types | How much Interest in Politics and Public affairs ||||  Total |
|---|---|---|---|---|---|---|
| | | Great | Some | None | N.A. | |
| 1 | 2 | 3 | 4 | 5 | 6 | 7 |
| BIHAR | Regular | 17.1 | 40.1 | 42.8 | — | (147)100.0 |
| | Shifter | 9.7 | 31.3 | 59.0 | — | ( 83)100.0 |
| | Indifferent | 5.4 | 30.3 | 64.3 | — | ( 56)100.0 |
| | Non-voter | — | 28.5 | 64.2 | 7.3 | ( 14)100.0 |
| | Total | (36)12.0 | (106)35.3 | (157)52.3 | (1)0.3 | (300)100.0 |
| PUNJAB | Regular | 26.3 | 34.0 | 39.7 | — | (176)100.0 |
| | Shifter | 33.8 | 29.0 | 35.5 | 1.7 | ( 62)100.0 |
| | Indifferent | 25.0 | 25.0 | 50.0 | — | ( 12)100.0 |
| | Non-voter | 33.3 | — | 66.7 | — | ( 3)100.0 |
| | Total | (70)27.6 | (80)31.6 | (102)40.3 | (1)0.5 | (253)100.0 |

(Contd.)

| 1 | 2 | 3 | 4 | 5 | 6 | 7 |
|---|---|---|---|---|---|---|
| UTTAR PRADESH | Regular | 21.6 | 35.1 | 42.5 | 0.8 | (148)100.0 |
| | Shifter | 13.7 | 54.3 | 32.0 | — | (103)100.0 |
| | Indifferent | 7.7 | 38.9 | 51.9 | 1.5 | (77)100.0 |
| | Non-voter | 8.8 | 23.5 | 64.7 | 3.0 | (34)100.0 |
| | Total | (55)15.3 | (146)40.3 | (158)43.7 | (3)0.7 | (362)100.0 |
| WEST BENGAL | Regular | 19.3 | 46.7 | 32.2 | 1.8 | (124)100.0 |
| | Shifter | 23.2 | 34.2 | 41.0 | 1.6 | (73)100.0 |
| | Indifferent | 15.9 | 31.5 | 52.6 | — | (19)100.0 |
| | Non-voter | 33.3 | — | 66.7 | — | (3)100.0 |
| | Total | (45)20.5 | (89)40.6 | (82)37.4 | (3)1.5 | (219)100.0 |

regular voters more than shifters or other types of voters will be highly partisan. To demonstrate this we use three separate items to measure the strength of party identification. It can reasonably be argued that an individual with firm party identification will be greatly concerned about electoral outcome. Similarly, he is most likely to vote for the party candidate even if the choice of the candidate does not conform to his own ideas, and will be willing to vote again for the party if called upon to do so. In other words, these are some of the areas in terms of which the strength of party identification of a voter can well be judged. Given the operational usefulness of these items for measuring the strength of partisanship, it can be expected that regular voters more than shifters, will manifest these attributes in greater proportion.

Having posed our hypothesis this way, let us now turn to the data presented in Table 4:7 in order to find whether or not our expectations of electoral behaviour are substantiated. The first item in the table concerns whether or not our respondents cared who won in the election.[17] It is to be again noted that higher the level of economic development, the larger is the proportion of voters caring quite a lot about electoral outcome. In Punjab, for example, 43.5 per cent of our respondents say that they cared quite a lot about who won in the constituency, in West Bengal 42.0 per cent, in Bihar 37.6 per cent and in U.P. only 25.9 per cent. Given this not quite a great interest in the electoral outcome, the fact remains that in all states a large proportion of regular voters, as compared to others, shows greater interest in electoral outcome. This is reflected in the fact that as we move down in the table, the proportion of voters indicating a great interest in the electoral outcome steadily decreases. As a matter of fact, in terms of percentage difference between various categories of voters expressing quite a lot of interest in election results and regular voters constitute a larger proportion than shifters. It is only in U.P. that the proportions of regulars and shifters are equal. The cases of indifferent voters and non-voters need no comments.

---

17. The question reads : "Generally speaking, would you say that you personally cared quite a lot, somewhat, or not at all about who won in the constituency in the elections just held ?"

It can, not unreasonably, be argued that whether or not a voter cares about who wins in the constituency is not a better indicator of strong partisanship. We therefore, present additional, evidence to support our hypothesis. As we indicated earlier, if a voter is strongly attached to a party, he will not think of leaving it even if the candidate put up by the party does not meet his approval.[18] This means that voters with weak partisan loyalty would be most likely to transfer their vote to other party if the candidate choice is wrong. This is very consistently reflected in our data. Note, for example, that in all the states more than 50 per cent of regular voters say that they would stick to the party even if the candidate choice were wrong. In contrast, only one-fourth to one-third of the shifters express their resolve to stick to the party.

We now come to the last item in the table. Through this item we intend to find whether or not the voter would vote the same party/candidate, if called upon to vote again. Admittedly, this pertains to the strength of partisan attachment and we use it as such. Again, we observe the same pattern we found operating with other items in the table. In each state more than 50 per cent of our respondents say that they would vote for the same party or candidate. Given this, however, a larger proportion of regular than other types of voters reflects firm partisan loyalty. Note, for example, that 72.8 per cent of regulars against 48.2 per cent of shifters in Bihar, 77.8 per cent as against 46.8 per cent in Punjab, 77.0 per cent as against 46.6 per cent in U.P. and 61.3 per cent as against 53.4 per cent in West Bengal indicate their willingness to vote for the same party or candidate. The proportions of indifferent and non-voters willing to vote for the same party or candidate are even smaller.

Uptill now our discussion has focussed on the relationship between strength of party identification and partisan stability. We should also examine the argument that one of the indicators of firm partisanship is the timing of voting decision. If a voter

---

18. The question reads, "Suppose there was an election when the party you support was running a candidate that you did not like. What would you do? Would you still vote for your party, or vote for another party or not vote at all in the election?"

TABLE 4 : 7

**Voter Types and Strength of Party Identification (in per cent)**

| States | Voter Types | Cared who won in the Constituency | | | | | What would you do, if you did not like the party candidate? | | | | If voting again, would vote same party? | | | |
|---|---|---|---|---|---|---|---|---|---|---|---|---|---|---|
| | | A lot | Some-what | Not at all | NA | Total | Vote same party | Not vote or vote other party | D.K. | Total | Yes | No and undecided | Others | Total |
| 1 | 2 | 3 | 4 | 5 | 6 | 7 | 8 | 9 | 10 | 11 | 12 | 13 | 14 | 15 |
| BIHAR | Regular | 46.3 | 18.3 | 34.7 | 0.7 | 147 100.0 | 60.5 | 27.2 | 12.3 | 147 100.0 | 72.8 | 26.5 | 0.7 | 147 100.0 |
| | Shifter | 36.1 | 22.9 | 39.8 | 1.2 | 83 100.0 | 33.7 | 49.4 | 16.9 | 83 100.0 | 48.2 | 51.8 | — | 83 100.0 |
| | Indifferent | 19.6 | 19.6 | 60.8 | — | 56 100.0 | 50.0 | 30.4 | 19.6 | 56 100.0 | 44.6 | 37.5 | 17.9 | 56 100.0 |
| | Non-voter | 28.6 | 42.8 | 14.3 | 14.3 | 14 100.0 | 28.6 | 50.0 | 21.4 | 14 100.0 | 28.6 | 14.3 | 57.1 | 14 100.0 |
| | Total | 113 37.6 | 63 21.0 | 120 40.0 | 4 1.4 | 300 100.0 | 149 49.6 | 105 35.0 | 46 15.4 | 300 100.0 | 176 58.7 | 105 35.0 | 19 6.3 | 300 100.0 |

(Contd.)

| 1 | 2 | 3 | 4 | 5 | 6 | 7 | 8 | 9 | 10 | 11 | 12 | 13 | 14 | 15 |
|---|---|---|---|---|---|---|---|---|---|---|---|---|---|---|
| PUNJAB | Regular | 44.9 | 27.9 | 26.1 | 1.1 | 176 100.0 | 54.0 | 33.5 | 12.5 | 176 100.0 | 77.8 | 22.2 | — | 176 100.0 |
|  | Shifter | 38.9 | 30.6 | 30.6 | — | 62 100.0 | 33.9 | 46.8 | 19.3 | 62 100.0 | 46.8 | 51.6 | 1.6 | 62 100.0 |
|  | Indifferent | 41.7 | 8.3 | 50.0 | — | 12 100.0 | 50.0 | 41.7 | 8.3 | 12 100.0 | 41.7 | 50.0 | 8.3 | 12 100.0 |
|  | Non-voter | 66.7 | — | 33.3 | — | 3 100.0 | 33.3 | — | 66.7 | 3 100.0 | — | 100.0 | — | 3 100.0 |
|  | Total | 119 43.5 | 69 27.3 | 72 28.4 | 2 0.8 | 253 100.0 | 123 48.6 | 93 36.8 | 37 14.6 | 253 100.0 | 171 67.6 | 80 31.6 | 2 0.8 | 253 100.0 |
| UTTAR PRADESH | Regular | 29.1 | 31.8 | 37.8 | 1.3 | 148 100.0 | 49.3 | 40.9 | 9.8 | 148 100.0 | 77.0 | 23.0 | — | 148 100.0 |
|  | Shifter | 29.1 | 45.6 | 24.3 | 1.0 | 103 100.0 | 24.3 | 64.1 | 11.6 | 103 100.0 | 46.6 | 53.4 | — | 103 100.0 |
|  | Indifferent | 19.5 | 28.6 | 49.3 | 2.6 | 77 100.0 | 36.4 | 35.1 | 28.5 | 77 100.0 | 42.9 | 37.6 | 19.4 | 77 100.0 |
|  | Non-voter | 17.6 | 8.8 | 70.6 | 3.0 | 34 100.0 | 55.9 | 23.6 | 20.5 | 34 100.0 | 35.3 | 38.1 | 26.6 | 34 100.0 |
|  | Total | 94 25.9 | 119 32.9 | 143 39.6 | 6 1.6 | 362 100.0 | 145 40.1 | 160 44.1 | 57 15.8 | 362 100.0 | 207 57.2 | 131 36.1 | 24 6.7 | 362 100.0 |

*(Contd.)*

| 1 | 2 | 3 | 4 | 5 | 6 | 7 | 8 | 9 | 10 | 11 | 12 | 13 | 14 | 15 |
|---|---|---|---|---|---|---|---|---|---|---|---|---|---|---|
| WEST BENGAL | Regular | 50.0 | 21.8 | 25.8 | 2.4 | 124 100.0 | 55.6 | 29.0 | 15.4 | 124 100.0 | 61.3 | 38.7 | — | 124 100.0 |
| | Shifter | 34.3 | 26.0 | 35.6 | 4.1 | 73 100.0 | 38.4 | 45.2 | 16.4 | 73 100.0 | 53.4 | 46.6 | — | 73 100.0 |
| | Indifferent | 21.1 | 26.3 | 47.4 | 5.2 | 19 100.0 | 52.6 | 26.3 | 21.1 | 19 100.0 | 21.1 | 52.6 | 26.3 | 19 100.0 |
| | Non-voter | 33.3 | — | 66.7 | — | 3 100.0 | 33.3 | 66.7 | — | 3 100.0 | 33.3 | 66.7 | — | 3 100.0 |
| | Total | 92 42.0 | 51 23.3 | 69 31.5 | 7 3.2 | 219 100.0 | 108 49.3 | 76 34.8 | 35 15.9 | 219 100.0 | 122 55.7 | 94 42.9 | 3 1.4 | 219 100.0 |

decides pretty early in the campaign, the strength of his party identification should be treated as high since he does not need other stimuli to come to a decision. In contradistinction to this, a voter who takes a longer time to decide must depend on other stimuli to make up his mind and, as a consequence, he is liable to shift his allegiance from one election to the next depending upon the salience and strength of election stimuli. What do our data suggest? A look at Table 4:8 will suggest that patterns differ from one state to another. If more than 60 per cent of respondents make up their mind even before the campaign starts in Punjab, only 40 per cent do so in U.P. In West Bengal and Bihar only 31 and 20 per cent of respondents respectively decide about their partisan choice much before the campaign starts. Given this, however, there seems to be some association between firm partisanship and earlier voting decision. Note, for example, that in each of the states a larger proportion of regular voters as compared to shifters make up their mind very early. To look at it from a different angle, our data reveal that among those who decide on the polling day itself about whom to vote, shifters constitute a larger proportion than regulars.

The discussion above, then, generally confirms the hypothesis that firm party identification is conducive to consistent voting. To say this, however, does not mean that such a relationship is either direct or quite perfect. Indeed some factors intervene to reinforce or attenuate the conversion of identification into firm partisan choice. What are these mediating factors? For our purposes, we specify two such factors. We assume, first that a voter who actively engages himself in an electoral campaign would be less likely to transfer his allegiance from one party to another. Considering the fact that less than 20 per cent of our respondents claim to have taken part in any electoral campaign, it is legitimate to assume that this small proportion which actively engages in such a campaign can be expected to have a greater degree of political interest and partisan intensity. Moreover, participation in a campaign reflects a forging of firmer identification with a party. Secondly, another mediating factor may possibly be the magnitude of satisfaction or dissatisfaction with the performance of the previous MLA in stabilizing or destabilizing firm partisanship. Our choice of these two indicators is deliberate. It is deliberate in the sense that we think them as

## TABLE 4:8

### Voter types and Timing of Voting Decision (in per cent)

| States | Voter Types | When Decided to Vote? | | | | Inap. | Total |
|---|---|---|---|---|---|---|---|
| | | On polling day | A few days before poll | Soon after campaign started | Before the campaign | | |
| 1 | 2 | 3 | 4 | 5 | 6 | 7 | 8 |
| BIHAR | Regular | 15.0 | 44.2 | 12.9 | 27.9 | — | 147<br>100.0 |
| | Shifter | 30.1 | 31.3 | 20.5 | 18.1 | — | 83<br>100.0 |
| | Indifferent | 23.2 | 35.7 | 14.2 | 7.2 | 19.7 | 56<br>100.0 |
| | Non-voter | — | 28.6 | 14.3 | 14.3 | 42.8 | 14<br>100.0 |
| | Total | 60<br>20.0 | 115<br>38.3 | 46<br>15.5 | 62<br>20.6 | 17<br>5.6 | 300<br>100.0 |

(Contd.)

| 1 | 2 | 3 | 4 | 5 | 6 | 7 | 8 |
|---|---|---|---|---|---|---|---|
| PUNJAB | Regular | 5.1 | 18.2 | 8.0 | 68.7 | — | 176<br>100.0 |
| | Shifter | 6.4 | 32.3 | 14.5 | 46.8 | — | 62<br>100.0 |
| | Indifferent | — | 25.0 | 16.7 | 50.0 | 8.3 | 12<br>100.0 |
| | Non-voter | 33.3 | 33.3 | — | — | 33.3 | 3<br>100.0 |
| | Total | 14<br>5.5 | 56<br>22.1 | 25<br>9.9 | 156<br>61.6 | 2<br>0.9 | 253<br>100.0 |
| UTTAR PRADESH | Regular | 12.8 | 18.9 | 17.6 | 50.0 | 0.7 | 148<br>100.0 |
| | Shifter | 16.5 | 25.2 | 19.4 | 38.9 | — | 103<br>100.0 |
| | Indifferent | 16.9 | 23.4 | 18.2 | 32.5 | 9.0 | 77<br>100.0 |
| | Non-voter | 5.9 | 17.6 | — | 20.6 | 55.9 | 34<br>100.0 |
| | Total | 51<br>14.1 | 78<br>21.5 | 60<br>16.6 | 146<br>40.3 | 27<br>7.5 | 362<br>100.0 |

(*Contd.*)

| 1 | 2 | 3 | 4 | 5 | 6 | 7 | 8 |
|---|---|---|---|---|---|---|---|
| WEST BENGAL | Regular | 13.7 | 32.2 | 20.2 | 33.9 | — | 124 100.0 |
| | Shifter | 27.4 | 28.8 | 10.9 | 32.9 | — | 73 100.0 |
| | Indifferent | 21.1 | 10.5 | 26.3 | 10.5 | 31.6 | 19 100.0 |
| | Non-voter | — | — | 33.3 | — | 66.7 | 3 100.0 |
| | Total | 41 18.7 | 63 28.7 | 39 17.9 | 68 31.0 | 8 3.7 | 219 100.0 |

of immediate significance to the voter. Also, since we have not as yet been able to analyze our data fully, we have to make do with these two factors. However, if these factors are seen to have some impact on the voter's partisanship, it will be enough to demonstrate the salience of mediating factors for partisan choice.

Keeping these limitations in mind, we now turn to Table 4:9 where we juxtapose the responses of our respondents to these two dimensions against voter types. The first item pertains to whether or not our respondents participated in the election campaign. The second refers to their satisfaction with the work their previous MLA did. Looking at the table, we note that the regular voters more than shifters take part in election campaigns. The only exception is West Bengal where more shifters than regulars participate in election campaigns. In Punjab, however, there is only a difference of about two percentage points between the regulars and the shifters who claim to have campaign experience. In other words, then, campaign experience does not seem to be very potent in reinforcing partisanship.

What about satisfaction with the previous MLA? In each of the states, it can be seen, operates a consistent pattern; a large proportion of voters who express satisfaction with the performance of their previous MLA are regular voters. Also, in all the four states, the proportion of the satisfied regular voters is larger than that of dissatisfied regular voters. Further, in each state the proportion of dissatisfied shifters is larger than that of dissatisfied regulars. This suggests that while making voting decision, a larger number of our respondents are also influenced by the consideration of how the previous MLA has performed. If dissatisfied with his performance, many of these voters are likely to vote for another candidate or party when they find their party putting up the same MLA as its candidate. Thus, the evaluation of the performance of the previous MLA seems to be a salient mediating factor.

Our discussion highlights some of the factors that impinge upon the phenomenon of partisan stability. In brief, we focussed our attention on two sets of such factors: socio-economic background variables and certain political attributes. We argued that socio-economic background variables are crucial conditioning factors that shape and influence, to a considerable extent, the political attributes of voters placed in different life situations.

## TABLE 4 : 9
### Voter Types, Campaign Participation, and Satisfaction with MLA (in per cent)

| States | Voter Types | Participated in Campaign ? | | | | Satisfaction with Previous MLA | | | |
|---|---|---|---|---|---|---|---|---|---|
| | | Yes | No | NA | Total | Yes | No | NA | Total |
| 1 | 2 | 3 | 4 | 5 | 6 | 7 | 8 | 9 | 10 |
| BIHAR | Regular | 25.2 | 74.8 | — | 147<br>100.0 | 57.1 | 36.0 | 6.9 | 147<br>100.0 |
| | Shifter | 8.5 | 91.5 | — | 83<br>100.0 | 46.9 | 45.7 | 7.4 | 83<br>100.0 |
| | Indifferent | 14.3 | 85.7 | — | 56<br>100.0 | 53.5 | 32.1 | 14.4 | 56<br>100.0 |
| | Non-voter | 21.5 | 78.5 | — | 14<br>100.0 | 42.8 | 28.6 | 28.6 | 14<br>100.0 |
| | Total | 55<br>18.3 | 245<br>81.7 | — | 300<br>100.0 | 159<br>53.0 | 113<br>39.6 | 28<br>9.3 | 300<br>100.0 |

(*Contd.*)

| 1 | 2 | 3 | 4 | 5 | 6 | 7 | 8 | 9 | 10 |
|---|---|---|---|---|---|---|---|---|---|
| PUNJAB | Regular | 24.4 | 75.6 | — | 176<br>100.0 | 65.3 | 29.5 | 5.2 | 176<br>100.0 |
| | Shifter | 22.6 | 77.4 | — | 62<br>100.0 | 45.1 | 40.3 | 14.6 | 62<br>100.0 |
| | Indifferent | 25.0 | 75.0 | — | 12<br>100.0 | 25.0 | 25.0 | 50.0 | 12<br>100.0 |
| | Non-voter | — | 100.0 | — | 3<br>100.0 | — | — | 100.0 | 3<br>100.0 |
| | Total | 60<br>23.7 | 193<br>76.3 | — | 253<br>100.0 | 146<br>57.7 | 80<br>31.5 | 27<br>10.8 | 253<br>100.0 |
| UTTAR<br>PRADESH | Regular | 20.9 | 78.3 | 0.8 | 148<br>100.0 | 66.2 | 27.0 | 6.8 | 148<br>100.0 |
| | Shifter | 10.6 | 82.3 | 1.1 | 103<br>100.0 | 57.3 | 30.1 | 12.6 | 103<br>100.0 |
| | Indifferent | 14.3 | 84.4 | 1.3 | 77<br>100.0 | 57.1 | 41.2 | 1.7 | 77<br>100.0 |
| | Non-voter | 2.9 | 94.1 | 2.9 | 34<br>100.0 | 32.3 | 35.5 | 32.4 | 34<br>100.0 |
| | Total | 54<br>14.9 | 304<br>83.9 | 4<br>1.2 | 362<br>100.0 | 212<br>58.8 | 105<br>29.0 | 45<br>12.2 | 362<br>100.0 |

(Contd.)

| 1 | 2 | 3 | 4 | 5 | 6 | 7 | 8 | 9 | 10 |
|---|---|---|---|---|---|---|---|---|---|
| WEST BENGAL | Regular | 16.9 | 82.2 | 0.9 | 124<br>100.0 | 53.2 | 35.5 | 11.3 | 124<br>100.0 |
| | Shifter | 19.2 | 80.8 | — | 73<br>100.0 | 41.1 | 42.3 | 16.6 | 73<br>100.0 |
| | Indifferent | 21.1 | 78.9 | — | 19<br>100.0 | 57.9 | 21.0 | 21.1 | 19<br>100.0 |
| | Non-voter | 33.3 | 66.7 | — | 3<br>100.0 | — | 66.7 | 33.3 | 3<br>100.0 |
| | Total | 40<br>18.2 | 178<br>81.3 | 1<br>0.5 | 219<br>100.0 | 107<br>48.8 | 81<br>36.9 | 31<br>14.3 | 219<br>100.0 |

Given this, however, political attributes are major determinants of regularity and consistency in voting. Our data amply suggest that strong party identification is one of the most crucial variables in influencing partisan stability. While the importance of party identification must be recognized, when we come to political interest, the evidence at our disposal points to two distinct patterns. In economically advanced states, shifters are much more likely to be greatly interested in politics than regular voters. In contrast, in economically backward states, the pattern is reversed. However, different types of voters are characterised by differential syndrome of socio-economic as well as political variables. Moreover, the differential patterning of these attributes in different states strongly suggests the crucial importance of contextual factors for partisan stability.

# CHAPTER FIVE
# *Political Profile of Voters*

IN chapter four we discussed some factors that impinge upon firmness in partisan choice. Our discussion underlined the very crucial conditioning effect of socio-economic background variables on the acquisition effect of certain political dispositions, on the one hand, and the firmness of partisan choice on the other. We also referred to two different ways in which such variables operate to shape political dispositions. In the first place, the differing socio-economic background in itself constitutes a resource base which allows an individual to acquire certain capabilities—a certain level of mental and social attainments. These capabilities symbolize certain orientations towards objects that impinge either remotely or intimately on the individual's self-defined realm of relevance.

In the second place, the location of the individual in a particular socio-economic situation defines for him not only the dominant interest of his life but also the pattern of his interaction with his immediate environment. Whether the individual is only vaguely aware of his interest or quite clear and articulate about it does not matter as long as he can relate the protection or advancement of his interest to certain categories of political tendencies, events, etc. With a change in the objective conditions influencing his conception of what serves his interest, the individual is likely to re-examine the implications of the changing situation and take suitable steps to protect his interest. Thus, at certain points in time, the individual may, due to certain contingencies, shift his ground and forge fresh alignments. That this happens is positively substantiated by our data. What is even more important in this regard is the fact that differing socio-economic backgrounds lead to different patterns of realignment.

This should all the more draw our attention to the fact that short-term factors affecting voters' choice are as, if not more, important as the long-term tendencies. After all, it is short-term factors that at crucial points in electoral politics determine the long-term trends in the development of the party system, in general, and lay the structure of party competition, in particular. Since the role of the electorate in influencing these developments is very crucial, the behaviour of the electorate in regard to the normal course of political processes in general, and electoral policies in particular, assumes a theoretical significance. In even more important a sense, despite the discouraging findings of empirical studies in voting behaviour that emphasize the generally low level of the citizens' interest in and concern with politics and public affairs and their vulnerability to demagogic manipulation of momentary passions and emotions, it is the electorate that sits in judgment on what competing political activitists and leaders promise to do and, more important, succeed or fail to do. It is certain that objective and dispassionate evaluation of promises fulfilled and broken is not possible since electoral verdict is generally the outcome of conflicting partisan passions.

Given the intimate relationship between electoral verdict and the quality of partisanship, we have noted the salience of socio-economic background for instilling and, when necessary, activating certain dispositions controlling behaviour. However, socio-economic background is only one part of the story. It is not rare to find persons breaking through the restraints created by their low socio-economic status, rising above their own level and forging new interests and concerns. It is also not rare to find persons who, though favoured by good fortune, fail to make good use of their resources and, therefore, slip back to a low level of mental attainment. In sum, then, socio-economic background can best be treated as a conditioning factor defining for an individual the range of opportunities he can or cannot exploit.

The recognition of the importance of socio-economic background, however, should not obscure the fact that it is the first, albeit a very important, landmark in the individual's journey of life. In the course of this journey he is exposed to new vistas, acquires new perspectives, and gathers new experiences. He increases his stock of information, gives an endurable shape to his interests and engages in actions that promise to protect or advance his interest. In other words, for a meaningful analysis of the electorates' role in sustaining and preserving a democratic form of political system, we have necessarily to go beyond the mere location of the individual in social geography. We have to take into consideration the crucial facts of his biographical situation which define for him the arena of his action, provide guidelines for interpreting its possibilities, and propel him to engage its challenges. As Natanson succinctly puts it:

...Even the determination of what the individual can modify or not modify is affected by his unique situation. The funded experience of a life, what a phenomenologist would call the 'sedimented' structure of the individual's experience, is the condition for subsequent interpretation of all new events and activities. 'The' world becomes transposed into 'my' world in accordance with the relevant elements of my biographical situation.[1]

This is simply to suggest that the range of experiences the individual goes through, the interest he has come to hold and works for, the capabilities he has developed to meaningfully interact with his environment—all these factors become relevant for the nature and quality of responses the individual makes to stimuli that are channelled in his direction. No matter what his interests and concerns are and how they are affected by environmental pressures, the individual is bound to endow his interests and concerns with relevance and interpret the implications of the impinging forces in the light of his primordial range of experiences. To quote Natanson again, "Although we have special concerns and interests in our roles, we are forever rooted in a primordial range of experience out of which these concerns and interests arise and to which they remain connected."[2]

The primordial range of experience of the individual then becomes a crucial guidepost for checking his orientations and attitudes towards political objects. We should also note the fact that it is through this primordial range of experiences that the individual attributes certain meaning to the social reality manifested in the institutional structures, cultural patterns and normative elements. This, then, constitutes for us a major dimension symbolizing the profile of the individual's subjective

---

1. Maurice Natanson in Alfred Schutz, *Collected Papers,* edited by Maurice Natanson, (The Hague: Martinus Nijhoff, 1962), Vol. I; Introduction, p. xxviii.
2. *Ibid.*

reality from which spring actions directed towards affecting, modifying or changing the environment. It is through the exploration of this subjective reality that we can gain some glimpses of how the individual views his interaction with the environment and in what ways he contemplates to set such interactions, if at all, on a new footing.

Formulated thus, the primordial range of experience points to the necessity of, first, ascertaining the nature of the individual's realm of relevance, his perception of his relationship with the environment, his evaluation of such a relationship for its implications for the realization of his own interests and concerns and the intention that all these lead him to articulate. Three importance facets of the individual's subjective reality can then be specified as having important bearings on the individual's interaction with his environment. In the first place, we must be clear about what the individual's perceptions are in respect of the external objects, both remote and near, and how they are relevant not only for him but also for the web of identifications he is encumbered with. In the second place, we must ascertain the extent to which the individual possesses information requisite for evaluating the relative importance of various events, processes and procedures as they impinge on his own realm of relevance. And, lastly, given the perceptual as well as the cognitive aspects of the individual's subjective reality, we should also explore the way he evaluates different objects in terms not only of how useful they are but also how effective they turn out to be in assuring the maintenance and further creation of certain facilities and services that make the life of the individual much more comfortable.

The relevance of these considerations for the research concern at hand cannot be overstressed. The unique biographical situation of the individual defines for him not only the interests and concerns he may have but also his relationship with the environment and a personalized salience of such a relationship for pursuit of his interests and concerns. The socio-economic background constitutes only a part of such a biographical situation. Not less important are factors that relate to the individual's perspective on the external objects, his understanding, of these objects as they relate to his own realm of relevance, and his capabilities to effectively cope with environmental pressures.

Given the crucial theoretical importance of these dimensions for reconstructing and appraising the nature of social reality, we need, however, to translate them into appropriate operational categories for the purpose at hand. Our concern, it may again be emphasized, relates to exploring the ways in which the unique biographical situation of each of the voters enters in his participation, through periodic elections, in shaping democratic institutions in a country like India. Besides his location in the social space, we are also interested in ascertaining his perspective on the democratic institutional structure which for him constitutes a significant environmental factor and whose functioning impinges on him in manifold ways. It may be that he is not aware either of this structure or the way it impinges on him. However, with the increasing penetration of these institutions into realms very close to the voter's life, he has to take note of them, respond to them and use them according to his own lights. In view of this, no matter what the salience of these institutions for the voter, he has to develop a perspective that relates his own interests and concerns with the adopted institutions. This perspective is, in the last analysis, composed of the voter's knowledge of, interest in, and affective orientations based on certain evaluative criteria towards these institutions. The last consideration is important inasmuch as institutional structures become meaningful when they appear to serve certain needs of the voter and seem to be doing so effectively.

To be more specific, we turn in this and subsequent chapters to examining the extent to which our respondents manifest certain of the attributes that are supposed to be essential for maintaining and preserving democratic institutions. In very general terms, it is suggested that the electorate must have at least a generalized awareness of and commitment to the basic principles of the functioning of democratic institutions.[3] Even if viewed from this perspective, a set of attributes relevant for exploring the degree of the electorate's awareness of and commitment to democratic norms can be identified. To specify these attributes, mention may be made of the electorate's level

---

3. Peter Y. Medding, "Elitist' Democracy : An Unsuccessful Critique of a Misunderstood Theory," *The Journal of Politics*, XXXI : 3 (August 1969), p. 650.

of politically relevant information, the level of its political interests, its identification with certain parties, involvement with politics, its understanding of the functioning of democratic political process, its sense of legitimacy of democratic institutions and a sense of political efficacy.

We begin this chapter with a discussion of the extent to which our respondents are politically informed, evince interest in political matters, engage themselves in electoral activities and manifest identification with a particular political party. We reserve the discussion of other themes for subsequent chapters. Our interest in these dimensions is not simply to indicate how our respondents score on these. More importantly, we are interested in finding out what, in fact, are some of the determinants of the differential configurations of politically relevant attributes in the case of different individuals.

We begin first with demonstrating the relationship, if any, between socio-economic status of our respondents and their levels of information, interests, electoral involvement and identification. We then go on to examine the relationship between these attributes themselves. In Table 5:1 is presented information on the socio-economic status of our respondents and the level of their political information.[4] It is at once apparent that the higher the socio-economic status, the higher, generally, is the level of information. Given this, however, there are variations from one state to the next. Note, for example, that more than two-thirds of our respondents in Punjab score high on the index of political information as compared to other states. Even in Bihar, quite a backward state from any standard, more than half (58.5 per cent) of our respondents are high on this index.

---

4. The index of political information is derived from two questions. (i) Who was the M. L. A. elected from your constituency in 1967? (ii) Who won the election recently held in your constituency? These two questions, it will be seen, refer only to items that are not difficult for a politically interested voter to answer in as much as the MLA as a political functionary is usually not only a well-known person in the constituency but also a crucial link between the voter and the citizen seeking to influence some administrative decision. We, therefore, selected these two items among several as being most salient for reflecting the level of our respondent's political information.

In contrast, only 51.4 per cent of respondents in both U.P. and West Bengal score high on this index.

Relating this to socio-economic status in each state gives us a somewhat different picture. It is in Punjab, again that we find 86.9 per cent of those who are high on SES are also high on information. U.P. and West Bengal show equal proportions of respondents high on SES scoring high also on information. It is in Bihar that the proportion of respondents coming from high socio-economic background scoring high on information is the lowest of all states. Viewed from a different angle, the proportion of those who are low both on SES and information is largest in West Bengal followed by U.P., Bihar and Punjab in that order.

It should, however, be pointed out that the differential impact of socio-economic status on the voters' level of political information seems to be least in Punjab and most in West Bengal. Notice that a large proportion of voters enjoying higher social status in Bihar seems not to care much about relevant political facts as compared to other states. In Punjab, socio-economic status does not make that much difference in regard to voter's acquisition of salient political facts inasmuch as a large proportion of voters from all social strata claim to know who their previous MLA was and who successfully fought the 1969 election. In U.P. and West Bengal, in contrast, voters at the lowest rung of social hierarchy are prone to be unconcerned about important political facts. This is probably indicative of the fact that a sizeable number of voters from socially depressed sectors feel less stake in politics than elsewhere. This is perhaps also indicative of the perception of their inability to effectively influence the course of public affairs in their own milieu.

Our data, then, adequately support the hypothesis that the socio-economic background of the respondent is very important for acquiring political information. Another important factor is age of the respondent. We referred earlier to the relationship between electoral experience and firm partisanship. It is argued that the forging of firm party identification is a function of habituation; that is, the more a person participates in electoral politics, the more likely he is to develop firm party loyalty. By the same token, it can also be argued that a voter voting for the first time may not be that interested in knowing about

TABLE 5 : 1

SES and Information (in per cent)

| SES | Bihar High | Bihar Medium | Bihar Low | Bihar Total | Punjab High | Punjab Medium | Punjab Low | Punjab Total | U.P. High | U.P. Medium | U.P. Low | U.P. Total | W.B. High | W.B. Medium | W.B. Low | W.B. Total |
|---|---|---|---|---|---|---|---|---|---|---|---|---|---|---|---|---|
| High | 69.7 | 21.1 | 9.2 | 76 / 100.0 | 86.9 | 11.5 | 1.6 | 61 / 100.0 | 78.9 | 17.1 | 3.9 | 76 / 100.0 | 78.7 | 11.5 | 9.8 | 61 / 100.0 |
| Medium | 59.9 | 25.4 | 14.8 | 142 / 100.0 | 79.1 | 18.2 | 2.7 | 148 / 100.0 | 53.4 | 32.3 | 14.3 | 189 / 100.0 | 52.0 | 32.8 | 15.2 | 125 / 100.0 |
| Low | 49.6 | 29.4 | 21.0 | 119 / 100.0 | 70.7 | 24.4 | 4.9 | 82 / 100.0 | 35.0 | 33.8 | 31.2 | 157 / 100.0 | 23.0 | 44.3 | 32.8 | 61 / 100.0 |
| NA | 66.7 | 33.3 | — | 3 / 100.0 | 100.0 | — | — | 1 / 100.0 | 66.6 | 16.7 | 16.7 | 6 / 100.0 | 50.0 | 50.0 | — | 2 / 100.0 |
| Total | 199 / 58.5 | 88 / 25.9 | 53 / 15.6 | 340 / 100.0 | 229 / 78.4 | 54 / 18.5 | 9 / 3.1 | 292 / 100.0 | 220 / 51.4 | 128 / 29.9 | 80 / 18.7 | 428 / 100.0 | 128 / 51.4 | 76 / 30.5 | 45 / 18.1 | 249 / 100.0 |

C = 0.164    C = 0.142    C = 0.322    C = 0.374

diverse political facts. However, with growing exposure to electoral politics, he may be expected to show greater awareness of these facts. We need to consider one further point in this connection. Advancing age means a greater collection of diverse experiences and, therefore, accumulation of a lot of information on diverse subjects. Would not this, then, mean that older the voter, greater the store of political information. Two considerations deserve our attention. In the first place, with advancing age is associated also the phenomenon of forgetfulness and a gradual attenuation of the intensity of political interest and, therefore, a lesser inclination to collect political facts. In the second place, with the gradual expansion in educational facilities, young voters are more likely to have gone through some schooling and, therefore, more inclined to equip themselves with relevant political facts.

What do our data suggest? Relevant information in this regard is presented in Table 5:2. Two distinct patterns emerge. First, a very large proportion of young voters score very high on the index of political information in each of the states. While in Punjab 81.7 per cent of voters in the age group 21-30 are high on political information, the corresponding figures for other states are also high: Bihar 61.6 per cent, West Bengal 56.1 per cent and U.P. 49.2 per cent. However, it is in the 31-40 age group that the largest proportion of highly informed voters can be located in three states: Bihar, Punjab and U.P. In the case of the former two states, as age of the voter advances, the proportion of highly informed voters declines after the age of 40. In other words, participation in elections tends to swell the ranks of politically informed voters. But, then, after one has crossed the age of forty, interest in things political seems to decline. In contrast, in U.P. and West Bengal there seems to operate another tendency. In West Bengal, for example, the largest proportion of highly informed voters is to be found among the youngest voters. After the age of thirty, however, the proportion of highly informed voters declines and then slowly rises in other age groups. In U.P., the proportion of highly informed voters increases in the 31-40 age group, then declines in the 41-50 and again rises in the 51-and-over age group. The fact, however, remains that younger voters are more likely to be politically informed than older voters.

TABLE 5:2

Age and Level of Political Information (in per cent)

| States | Bihar | | | | Punjab | | | | U.P. | | | | W.B. | | | |
|---|---|---|---|---|---|---|---|---|---|---|---|---|---|---|---|---|
| Level of Political Information / Age (in years) | High | Medium | Low | Total | High | Medium | Low | Total | High | Medium | Low | Total | High | Medium | Low | Total |
| Below 21 | 86.6 | 6.7 | 6.7 | 15 / 100.0 | 20.0 | 60.0 | 20.0 | 5 / 100.0 | — | 50.0 | 50.0 | 4 / 100.0 | — | — | — | — |
| 21—30 | 61.6 | 26.8 | 11.6 | 112 / 100.0 | 81.7 | 16.5 | 1.8 | 109 / 100.0 | 49.2 | 35.3 | 15.5 | 136 / 100.0 | 56.1 | 30.1 | 13.8 | 96 / 100.0 |
| 31—40 | 64.0 | 22.1 | 13.9 | 95 / 100.0 | 82.0 | 18.0 | — | 61 / 100.0 | 55.6 | 27.3 | 17.1 | 99 / 100.0 | 47.0 | 33.0 | 20.0 | 70 / 100.0 |
| 41—50 | 49.0 | 26.3 | 24.7 | 57 / 100.0 | 78.5 | 19.6 | 1.9 | 51 / 100.0 | 50.1 | 29.9 | 20.0 | 80 / 100.0 | 48.6 | 27.0 | 24.4 | 37 / 100.0 |
| 51+ | 46.0 | 34.4 | 19.6 | 61 / 100.0 | 74.3 | 18.9 | 6.8 | 66 / 100.0 | 52.3 | 25.7 | 22.0 | 109 / 100.0 | 50.0 | 30.3 | 19.7 | 40 / 100.0 |
| Total | 199 / 58.5 | 88 / 25.9 | 53 / 15.6 | 340 / 100.0 | 229 / 78.4 | 54 / 18.5 | 9 / 3.1 | 292 / 100.0 | 220 / 51.4 | 128 / 29.9 | 80 / 18.7 | 428 / 100.0 | 128 / 51.4 | 76 / 30.5 | 45 / 18.1 | 249 / 100.0 |

We have noted the effect of socio-economic status and age on the acquisition of political information. The index of socio-economic status, as we have already pointed out, is composed of caste, education, land/income. As such, the inclusion of education in the index may be responsible for producing higher proportion of voters who are high both on status and information. But it would be only partially true since education by itself would not place a voter in the high status category. To be so placed, the voter needs to belong to higher castes and higher income or land-ownership brackets. It is the conjunction of all these factors that accounts for the location of an individual in a particular status category. It follows, then, that, by virtue of being placed in the high category of the socio-economic status, the individual is assured of the availability of certain resources that help him acquire certain knowledge. Given the salience of socio-economic status for disposing towards or enabling for acquiring politically relevant information, the young age becomes another crucial factor in this connection.

If the acquisition of political information is so dependent on socio-economic status and age, what about political interest? Information on this aspect of our enquiry is presented in Table 5:3. Our index of political interest, as pointed out earlier, refers to general interest in politics and public affairs and is, therefore, distinct from the index of electoral involvement inasmuch as the latter purports to tap actual involvement of our respondents in campaigns and other election activities. As will be seen from the table, only a very small proportion of our respondents is high on political interest: only 26.0 per cent in Punjab, 19.7 per cent in West Bengal and a little over 12 per cent in both U.P. and Bihar.

Given this, however, socio-economic status does make a difference in respect of general interest in politics and public affairs. Notice that in each of the states a pattern indicating a relationship between high SES and a high level of political interest operates consistently. To be more specific, the percentage difference between high and low-statused respondents in terms of high political interest is 19 per cent, in Punjab 36 per cent, in U.P. 28 per cent and in West Bengal 24 per cent. Also interesting is the fact that even in the case of medium level of political interest, status differences make quite an impact.

TABLE 5 : 3

SES and Political Interest (in per cent)

| States | Bihar | | | | Punjab | | | | U.P. | | | | W.B. | | | |
|---|---|---|---|---|---|---|---|---|---|---|---|---|---|---|---|---|
| Political Interest \ SES | High | Medium | Low | Total | High | Medium | Low | Total | High | Medium | Low | Total | High | Medium | Low | Total |
| High | 23.7 | 44.7 | 31.6 | 76 100.0 | 41.0 | 41.0 | 18.0 | 61 100.0 | 31.6 | 55.3 | 13.2 | 76 100.0 | 32.8 | 52.5 | 14.8 | 16 100.0 |
| Medium | 13.4 | 33.1 | 53.5 | 142 100.0 | 31.8 | 39.2 | 29.1 | 148 100.0 | 12.7 | 51.9 | 35.4 | 189 100.0 | 19.2 | 45.6 | 35.2 | 125 100.0 |
| Low | 3.4 | 36.1 | 60.5 | 119 100.0 | 4.9 | 24.4 | 70.7 | 82 100.0 | 3.8 | 42.7 | 53.5 | 157 100.0 | 8.2 | 39.2 | 52.5 | 61 100.0 |
| NA | — | 33.3 | 66.7 | 3 100.0 | — | 100.0 | — | 1 100.0 | — | 83.3 | 16.7 | 6 100.0 | — | 100.0 | — | 2 100.0 |
| Total | 41 12.1 | 125 36.8 | 174 51.2 | 340 100.0 | 76 26.0 | 104 35.6 | 112 38.4 | 292 100.0 | 54 12.6 | 212 49.5 | 162 37.9 | 428 100.0 | 49 19.7 | 115 46.2 | 85 34.1 | 249 100.0 |
| | C=0.269 TC=0.201 | | | | C=0.411 TC=0.307 | | | | C=0.348 TC=0.352 | | | | C=0.306 TC=0.141 | | | |

Except in the case of Bihar as status level decreases the proportion of respondents also diminishes. Moreover, on the basis of contingency coefficients and Kendall's Tau—two different measures of association between ordinal scales—the relationship between SES and political interest must be inferred to be quite strong.

It is then beyond doubt that the socio-economic status both as a conditioning factor and as a resource base has a great amount of influence on a voter's interest in public affairs. Can this be said of the relationship between age and political interest? As will be seen from Table 5:4, there are discernible two patterns of relationship between age and political interest. First, in the case of Bihar and West Bengal, as the voter grows older he seems to be less interested in public affairs. To put it differently, it is only in the younger age cohorts that a larger proportion of voters taking greater interest in political matters is to be found. This suggests that it is largely in the early stages of electoral participation that a sizeable number of voters show interest in public affairs. This interest, however, declines when one goes through the excitement of electoral process once or twice. It should, however, be noted that relatively more younger voters score high on the index of political interest in West Bengal than is the case in Bihar. While in Bihar only about 18 per cent of young voters are high on interest, their proportion shoots up to 27 per cent in West Bengal.

In contradistinction to this, in Punjab and U.P. advancing age does not seem to dim our respondents' interest in public affairs. Note, for example, that while only 26.7 per cent of young voters in the age group 21-30 are high on political interest, 28.0 per cent in the 31-40 age group and 29.5 per cent in the 41-50 age group manifest high interest in politics. It is only in the 51 plus age group that the proportion of voters high on interest drops down to 22.7 per cent. In U.P., on the other hand, it is in the 31-40 age group that the largest proportion of our respondents expressing a greater degree of interest in politics is to be found. However, compared to voters in the 21-30 age group, the proportion of voters with high interest in politics is larger in other age groups.

Given the variations in the amount of political interest our respondents in different states manifest, it should once again

TABLE 5 : 4

Age and Political Interest (in per cent)

| States | Bihar | | | | Punjab | | | | U.P. | | | | W.B. | | | |
|---|---|---|---|---|---|---|---|---|---|---|---|---|---|---|---|---|
| Level of Political Interest / Age (in years) | High | Medium | Low | Total | High | Medium | Low | Total | High | Medium | Low | Total | High | Medium | Low | Total |
| Below 21 | 6.7 | 46.7 | 46.7 | 15 100.0 | — | 20.0 | 80.0 | 5 100.0 | — | 25.0 | 75.0 | 4 100.0 | — | — | — | — |
| 21—30 | 17.9 | 39.3 | 42.8 | 112 100.0 | 26.7 | 37.6 | 35.7 | 109 100.0 | 11.8 | 58.8 | 29.4 | 136 100.0 | 27.0 | 5.0 | 23.0 | 96 100.0 |
| 31—40 | 15.8 | 35.8 | 48.4 | 95 100.0 | 28.0 | 40.9 | 31.1 | 61 100.0 | 14.2 | 56.6 | 29.2 | 99 100.0 | 18.6 | 47.1 | 34.3 | 70 100.0 |
| 41—50 | 7.1 | 35.0 | 57.9 | 57 100.0 | 29.5 | 33.3 | 37.2 | 51 100.0 | 12.5 | 45.0 | 42.5 | 80 100.0 | 18.9 | 37.9 | 43.2 | 37 100.0 |
| 51+ | 2.6 | 32.8 | 65.6 | 61 100.0 | 22.7 | 30.3 | 47.0 | 66 100.0 | 12.9 | 35.7 | 51.4 | 109 100.0 | 6.5 | 43.5 | 50.0 | 46 100.0 |
| Total | 41 12.1 | 125 36.8 | 174 51.2 | 340 100.0 | 76 26.0 | 103 35.6 | 112 38.4 | 292 100.0 | 54 12.6 | 212 49.5 | 162 37.9 | 428 100.0 | 49 19.7 | 115 46.2 | 85 34.1 | 249 100.0 |

be emphasized, that, by any standard, voters in these states seem less interested in public affairs. The gap between their level of information and that of interest is quite marked. This is indicative of the fact that mere acquisition of information on politically relevant facts is not enough to arouse an enduring interest in public affairs. This can be verified from Table 5:5. Notice that, in Bihar, as against only 12.1 per cent of respondents high on interest, 58.5 per cent are high on information. This wide gap between the level of information and that of interest is noticeable in the case of other states too. In Punjab, only 26 per cent of respondents are high on political interest while 78.4 per cent are high on information, in U.P., 12.6 per cent versus 57.4 per cent and in West Bengal 19.7 per cent as against 51.4 per cent. Note also the fact that out of those high on information, only 17.1 per cent of respondents in Bihar are high on political interest. The highest incidence of highly informed voters showing also a high degree of interest in politics is discernible only in Punjab. While West Bengal follows closely the pattern in Punjab, U.P. is closer to Bihar.

That possession of politically relevant information does not necessarily insure a high level of interest in politics and public affairs is quite clear. On the contrary, our data suggest that it is rather the level of political interest that determines the quantum of information a voter may have. This can be ascertained by examining column percentages in Table 5:5. Note, for example, that out of those in Bihar who manifest a high degree of political interest, 82.9 per cent are also high on the level of information. This observation is equally applicable to other states. In Punjab, 86.8 per cent of those high on interest are also high on information, in U.P. 72.2 per cent and in West Bengal 63.3 per cent—the lowest incidence so far. It is, then, apparent that once a voter begins taking interest in politics, he is likely to acquire relevant political information to keep his interest alive.

We have so far discussed the relationship between SES, age, level of information and that of political interest. The exploration of the two dimensions, i.e., the level of our respondent's information and interest does not allow us to determine the degree to which voters may be disposed to actively engage in politics. Even politically inert or alienated citizens

TABLE 5 : 5

Information and Political Interest (in per cent)

| Information \ Interest | Bihar | | | | Punjab | | | | U.P. | | | | W.B. | | | |
|---|---|---|---|---|---|---|---|---|---|---|---|---|---|---|---|---|
| | High | Medium | Low | Total | High | Medium | Low | Total | High | Medium | Low | Total | High | Medium | Low | Total |
| High | 17.1 (82.9)* | 40.7 (64.8) | 42.2 (48.3) | 199 100.0 | 28.8 (86.8) | 39.3 (86.5) | 31.9 (65.2) | 229 100.0 | 17.7 (72.2) | 54.5 (56.6) | 27.7 (37.7) | 220 100.0 | 24.2 (83.3) | 53.1 (59.1) | 22.7 (34.1) | 128 100.0 |
| Medium | 6.8 (14.6) | 34.1 (24.0) | 59.1 (29.9) | 88 100.0 | 16.7 (11.8) | 25.9 (13.5) | 57.4 (27.7) | 54 100.0 | 8.6 (20.4) | 50.8 (30.7) | 40.6 (32.1) | 128 100.0 | 14.5 (22.4) | 46.1 (30.4) | 39.5 (35.3) | 76 100.0 |
| Low | 1.9 (2.4) | 26.4 (11.2) | 71.7 (21.8) | 53 100.0 | 11.1 (1.3) | — | 88.9 (7.1) | 9 100.0 | 5.0 (7.4) | 33.7 (12.7) | 61.2 (30.2) | 80 100.0 | 15.6 (14.3) | 26.7 (10.4) | 57.8 (30.6) | 45 100.0 |
| Total | 41 12.1 | 125 36.8 | 174 51.2 | 340 100.0 | 76 26.0 | 104 35.6 | 112 38.4 | 292 100.0 | 54 12.6 | 212 49.5 | 162 37.9 | 428 100.0 | 49 19.7 | 115 46.2 | 85 34.1 | 249 100.0 |
| | C=0.246 | | | | C=0.267 | | | | C=0.267 | | | | C=0.277 | | | |
| | TC=0.199 | | | | TC=0.159 | | | | TC=0.220 | | | | TC=0.119 | | | |

* Figures in parentheses denote percentages calculated from column totals.

may be better politically informed and may evince a greater interest in political matters. The spirit of democratic institutions, stipulates one further condition besides requiring citizens to be politically well-informed and to take sustained interest in public affairs. This stipulation refers to the necessity of their active participation in decision-making processes so that they may exert influence on political rulers and prevent any tendency in the rulers towards self-aggrandizement. It is, therefore, necessary to ascertain the degree to which our respondents manifest the attribute of political activeness.

As a host of studies in voting behaviour reveals, despite the legal norm of universal adult citizenship in democratic politics, the actual level of political activeness of the citizen is quite low.[5] The voters in India are no exception to this. And yet the vigour of democratic institutions depends on the degree to which voters engage themselves in diverse political activities. These political activities may range from a deliberate attempt to influence the formulation of a particular policy to the ritualistic act of voting. Given this wide range of activities through which citizens may participate in political processes, it is also of interest to indicate that citizen participation is aimed either at bringing about, or preventing the bringing about, of a particular state of affairs. Also, this purposive action must take effect through a complex network of institutional arrangement in which political parties occupy a crucial position. As a matter of fact, for most voters strong identification with a particular party seems to be a very weak relationship between the socio-economic status of a voter and the strength of his partisan identification. It is only in the case of Punjab that a consistent pattern reflecting high status leading to a greater degree of partisan identification can be observed. It is true that a larger proportion of strong identifiers can be found in high-status group than in the low one, the pattern is not consistent.

Given these considerations, we turn in the following pages to discussing, first some of the determinants of the voter's party identification and, second the degree to which he is involved in

---

5. See Robert A. Alford and Harry M. Scoble, "Sources of Local Political Involvement", *American Political Science Review*, LXII : 4 (December 1968), p. 1,192. For other references, see footnotes therein.

different political activities. In Table 5:6 is presented information on the relationship between the socio-economic status of our respondents and their strength of party identification.[6] A glance at the table suggests that only a small proportion of voters in each state is strongly partisan. It is in Punjab that the largest proportion (32.5 per cent) of strong identifiers is located. In the rest of the states, the proportion of strong identifiers is smaller: Bihar 9.2 per cent, U.P. 18.9 per cent and West Bengal 16.5 per cent. Also interesting is the fact that it is in West Bengal that the largest proportion of very weak identifiers is to be found. Apart from this, identification offers not only a guide to what concrete issues will be canvassed for or against but also the channels of participation. It is party identification that colours the perspective of many voters. As such, it is highly relevant to examine the degree to which our respondents identify themselves with political parties.

In terms of the relationship between SES and partisan identification, it can be seen that in Bihar and West Bengal it is the voters with medium level of SES that constitute the largest proportion of strong party identifiers: 28.2 and 19.2 per cent, respectively. In U.P., it is mostly the voters in the high-status category that manifest strong partisanship. Note, for example, that there is a big drop in the percentage of strong identifiers in the medium-status category in U.P. Similarly, in Punjab, voters in both high and medium status categories are relatively more identified than their counterparts in the low-status category. In sum, then, unlike other political attributes, partisan identification does not seem to be so strongly influenced by socio-economic status. It is true that voters enjoying higher status do tend to be strong identifiers; however, the need to identify oneself with a particular party spills over status boundaries indicating the spread effect in varying degrees of the phenomenon of politicization in different status groups.

Given the low salience of SES for party identification, what

---

6. Our index of identification is derived from four questions: 1. If you could vote again, would you still vote for the same party candidate? 2. (If not a member of any party), would you consider joining a political party? 3. Generally speaking, which party do you feel closest to? 4. Is your preference for this party (if party mentioned) very strong?

## TABLE 5:6
### SES and Party Identification (in per cent)

| States | Bihar | | | | Punjab | | | | U.P. | | | | W.B. | | | |
|---|---|---|---|---|---|---|---|---|---|---|---|---|---|---|---|---|
| Identification / SES | High | Medium | Low | Total | High | Medium | Low | Total | High | Medium | Low | Total | High | Medium | Low | Total |
| High | 27.6 | 43.4 | 28.9 | 76 100.0 | 39.3 | 47.6 | 13.1 | 61 100.0 | 31.6 | 59.2 | 9.2 | 76 100.0 | 16.4 | 41.0 | 42.6 | 61 100.0 |
| Medium | 28.2 | 50.7 | 21.1 | 142 100.0 | 37.2 | 52.0 | 10.8 | 148 100.0 | 15.3 | 69.4 | 15.3 | 189 100.0 | 19.2 | 56.0 | 24.8 | 125 100.0 |
| Low | 13.4 | 60.5 | 26.1 | 119 100.0 | 19.5 | 62.2 | 18.3 | 82 100.0 | 17.8 | 65.0 | 17.2 | 157 100.0 | 9.8 | 55.8 | 34.4 | 61 100.0 |
| NA | 33.3 | 66.7 | — | 3 100.0 | — | 100.0 | — | 1 100.0 | — | 50.0 | 50.0 | 6 100.0 | 50.0 | 50.0 | — | 2 100.0 |
| Total | 78 22.9 | 179 52.7 | 83 24.4 | 340 100.0 | 95 32.5 | 158 54.1 | 39 13.4 | 292 100.0 | 81 18.9 | 281 65.7 | 66 15.4 | 428 100.0 | 41 16.5 | 130 52.2 | 78 31.3 | 249 100.0 |
| | C=0.186 | | | | C=0.189 | | | | C=0.195 | | | | C=0.201 | | | |

can be said of the relationship between age and partisanship? If the thesis that firmer party identification develops through habituation crystallized by repeated participation in electoral processes is valid, we will expect that the younger the age of a voter, lesser would be the strength of partisanship. In order to test this, we worked out the mean strength of partisanship by age cohorts.[7] The result is presented in Figure 5.1 whose vertical axis measures mean strength of partisanship and the horizontal, the age in years of our respondents. A look at the figure discloses that there is no set pattern in the postulated relationship between age and the strength of partisanship. It is true that two high peaks of the strength of partisanship, one in the case of 40-45 and the other in that of the 50-55 age cohorts, both after the ripe age of 40, in any case—can be discerned, this does not indicate a straight and unequivocal association between advancing age and strength of partisanship.

Even more important, state variations as reflected in the graph are quite considerable. Note, for example, that if the young voters in U.P. participate in their first election with quite a low strength of partisanship, as they go through the experience of successive elections, the mean strength of their partisanship increases till it reaches the highest point between the age of 30-35. After that a pattern of alternate fall and rise becomes operative. However, the mean strength of partisanship never falls precipitously; it remains more or less on a high level. The contrasting case is that of West Bengal where young voters (20-25 age cohorts) vote in the first election with a strong partisan identification but, from then on, partisan strength declines as we move on to age cohorts in the early thirties and reaches a low point between 30-35, then rises again and attains the highest peak in the age group 40-45, registers a precipitous drop in 45-50 age group and so on. In other words, there is quite a considerable amount of variation in the mean strength of partisanship from one age cohort to another. Punjab and Bihar mainfest quite different patterns.

Our discussion of the relationship between age and partisan

---

7. The same items as used in deriving the index of identification have also been used in this case.

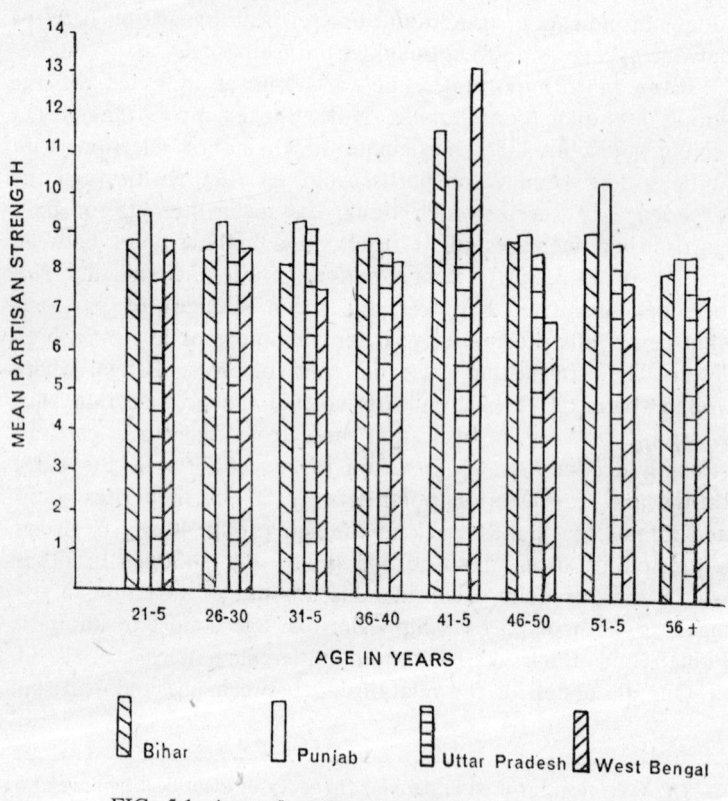

FIG. 5.1 Age and partisan strength in the four states

strength does not reveal any clear pattern. What about the relationship between the level of information and party identification? As can be seen from Table 5:7, there appears to be some relationship between these two attributes. It can, for instance, be seen that in each of the states a large number of those who score high on the index of information are also high on party identification. As the level of information goes down, the proportion of strong identifiers also goes down. In terms of state variations, Bihar and Punjab contain the largest proportions of highly informed voters who are also strong identifiers. But while in Bihar the proportion of strong identifiers decreases with each decrease in the level of information, in Punjab, level of information does not seem to make any difference to the strength of partisanship. Almost an equal proportion of strong identifiers can be found at all levels of information in Punjab.

That the level of information has some influence on the strength of partisanship cannot be doubted. However, a close look at the table suggests that instead of the level of information being the independent catalyst of party identification, it is the latter that seems to be instrumental in inclining partisans to acquire relevant political information. This is what an examination of column percentages in Table 5:7 suggests. In each state more than 50 per cent of those who are strongly partisan are also well-informed. As a matter of fact, in Bihar and Punjab close to four-fifth of our respondents claiming to be strongly partisan also score high on the index of information. In West Bengal and U.P., however, the proportion of well-informed party identifiers goes down: West Bengal 55.2 per cent, and U.P., 56.8 per cent. Note also that as the strength of partisanship decreases, the level of our respondents' information also declines. This is enough to suggest that the strength of identification is much more salient for promoting receptivity to politically relevant information.

The low salience of information for the formation of strong party identification is thus reflected in our data. However, somewhat more salient in this regard seems to be the interest the voters take in politics and public affairs. We have already noted the fact that if the level of interest is high, the level of information also tends to be high. Similar is the case with the

TABLE 5 : 7

Information and Party Identification (in per cent)

| Party | Bihar | | | | Punjab | | | | U.P. | | | | W.B. | | | |
|---|---|---|---|---|---|---|---|---|---|---|---|---|---|---|---|---|
| Party Identification → | High | Medium | Low | Total | High | Medium | Low | Total | High | Medium | Low | Total | High | Medium | Low | Total |
| Level of Information ↓ | | | | | | | | | | | | | | | | |
| High | 30.7 (78.2)* | 53.3 (59.2) | 16.1 (38.6) | 199 100.0 | 32.8 (78.9) | 55.9 (81.0) | 11.4 (66.7) | 229 100.0 | 20.9 (56.8) | 70.5 (55.2) | 8.6 (28.8) | 220 100.0 | 20.3 (63.4) | 52.3 (51.5) | 27.3 (44.9) | 128 100.0 |
| Medium | 13.6 (15.4) | 59.1 (29.1) | 27.3 (28.9) | 88 100.0 | 31.5 (17.9) | 50.0 (17.1) | 18.5 (25.6) | 54 100.0 | 22.7 (35.8) | 58.6 (26.7) | 18.8 (36.4) | 128 100.0 | 13.2 (24.4) | 57.9 (33.8) | 28.9 (28.2) | 76 100.0 |
| Low | 9.4 (6.4) | 39.6 (11.7) | 50.9 (32.5) | 53 100.0 | 33.3 (3.2) | 33.3 (1.9) | 33.3 (7.7) | 9 100.0 | 7.5 (7.4) | 63.7 (18.1) | 28.7 (34.8) | 80 100.0 | 11.1 (12.2) | 42.2 (14.6) | 46.2 (26.9) | 45 100.0 |
| Total | 78 22.9 | 179 52.6 | 83 24.4 | 340 100.0 | 95 32.5 | 158 54.1 | 39 13.4 | 292 100.0 | 81 18.9 | 281 65.1 | 66 15.4 | 428 100.0 | 41 16.5 | 130 52.2 | 78 31.3 | 249 100.0 |
| | C=0.311 | | | | C=0.136 | | | | C=0.237 | | | | C=0.176 | | | |

*Figures in parentheses denote percentages calculated from column totals.

relationship between the level of interest and that of identification. This can be easily verified by a reference to Table 5:8. The consistency of the relationship between interest and identification is confirmed by the table. As the level of interest declines, the proportion of strong identifiers also decreases in all the states. In U.P. the largest coincidence of a high level of interest leading to strong partisan identification can be identified. The percentage difference between highly interested strong identifiers and moderately interested strong identifiers is about 40 per cent. In West Bengal and Punjab also. the difference between these two categories of our respondents is quite high— that is, 26 per cent and about 23 per cent, respectively.

It is also to be noted that strong identification does seem to be a crucial factor in inducing a high degree of interest in politics and public affairs. Note, for example, that, taking column percentages into account, the voters expressing a sense of strong party identification are not necessarily high on the index of political interest. In U.P., where we noted a high degree of convergence between political interest and party identification, only 38.3 per cent of those high on party identification are also high on political interest. It is only in West Bengal and, to a lesser degree in Punjab, that a larger proportion of strong identifiers can be seen also to manifest a high degree of political interest. Given this, however, the fact remains that more people with greater interest in politics are strong identifiers. The reverse is only true in West Bengal.

We have so far been concerned with certain political attributes that specifically relate to the voters' dispositional and attitudinal properties. The salience of all these attributes lies in the fact that they are related to the action propensity of the voters. The quantum of information, interest and party identification are necessary conditions for disposing voters to participate in political processes that relate to decision-making aspects of a political system. If the voter remains inert and passive even though he may be endowed with other necessary attributes, it would lend capricious overtones to the functioning of democratic institutions. It need not be over-emphasized that it is through the efforts to make strongly held views widely acceptable that democratic institutions draw their sustenance. And this necessarily involves action consisting of the effort to

TABLE 5 : 8

Political Interest and Party Identification (in per cent)

| States | Bihar | | | | Punjab | | | | U.P. | | | | W.B. | | | |
|---|---|---|---|---|---|---|---|---|---|---|---|---|---|---|---|---|
| Party Identification / Level of Political Interest | High | Medium | Low | Total | High | Medium | Low | Total | High | Medium | Low | Total | High | Medium | Low | Total |
| High | 43.9 (23.1)* | 41.5 (9.5) | 14.6 (7.2) | 41 100.0 | 55.3 (44.2) | 32.9 (15.8) | 11.8 (23.1) | 76 100.0 | 57.4 (38.3) | 38.9 (7.5) | 3.7 (3.0) | 54 100.0 | 40.8 (48.8) | 44.9 (16.9) | 14.3 (9.0) | 41 100.0 |
| Medium | 33.6 (53.8) | 48.8 (34.1) | 17.6 (26.5) | 125 100.0 | 32.7 (35.8) | 56.7 (37.3) | 10.6 (28.2) | 104 100.0 | 17.9 (46.9) | 71.3 (53.7) | 10.8 (34.8) | 212 100.0 | 14.8 (41.5) | 53.9 (47.7) | 31.3 (46.2) | 130 100.0 |
| Low | 10.3 (23.1) | 58.1 (56.4) | 31.6 (66.3) | 174 100.0 | 17.0 (20.0) | 66.0 (46.8) | 17.0 (48.7) | 112 100.0 | 7.4 (14.8) | 67.3 (38.8) | 25.3 (62.1) | 162 100.0 | 4.7 (9.8) | 54.1 (35.4) | 41.2 (44.9) | 28 100.0 |
| Total | 22.9 | 52.6 | 24.4 | 340 100.0 | 32.5 | 54.1 | 13.4 | 292 100.0 | 18.9 | 65.7 | 15.4 | 428 100.0 | 16.5 | 15.2 | 31.3 | 249 100.0 |
| | 78 C=0.310 | 179 | 83 | | 95 C=0.313 | 158 | 39 | | 81 C=0.394 | 281 | 66 | | 41 C=0.341 | 130 | 78 | |

*Figures in parentheses denote percentages calculated from column totals.

persuade others, canvass support, see that right type of representatives are elected, etc. Therefore, action propensity is one of the essential attributes of a committed citizen not because the action is an end in itself but because it is through action that different view points are brought to public attention. In the remainder of this chapter, we turn to this aspect of our discussion taking the index of electoral involvement[8] as a measure of action propensity.

We present in Table 5:9 information on the voters' SES and their level of electoral involvement. It is readily apparent that very few of our respondents involve themselves in electoral activities. The largest proportion of voters taking active part in electoral campaigns can be identified in Punjab (24.3 per cent) followed by West Bengal (20.1 per cent). In Bihar and U.P., only 14.4 and 11.9 per cent of respondents, respectively, score high on the index of electoral involvement. In other words, about 50 to 80 per cent of our respondents seldom take part in electoral activities. Given this very low-keyed action propensity of our respondents, the influence of SES on electoral involvement appears to be considerable. In three states—Punjab, U.P. and West Bengal—a sizeable number of voters in the high socio-economic status is high on electoral involvement. As we move down the status gradation, the proportion of those who claim to participate in electoral activities declines. This is also true of Bihar where electoral involvement is the lowest. More or less the same pattern obtains in the case of those who occupy medium social status. To look at it differently, in each of the states, the proportion of those who score low on this index steadily goes down as the level of socio-economic status declines.

---

8. Our index of electoral involvement is derived from a set of five questions. They are: 1. Generally speaking, would you say that you personally cared quite a lot, somewhat, or not at all, about who won in the constituency in the elections just held? 2. Have you ever engaged in any activity during a political campaign to elect some candidate? 3. Have you ever attended a political meeting or rally during an election or at any other time? 4. Have you ever tried to tell anyone why he should vote for one of the parties, or candidates? 5. Have you ever done anything to help a party or candidate get elected?

TABLE 5 : 9

ES and Electoral Involvement (in per cent)

| States | Bihar | | | | Punjab | | | | U.P. | | | | W.B. | | | |
|---|---|---|---|---|---|---|---|---|---|---|---|---|---|---|---|---|
| Electoral Involvement → <br> Level of SES ↓ | High | Medium | Low | Total | High | Medium | Low | Total | High | Medium | Low | Total | High | Medium | Low | Total |
| High | 21.1 | 17.1 | 66.8 | 76 <br> 100.0 | 34.4 | 34.4 | 31.1 | 61 <br> 100.0 | 34.2 | 26.3 | 39.5 | 76 <br> 100.0 | 34.4 | 26.2 | 39.3 | 61 <br> 100.0 |
| Medium | 15.5 | 22.5 | 62.0 | 142 <br> 100.0 | 29.1 | 25.7 | 45.3 | 148 <br> 100.0 | 9.0 | 16.4 | 74.6 | 189 <br> 100.0 | 18.4 | 20.8 | 60.8 | 125 <br> 100.0 |
| Low | 8.4 | 18.5 | 73.1 | 119 <br> 100.0 | 8.5 | 18.3 | 73.2 | 82 <br> 100.0 | 5.1 | 13.4 | 81.5 | 157 <br> 100.0 | 6.6 | 14.8 | 78.7 | 61 <br> 100.0 |
| NA | 33.3 | — | 66.7 | 3 <br> 100.0 | — | 100.0 | — | 1 <br> 100.0 | — | — | 100.0 | 6 <br> 100.0 | 100.0 | — | — | 2 <br> 100.0 |
| Total | 49 <br> 14.4 | 67 <br> 19.7 | 224 <br> 65.9 | 340 <br> 100.0 | 71 <br> 24.3 | 75 <br> 25.7 | 146 <br> 50.0 | 292 <br> 100.0 | 51 <br> 11.9 | 72 <br> 16.8 | 305 <br> 71.3 | 428 <br> 100.0 | 50 <br> 20.1 | 51 <br> 20.5 | 148 <br> 59.4 | 249 <br> 100.0 |
| | C=0.162 | | | | C=0.317 | | | | C=0.357 | | | | C=0.327 | | | |

Apart from the salience of SES for electoral involvement, age of the voter also seems to play some role in inducing him to take active part in electoral activities. As Table 5:10 reveals, different states manifest different patterns. In the case of West Bengal, for example, while the largest proportion of young voters can be observed to have taken active part in campaign activities, the proportion of older voters scoring high on the index of electoral involvement declines steadily. If 30.1 per cent of 21–30 age cohorts are high on the index of electoral involvement, only 18.6 per cent in the 31–40 age cohorts, 16.4 per cent in the 41–50 age groups and only 4.0 per cent in 50+ age group are high on this index. In other words, the voters of advanced age groups tend to lose their interest in electoral activities. In contrast, the remaining three states present entirely a different picture. Broadly speaking, with growing experience of elections, the level of electoral involvement rises. In Bihar, for example, as against 13.4 per cent of young voters high on electoral involvement, 18.9 per cent in the 31–40 age group and 17.6 per cent in the 41–50 age group are high on electoral involvement. It is only on the 51+age group that the proportion of electorally highly active voters drops down to 3.3 per cent. More or less the same pattern obtains in other two states also.

The demography of electoral involvement underlines the crucial importance of SES and age for electoral involvement. What about other attributes? In Table 5:11 is presented information on the relationship between the level of information and electoral involvement. The first thing that strikes us is the fact that while a large proportion of our respondents is high on the index of information, only a small proportion of voters is high on electoral involvement. Given this, however, Punjab, followed by West Bengal, contains the largest proportions of those voters who are high both on the index of information and that of electoral involvement. In Bihar and U.P., on the contrary, smaller proportions of highly informed voters actively participate in election campaign. In the second place, the level of information does not seem to be a crucial determinant in promoting active interest in election campaigns. Note, for example, that in Punjab where we find the largest proportion of electorally active voters, only 26.2 per cent of well-informed voters are also high on electoral involvement. And, yet, our data

TABLE 5 : 10

Age and Electoral Involvement (in per cent)

| States | Bihar | | | | Punjab | | | | U.P. | | | | W.B. | | | |
|---|---|---|---|---|---|---|---|---|---|---|---|---|---|---|---|---|
| Electoral Involvement | High | Medium | Low | Total | High | Medium | Low | Total | High | Medium | Low | Total | High | Medium | Low | Total |
| Age in years | | | | | | | | | | | | | | | | |
| Below 21 | 33.3 | 13.3 | 53.4 | 15 100.0 | — | — | 100.0 | 3 100.0 | — | 25.0 | 75.0 | 4 100.0 | — | — | — | — |
| 21—30 | 13.4 | 24.1 | 62.5 | 112 100.0 | 22.1 | 24.7 | 53.2 | 109 100.0 | 11.1 | 17.6 | 71.3 | 136 100.0 | 30.1 | 23.0 | 46.9 | 96 100.0 |
| 31—40 | 18.9 | 18.9 | 62.2 | 95 100.0 | 21.4 | 36.0 | 42.6 | 61 100.0 | 14.1 | 18.2 | 67.7 | 99 100.0 | 18.6 | 17.1 | 64.3 | 70 100.0 |
| 41—50 | 17.6 | 17.6 | 64.8 | 57 100.0 | 29.4 | 15.7 | 54.9 | 51 100.0 | 13.7 | 17.5 | 68.8 | 80 100.0 | 16.4 | 13.3 | 70.3 | 73 100.0 |
| 51+ | 3.3 | 18.0 | 78.7 | 61 100.0 | 25.7 | 27.3 | 47.0 | 66 100.0 | 10.0 | 13.9 | 76.1 | 109 100.0 | 4.0 | 26.1 | 69.9 | 46 100.0 |
| Total | 49 14.4 | 67 19.7 | 224 65.9 | 340 100.0 | 71 24.3 | 75 25.7 | 114 50.0 | 292 100.0 | 51 11.9 | 72 16.8 | 305 71.3 | 428 100.9 | 50 20.1 | 51 20.5 | 148 59.4 | 249 100.0 |

TABLE 5 : 11

Information and Electoral Involvement (in per cent)

| States | Bihar | | | | Punjab | | | | U.P. | | | | W.B. | | | |
|---|---|---|---|---|---|---|---|---|---|---|---|---|---|---|---|---|
| Electoral Involvement → | High | Medium | Low | Total | High | Medium | Low | Total | High | Medium | Low | Total | High | Medium | Low | Total |
| Level of Information ↓ | | | | | | | | | | | | | | | | |
| High | 19.6 (79.6)* | 21.1 (62.7) | 59.3 (52.7) | 199 100.0 | 26.2 (84.5) | 47.9 (85.3) | 45.9 (71.9) | 229 100.0 | 16.4 (70.6) | 22.7 (69.4) | 60.9 (43.9) | 220 100.0 | 25.0 (64.0) | 24.2 (60.8) | 50.8 (43.9) | 128 100.0 |
| Medium | 8.0 (14.3) | 21.6 (28.4) | 70.5 (27.7) | 88 100.0 | 20.4 (15.5) | 16.7 (12.0) | 63.0 (23.3) | 54 100.0 | 9.4 (23.5) | 11.7 (20.8) | 78.9 (33.1) | 128 100.0 | 18.7 (28.0) | 19.7 (29.4) | 61.8 (31.8) | 76 100.0 |
| Low | 5.7 (6.1) | 11.3 (9.0) | 83.0 (19.6) | 53 100.0 | — | 22.7 (2.7) | 77.8 (4.8) | 9 100.0 | 3.7 (5.9) | 8.7 (9.7) | 87.5 (23.0) | 80 100.0 | 8.9 (8.0) | 11.1 (9.8) | 80.0 (24.3) | 45 100.0 |
| Total | 49 | 67 | 224 | 340 100.0 | 71 | 75 | 146 | 292 100.0 | 51 | 72 | 305 | 428 100.0 | 50 | 51 | 148 | 249 100.0 |
| | C=0.240 | | | | C=0.174 | | | | C=0.238 | | | | C=0.216 | | | |

*Figures in parentheses denote percentages calculated from column totals.

suggest that larger the intake of politically relevant information, it is highly likely that the voter would actively engage himself in electoral processes. This is reflected by the fact that lower the level of information, smaller becomes the proportion of those who claim to be greatly active in electoral campaigns. The relationship is, however, very weak. It will, therefore, be more appropriate to say that electoral involvement is much more instrumental in inducing voters to inform themselves politically. This is what the perusal of column percentages suggests. Taking the case of Punjab again, it will be seen that 84.5 per cent of those who are high on electoral involvement are also high on information. In the case of other states also the proportion of such voters does not go below 64 per cent.

If the contribution of the level of information to electoral involvement is quite low, what can we say about party identification? A perusal of Table 5:12 will suggest that party identification is relatively more salient for electoral involvement. First, looking at the totals, we notice that it is only in the case of West Bengal that the proportion of those who are high on the index of electoral involvement surpasses that of strong identifiers. In the rest of the states, the proportion of strong identifiers is always larger than that of electorally highly active voters. Secondly, it will also be seen that the stronger the party identification, larger is the proportion of those who claim to take very active part in electoral campaign. In West Bengal, for example, 68.3 per cent of strong identifiers take active part in election campaigns. More or less similar is the case in Punjab. It is only in Bihar and U.P. that the proportion of these voters drops down to about 39 per cent. Also, in each of the states, as the strength of identification decreases, the proportion of electorally active voters also drops. Further, apart from this decline, there yawns a big gap between those who are strong identifiers as well as highly active and those who are only moderately so but highly active. In the last place, we again encounter the phenomenon of greater salience of electoral involvement for forging stronger identification. Note, for example, that in Punjab more than two-thirds of our respondents actively engaging in electoral activities are high on party identification. Although proportions vary from one state to the next, the fact, however, remains that, relatively speaking, a large number of highly active voters are

TABLE 5 : 12

Party Identification and Electoral Involvement (in per cent)

| States | Bihar | | | | Punjab | | | | U.P. | | | | W.B. | | | |
|---|---|---|---|---|---|---|---|---|---|---|---|---|---|---|---|---|
| Electoral Involvement → | High | Medium | Low | Total | High | Medium | Low | Total | High | Medium | Low | Total | High | Medium | Low | Total |
| Level of Party Identification ↓ | | | | | | | | | | | | | | | | |
| High | 39.7 (63.2)* | 24.4 (28.4) | 35.9 (12.5) | 78 100.0 | 57.9 (77.5) | 26.3 (33.3) | 15.8 (10.3) | 95 100.0 | 38.3 (60.7) | 32.1 (36.2) | 29.6 (7.9) | 81 100.0 | 68.3 (56.0) | 14.6 (11.8) | 17.1 (4.7) | 41 100.0 |
| Medium | 8.9 (32.7) | 21.8 (58.2) | 69.3 (55.4) | 179 100.0 | 7.6 (16.9) | 25.9 (54.7) | 66.5 (71.9) | 158 100.0 | 6.8 (37.3) | 14.6 (56.9) | 78.6 (72.4) | 281 100.0 | 14.6 (38.0) | 24.6 (62.7) | 60.8 (53.4) | 130 100.0 |
| Low | 2.4 (4.1) | 10.8 (13.4) | 86.8 (32.1) | 83 100.0 | 10.3 (5.6) | 23.1 (12.0) | 66.7 (17.8) | 39 100.0 | 1.5 (2.0) | 7.6 (6.9) | 90.9 (19.7) | 66 100.0 | 3.8 (6.0) | 16.7 (25.5) | 79.5 (41.9) | 78 100.0 |
| Total | 49 14.4 | 67 19.7 | 224 65.9 | 340 100.0 | 71 24.3 | 75 25.7 | 146 50.0 | 292 100.0 | 51 11.9 | 72 16.8 | 305 71.3 | 428 100.0 | 50 20.1 | 51 20.5 | 148 59.4 | 249 100.0 |
| | C=0.408 | | | | C=0.502 | | | | C=0.436 | | | | C=0.492 | | | |

*Figures in parentheses denote percentages calculated from column totals.

TABLE 5 : 13

Political Interest and Electoral Involvement (in per cent)

| States | Bihar | | | | Bihar | | | | U.P. | | | | W.B. | | | |
|---|---|---|---|---|---|---|---|---|---|---|---|---|---|---|---|---|
| Electoral Involvement → | High | Medium | Low | Total | High | Medium | Low | Total | High | Medium | Low | Total | High | Medium | Low | Total |
| Level of Political Interest ↓ | | | | | | | | | | | | | | | | |
| High | 41.5 (34.7)* | 26.8 (16.4) | 31.7 (5.8) | 41 / 100.0 | 55.3 (59.2) | 28.9 (29.3) | 15.8 (8.2) | 76 / 100.0 | 57.4 (60.8) | 22.2 (16.7) | 20.4 (3.6) | 54 / 100.0 | 55.1 (54.0) | 22.4 (21.6) | 22.4 (7.4) | 49 / 100.0 |
| Medium | 25.6 (65.3) | 23.2 (43.3) | 51.2 (28.6) | 125 / 100.0 | 23.1 (33.8) | 33.7 (46.7) | 43.3 (30.8) | 104 / 100.0 | 8.0 (33.3) | 25.0 (73.6) | 67.0 (46.6) | 212 / 100.0 | 19.1 (44.0) | 24.3 (54.9) | 56.5 (43.9) | 115 / 100.0 |
| Low | — | 15.5 (40.3) | 84.5 (65.6) | 174 / 100.0 | 4.5 (7.0) | 16.1 (24.0) | 79.5 (61.0) | 112 / 100.0 | 1.9 (5.9) | 4.3 (9.7) | 93.8 (49.8) | 162 / 100.0 | 1.2 (2.0) | 14.1 (23.5) | 84.7 (48.6) | 85 / 100.0 |
| Total | 49 / 14.4 | 67 / 19.7 | 224 / 65.9 | 340 / 100.0 C=529 | 71 / 24.3 | 75 / 25.7 | 146 / 50.0 | 292 / 100.0 C=492 | 51 / 11.9 | 72 / 16.8 | 305 / 71.3 | 428 / 100.0 C=438 | 50 / 20.1 | 51 / 20.5 | 148 / 59.4 | 249 / 100.0 C=464 |

* Figures in parentheses denote percentages calculated from column totals.

also strongly partisan: Bihar 63.3 per cent, U.P. 60.8 per cent and West Bengal 56.0 per cent.

It now remains for us to examine the relationship between the level of political interest and that of electoral involvement. Table 5:13 presents information in this regard. Given the fact that the levels of both political interest and electoral involvement are low, however, there seems to be quite a large degree of convergence between them. Note, for example, that among those who are high on interest, say, in Punjab, 55.3 per cent are also high on electoral involvement. Similar patterns obtain in other states also. Also interesting is the fact that those who are high on electoral involvement are, to a great extent, also high on political interest. To cite the example of Punjab again, out of those who are high on political involvement, 59.2 per cent are also high on political interest. In other words, political interest and electoral involvement are mutually reinforcing factors.

To sum up, our discussion brings out the salience of SES for acquiring certain political attributes. We have also shown that age plays a differential role in the manifestations of these attributes. What is more important, our discussion throws light on how different attributes are interrelated. Our analysis underlines, for instance, the greater saliences of political interest and electoral involvement for the acquisition of other traits such as political information and identification. To be more specific, the higher the social status of a voter, higher will generally be his level of political interest as well as electoral involvement. It is yet not clear whether it is political interest that leads a voter to participate actively in election campaigns or the latter leads to the former. For the present, we will assume interdependence between them. Once a voter either develops high interest in politics and public affairs or, due to one reason or other, comes to be actively engaged in election campaigns, he is most likely to acquire politically relevant information and forge stronger party identification.

# CHAPTER SIX
# *Political Comprehension and the Voter*

WE discussed in the last chapter some of the attributes of our respondents focussing particularly on the levels of political information, party identification and electoral involvement. It is true that quite a large number of our respondents are politically well-informed. However, in respect of their interest in and involvement with politics and public affairs, measured in terms of their participation in election campaigns, the proportion of the interested and active voters comes down sharply. It is interesting to note in this connection that only about 16 per cent of our respondents claim to be members of a political party. This does not, however, mean that our respondents have no partisan preference. As a matter of fact, about 80 per cent of our respondents claim that they feel closest to some party or the other. In other words, for most of the voters it is possible to be partisan without formally joining a party.

Given this, however, it can also be noted that less than a third of our respondents manifest a strong sense of partisanship. In terms of political interest and electoral involvement, the pattern remains more or less the same, that is, the proportion of interested and active voters ranges between 12 and 26 per cent. This underlines the important fact that the basic assumptions of the classical theory of democracy do not find empirical confirmation inasmuch as a large proportion of the *demos* lacks postulated attributes, such as, informed interest in public affairs and active participation in decision-making processes, to mention only two. This discrepancy between the expected and the observed attributes of the electorate has forced social scientists to reformulate the essential characteristics of individual citizens as they pertain to the preservation and sustenance of democratic institutions.

We have already alluded to the fact that the reformulation of democratic theory postulates a generalized sense of commitment on the part of citizens to the principles of democratic politics. This revision has both theoretical and practical implications. As Key observes,

> Conceptions and theories of the way voters behave do not raise solely arcane problems to be disputed among the democratic and anti-democratic theories or questions to be settled by the elegant techniques of the analysts of electoral behaviour. Rather, they touch upon profound issues at the heart of the problem of the nature and workability of systems of popular government.[1]

It is the electorate that selects rulers in a democracy and performs the role of controlling the rulers in order to assure their conformity to democratic principles. It is true that this control mechanism operates, in part, through open competition among contenders for political power and, in part, through the institutional complex devoted to decision-making. However, in the ultimate analysis, it is the electorate's responsibility to control the rulers. As is well known, this control function is performed through renewal of consent of the governed. However, this consent is expressed only periodically and is often vague about the scope of the mandate for governance. For want of an alert citizen body, therefore, politics of manipulation and coterie rule may become a prevalent practice.

The democratic theory, therefore, postulates the notion of active, well-informed and politically aware citizens as the only effective check on the self-aggrandizing tendencies of the political elites and activists. The very low level of citizen's interest and involvement in politics and public affairs, however, should not obscure the importance of the citizen's role in determining the mandate of governance. The nature of this mandate is inexorably linked up with the orientations and perspectives that condition the citizen's perception and evaluation of the political system. The individual characteristics, such as, the degree to which a voter is politically informed, interested and active are, it is true, one measure of ascertaining, as it were, the resource base of a representative government. What is even more important in this regard is the substantive concerns that illumine these attributes.

---

1. V.O. Key, Jr., *The Responsible Electorate, op. cit.,* pp. 5-6.

To put it differently, politics is a strange combination of rational and non-rational considerations and calculations. It is not simply a case of oringing expert knowledge to bear on a particular problem and identifying the most suitable alternative—an alternative that is objectively valid. Nor is it simply a matter of ascertaining the most popular fashion of issues, ideas, policies and programmes. Undeniably, both of these elements enter into politics but their mixes are never invariant. Political processes concern the evolving of action programmes out of issues that involve both factual judgements and value commitments. Often, political values are strongly held and are likely to survive momentary storms of contrary opinions. Men commit themselves to values and to action programmes emerging out of these values in a way that may remain unchanged and inaccessible to rational argument. And yet, such commitments shape the perception and action. Politics is, therefore, primarily concerned with bringing reconciliation among or forging consensus out of deep-seated but conflicting value commitments and using such a conciliation or consensus for developing action programmes. "It is always a combination of bargaining and compromise where there are irresolute and conflicting commitments and common deliberation about public policy, to which facts and rational arguments are relevant."[2]

Given the conflicting perspectives on what politics should be concerned with, the mediating structures, institutions and processes—both political and non-political—shape the articulation of these perspectives in so far as they impinge upon political processes. It is, therefore, necessary to go beyond the mere delineation of certain attributes and focus our attention on the substance which makes them relevant. That is to say, we must ask about what is it that citizens show some interest, try to acquire some information and join a party. This, however, raises another issue. In order to take a stand, acquire relevant information and engage in political activities, a voter must have the comprehension of how his own perspective and action are linked with broader political processes. He must have at least

---

2. Hanna F. Pitkin, *The Concept of Representation* (Berkeley : University of California Press, 1967), p. 212.

a general sense of what goes on in politics, how it is structured and how it functions. In other words, it is of interest for us to explore the extent to which the voter manifests comprehension of the political system, its essential components and the issues that give direction to politics.

To elaborate the idea of political comprehension, we intend to include in it such factors as the conception of politics as a legitimate activity that should engage the attention and energy of the citizens, the relevance of different political institutions, the salience of different political issues and the extent to which citizens are disposed to permit the government the liberty of initiative and action in certain issue areas. Our selection of these dimensions is not arbitrary. When we consider the fact that political development in the developing countries is characterized by a confrontation between the traditional and the modern, leading, not infrequently, to the crises of development, the relevance of these dimensions can readily be appreciated. After all, politics as a leveller of distinctions and a promoter of horizontal and vertical integration breaking the separation of distinct communities and sub-communities is a new phenomenon. Moreover, the emphasis on consensus and equity as principles of decision-making and conflict-resolution throws some doubt on the legitimacy of politics that, to many, is based on unrestrained competition.

If it is true of politics, understood very generally as a playground of conflicting parochial and primordial forces and interests, it is also true of other components of democratic institutional set up. The elections, political parties, legislative bodies, representatives and so on—all these institutions are not easily comprehended as of immediate relevance to an ordinary citizen. If the citizens in the developing countries cannot easily relate the functioning of these institutions to their own world, it is all the more hard for them to comprehend their importance for the national political system. And, yet, unless such a comprehension informs their participation in political decision-making process, the functioning of a democratic system will, in all probability, reflect a plebiscitary character.

These considerations, then, point to the necessity of investigating the degree to which voters have come to comprehend the nature and functions of political institutions and their unique characteristics that lend viability to a democratic polity. The greater diffusion of such a comprehension is a reflection of the maturation process of democratic politics. The concept of political comprehension is, therefore, a very relevant tool for examining and exploring the depth of the roots that democratic institutions have been able to strike in an alien soil. As we indicated earlier, we propose to examine the extent to which politics is supposed to be a legitimate activity for shaping the destiny of the nation. However, this serves for us only as a starting point for conducting our enquiry. It may be that under the influence of certain normative conditioning, voters may not approve of the way politics are generally conducted. However, they may be prepared to consider it as a necessary instrument for carrying on the tasks of government.

What is even more important, the dissatisfaction with the conduct of politics may not be reflected in the voters' perception of the role of government in conducting the affairs of the nation in a particular way. The voters may, for example, perceive the necessity of giving more powers to the government in order to initiate action in certain areas. This will necessarily increase the scope of politics although it may be looked at with suspicion. This is no doubt symptomatic of the inconsistency in the voters' perspective. But again, it may not be so. It is possible that the voters may react only to the seamy side of politics and at the same time be convinced of the necessity of the enlarged role of the government in managing national affairs. Whatever may be the case, our interest lies primarily in ascertaining the degree to which our respondents consider politics as a legitimate activity.

Given the centrality of politics, the question of the boundary within which the government can legitimately act becomes very important. It is true that citizen compliance to the *dictat* of the state is usually habitual and, therefore, normally taken for granted. However, the slumbering masses do sometimes wake up, take note of the doings of the government, and decide to put things right. The ruling elite has, therefore, to put its ears to the rumblings of the shifting public opinion and respond to the prevalent public mood before it gets thrown out. Whether the divination of the prevalent public mood is based on informed judgement or intuition, the main point is that the rulers define for themselves the area of permissiveness within which to conduct and manage the affairs of the nation. As such, the area of permissiveness bears a great relevance to our enquiry and we shall be concerned with exploring the extent to which voters in all the four states are inclined to allow a greater or smaller lee-way to the government for taking appropriate actions in a particular issue area. To be precise, we are interested in finding out the extent to which our respondents favour or disfavour the phenomenon of statism.

Once the priority of governmental action in certain fields or the pre-empting of certain fields for governmental action is recognized, the role of certain political institutions in proposing certain action programmes, deliberating over them and bringing to bear competing approaches, interests and outlooks on them assumes a crucial importance. An informed citizen is expected to have at least some general notions about the nature and functioning of these institutions and their contribution to the totality of the functioning political system. We can, for example, refer to two crucial institutional props of a democratic polity, viz., political parties and representatives. Political parties are organized groups that have the functions of providing rulers, articulating and organizing discontent against the government, etc. Even more important is the role of political parties in providing linkage between the functioning organs of the political system and the common man. Political parties can be distinguished and differentiated on the basis of their ideological orientation, programmatic values and social bases of recruitment. These differences and their reflection in the awareness of the voters make politics interesting as well as partisan. If the voters are not aware of these differences, politics becomes a dull and depressing affair of one political activist trying to outwit another. It is these differences—or, their perception by the voters—that induce partisan loyalty. It is, therefore, necessary to explore and examine the notions prevalent among the voters about political parties.

In addition to this, we are also interested in probing into the perceptions of the voters about representative bodies, such as, legislative assembly, and the representatives themselves. We are particularly interested in the latter inasmuch as the phenomenon of defection, i.e., frequent change of party label by legislators, witnessed in the last three years, has raised questions about the stability of government. This has highlighted the question of the relationship between the legislator and the party on whose ticket he has been elected, on the one hand, and the electorate's conception of the role of the representative, on the other. In other words, the role of the representative, the claim over him of the party he represents and his responsibility towards his constituents that he is supposed to represent are some of the issues that the decline in the Congress dominance has brought to the fore and we wish to explore the electorate's reaction to and understanding of these issues.

The concept of representation, as Pitkin has very ably demonstrated,[3] has mainly been discussed from the vantage point of an approach that emphasizes various individual-representation analogies—agent and trustee and deputy. According to Pitkin, where representation is conceived as that of unattached abstractions, the representative need not consult any one in his role performance. Depending upon the conception of interest—conceived in terms of whether something can be objectively determined or defined only by the person who has the interest—the concept of representation ranges between the autonomous and the subservient role of the representative. These extreme conceptions are unrealistic since "political representation is primarily a public, institutionalized arrangement involving many people and groups, and operating in the complex ways of large-scale social arrangements." The analogies of acting for others on the individual level do not, therefore, seem satisfactory for explaining the relationship between a political representative and his constituents. "He is neither agent, nor trustee, nor deputy, nor commissioner; he acts for a group without a single interest, most of whom seem incapable of forming an explicit will on political questions."[4]

We select for an extended discussion two aspects of the phenomenon of political representation. The role of the representative is inexorably linked up with two components of a democratic system, periodical elections and party system. If the party sponsors a candidate, mobilizes support for his

---

3. *Op. cit.*, see especially Chapter 10.
4. Pitkin, *op. cit.*, p. 221.

election and disciplines his conduct in and out of the legislature, his subsequent election is meant to facilitate the representation of a particular section of the electorate. In this context, the question as to whom the representative is finally responsible to assumes a critical importance.

That this question is not simply a theoretical one is suggested by the anxiety expressed in various quarters about the growing phenomenon of defection. Nor is it likely that this question can be resolved by theoretical debate inasmuch as there is always the possibility of conflicting points of view preventing agreement. If we accept the primacy of the party as the kingpin of a democratic polity in defining the interests that need to be protected and advanced, the role of the representative must then be subservient to the party. If, on the other hand, we consider the electorate as being supreme and whose interests the representative protects and advances, the party then becomes only an intermediary body that facilitates the act of representation. Yet, the perspective that endows the representative with individuality, knowledge and independent judgement cannot lightly be shelved. There may be occasions when he experiences a genuine conflict between what he himself considers to be the right and appropriate course of action and what either his party or his constituents perceive to be the best thing to do. Is the representative to acquiesce to his party's discipline against his own best judgment or is he to spurn such a control and act according to his own lights?

These are some of the issues involved in the intricate relationship between the function of representation and the relative importance of the party as well as the constituents in defining the boundary of the representational act. We do not propose to seek solutions to these questions: what we do propose is to empirically ascertain what views our respondents hold on these questions. Even if the representative is not aware of his constituents' conception of his role or, if aware, does not conform to it, what the electorate thinks the representative's role to be, still remains important since it is this perception that enters into the electorate's evaluation of the representative's role performance. The exploration of the constituent's conception of the representative's role helps us in understanding the mood of the electorate.

In short, then, our dimension of political comprehension includes certain perceptual, cognitive and evaluative categories that enter into the electorate's understanding of the political system. To state once again, we examine in particular the electorate's understanding of the relevance of politics, the basic institutional fabric of the political system, certain political issues and the role of the representative. It is to a discussion of these dimensions that we now turn.

We begin with a discussion of how our respondents view the widening circle of participation facilitated through periodical countrywide elections and the penetration of the rural areas by political parties. One of the factors leading to political instability in the four states is undoubtedly the result of the widening circle of political participation, the proliferation of political parties and groups and a tendency on their part to dominate the political scene at the cost of others. Whatever may be the long-term consequences of the interplay of political forces today, the general public all too frequently remains critical of politics thinking it corrupt and degrading. At yet another level, politics may be supposed to be mainly the concern of a few knowledgeable and dedicated persons. The widespread political participation in political processes may, then, be supposed to be dysfunctional for the system. Whether the data presented in Table 6:1 justifies the former or the latter inference is not at all clear. However, it is interesting to note that 50.3 per cent of our respondents say that the country would be much better off if so many people did not show interest in politics and, instead, attended to their own business. Only 28.1 per cent of respondents approve of people taking interest in politics.

Given the disapproval by half of our respondents of interest in politics, the state patterns are all the more interesting. Notice that about 60 per cent of respondents in U.P. and 52.6 per cent in Bihar think that people should not take an interest in politics. Even in West Bengal where left tendencies are quite strong, the opinion is divided: 44.2 per cent disapprove and 44.6 per cent approve. In Punjab again there seems to be no consensus on the issue. Apart from state variations, the relationship between SES and approval of politics is also interesting. Note, for example, that in Bihar higher the status, more likely it is that people will disapprove of a large number of people showing interest in

## TABLE 6:1

### SES and Approval of Politics (in per cent)

(Q: Do you think that the country would be much better off if so many people did not show interest in politics and attended to their own business?)

| States | Bihar | | | | | | Punjab | | | | | | U.P. | | | | | | W.B. | | | | | |
|---|---|---|---|---|---|---|---|---|---|---|---|---|---|---|---|---|---|---|---|---|---|---|---|---|
| Responses → SES ↓ | Yes | Undecided | No | D.K. | N.A. | Total | Yes | Undecided | No | D.K. | N.A. | Total | Yes | Undecided | No | D.K. | N.A. | Total | Yes | Undecided | No | D.K. | N.A. | Total |
| High | 61.8 | 13.2 | 23.7 | 1.3 | — | 76 / 100.0 | 27.9 | 21.3 | 50.8 | — | — | 61 / 100.0 | 67.1 | 7.9 | 25.0 | — | — | 76 / 100.0 | 42.6 | 9.8 | 47.6 | — | — | 61 / 100.0 |
| Medium | 54.2 | 21.8 | 19.7 | 4.3 | — | 142 / 100.00 | 39.9 | 16.9 | 42.6 | 0.6 | — | 148 / 100.0 | 55.6 | 19.0 | 23.3 | 2.1 | — | 189 / 100.0 | 47.2 | 8.0 | 44.0 | 0.8 | — | 125 / 100.0 |
| Low | 44.6 | 34.5 | 15.1 | 5.8 | — | 119 / 100.0 | 46.3 | 35.4 | 18.3 | — | — | 82 / 100.0 | 59.9 | 26.1 | 12.1 | 1.9 | — | 157 / 100.0 | 39.3 | 11.5 | 42.6 | 6.6 | — | 61 / 100.0 |
| NA | 66.7 | — | 33.3 | — | — | 3 / 100.0 | — | — | — | 100.0 | — | 1 / 100.0 | — | — | — | — | — | 6 / 100.0 | 50.0 | — | — | 50.0 | — | 2 / 100.0 |
| Total (N) | 179 | 82 | 65 | 14 | — | 340 | 114 | 67 | 110 | 1 | — | 292 | 256 | 83 | 82 | 7 | — | 428 | 110 | 23 | 111 | 5 | — | 249 |
| Total (%) | 52.6 | 24.1 | 19.1 | 4.2 | — | 100.0 | 39.0 | 22.9 | 37.7 | 0.4 | — | 100.0 | 59.8 | 19.4 | 19.2 | 1.6 | — | 100.0 | 44.2 | 9.2 | 44.6 | 2.0 | — | 100.0 |

politics. Whereas 61.8 per cent of our respondents falling in high-status category disapprove of widespread interest in politics, only 44.5 per cent of those in the low-status category do so. We observe the obverse of this tendency in Punjab where a larger proportion of higher statused as compared to low-statused respondents approve of wider participation in politics. In other words, higher the status, greater the likelihood that people in Punjab will approve of wider political participation. In the case of U.P. and West Bengal, although it is true that a larger proportion of higher statused respondents tends to disapprove of wider political participation, a contrasting feature can be noted. The largest proportion of voters disapproving of politics can be identified in West Bengal among voters in the medium-status category.

That a little over 50 per cent of our respondents do not approve of interest in politics is a reflection of the growing dissatisfaction with the way politics in these states is run. This is possibly due to the unstabilizing tendencies characterizing the functioning of popular government in these states. Its plausibility is suggested by our respondent's response to the question. "How would you rate the performance of the President's rule in your state when compared with the previous elected government?" As much as 38.5 per cent of respondents said it was better as against 29.4 per cent who said it was worse.[5]

The disapproval of politics does not necessarily imply that everything connected with it would be condemned. People may, as a matter fact, favour greater powers in the hands of the government and yet look askance at the way these powers are used or disapprove of the way parties compete for gaining power. Undoubtedly, enhancement of the powers and functions of the government in a democratic polity means more politics and, therefore, more scope for conflict generated by the push and pull of parochial and particular interests. But the general public may not be aware of this implication of enlarged state functions and due to ethos produced by the ideology of development may be quite willing to allow the expansion of governmental functions. Whatever the case, it is of interest to explore the extent to

---

5. The rest of the respondents said it did not make any difference.

which our respondents are willing to allow increased powers to the government. In a very important sense, this will provide us with an opportunity to examine the way our respondents react to the question of the appropriate role of the government in managing national affairs. The questions through which we propose to explore this enable us to characterize our respondents in terms of their location on "individualism-statism" dimension. We concentrate our attention on three basic issues, viz., our respondents' opinion about tax, control over industries and the abolition of private property.

With the growing accent on socialism as a desirable objective for Indian people to work for, all these three issues have, in one form or the other, been frequently emphasized in political propaganda. Moreover, in the context of the need of rapid economic growth for meeting the welfare needs of the people, on the one hand, and reducing the gap between privileged and the non- or under-privileged classes, on the other, the central role of the government as an energizer of the economy is recognized. The paucity of resources and the tenacity of the vested interests in defeating or, at least, delaying the realization of systemic goals cannot be overcome unless resources are raised internally by increasing taxes, on the one hand, and imposing controls over industries and private properties, on the other. However, the success in realizing these objectives is, to a great extent, dependent on the extent to which the general public is convinced of the desirability of these measures and is willing to support the government in implementing them. Questions relating to these dimensions, therefore, help us in determining the way the electorate thinks about these issues and, through this, the extent to which it manifests ideological orientation that supports development efforts.

We present, first, the opinion of our respondents (entire sample) in regard to these issue areas against their socio-economic status; we then move on to discuss the differential patterns of opinion configuration in different states; and, lastly, we present a summary measure of statism against the level of our respondent's socio-economic status by state. As will be seen from Table 6:2, as much as 47.4 per cent of our respondents think that taxes should not be cut if it meant postponing the implementation of some important programmes. Only 42.3 per

## TABLE 6 : 2

**SES and Issue-Orientation: Tax**
(Q: Do you think government ought to cut taxes even
if it means putting off some important things?)

| SES level | Responses | | | | |
|---|---|---|---|---|---|
| | Yes | Undecided | No | NA | Total |
| High | 75 (27.4) | 22 (8.0) | 176 (64.2) | 1 (0.4) | 274 (100.0) |
| Medium | 256 (42.4) | 50 (8.2) | 292 (48.7) | 3 (0.7) | 604 (100.0) |
| Low | 218 (52.0) | 50 (11.9) | 144 (34.4) | 7 (1.7) | 419 (100.0) |
| NA | 6 (50.0) | — | 6 (50.0) | — | 12 (100.0) |
| Total | 555 (42.3) | 122 (9.4) | 621 (47.4) | 11 (0.9) | 1,309 (100.0) |

cent of the respondents feel that taxes ought to be cut. It is clear then that a majority of our respondents supports the increasing burden of tax in order to facilitate the implementation of important programmes. However, the opposition of an equally large number of voters (42.3 per cent) to the heavy tax burden cannot be treated lightly. Our data also belie the expectation that mostly the voters falling in low-status category favour reduction in tax. Note, for example, that as status level rises, the proportion of those who oppose reduction of tax increases. Yet another interesting observation pertains to state variation in the responses. As will be seen from the table below, the level of development does seem to have some influence on how voters react to a particular issue area. Note, for example, that in economically backward states like Bihar and U.P., closer to 50 per cent of the respondents favour reduction in the tax burden. In contrast, only 36.0 per cent and 31.7 per cent of respondents in Punjab and West Bengal, respectively, are in favour of tax reduction.

If the respondents are divided in regard to the question of

| States | Responses | | | | |
|---|---|---|---|---|---|
| | Taxes ought to be cut | Undecided | Ought not to be cut | NA | Total |
| Bihar | 165(48.5) | 33( 9.7) | 142(41.8) | — | 340(100.0) |
| Punjab | 105(36.0) | 15( 5.1) | 172(58.9) | — | 292(100.0) |
| U.P. | 206(48.1) | 39( 9.1) | 173(40.4) | 10(2.4) | 428(100.0) |
| W.B. | 79(31.7) | 35(14.1) | 134(53.8) | 1(0.4) | 249(100.0) |
| Total | 555(42.3) | 122( 9.4) | 621(47.4) | 11(0.9) | 1,309(100.0) |

reducing tax burden, what about their opinion on control over industries? In Table 6:3 is presented the response of our respondents to this question. It is interesting that as much as 54.0 per cent of our respondents favour the idea of government itself controlling and managing the industries in the country.

TABLE 6 : 3

SES and Issue-Orientation: Control on Industries (Entire Sample)

(Q: Some people think that the government should itself control and manage the industries of the country, others say they should be left in private hands. On the whole, what do you yourself think ?)

| SES | Responses | | | | |
|---|---|---|---|---|---|
| | Control over none | Control over some | Control over all | D.K., N.A. | Total |
| High | 40(14.6) | 87(31.8) | 143(52.2) | 4( 1.4) | 274(100.0) |
| Medium | 111(18.4) | 123(20.4) | 333(55.1) | 37( 6.1) | 604(100.0) |
| Low | 70(16.7) | 70(16.7) | 223(53.2) | 56(13.4) | 419(100.0) |
| NA | 3(25.0) | 2(16.7) | 7(58.3) | — | 12(100.0) |
| Total | 224(17.1) | 282(21.6) | 706(53.9) | 97(7.4) | 1,309(100.0) |

Only 17.1 per cent of our respondents favour the idea of leaving the industries entirely in private hands. It may further be noted that difference in the level of status of the respondents does not make any appreciable impact on our respondents' opinion on this issue. Note, for example, that if 52.2 per cent of respondents in the high-status category opt for government control and management of industries, 53.9 per cent of respondents in the low-status category also prefer it.

| States | Responses | | | | |
|---|---|---|---|---|---|
| | Control over none | Control over some | Control over all | D.K. | Total |
| Bihar | 38(11.2) | 55(16.2) | 218(64.1) | 29( 8.5) | 340(100.0) |
| Punjab | 18( 6.2) | 39(13.4) | 223(76.3) | 12( 4.1) | 282(100.0) |
| U.P. | 136(31.8) | 110(25.7) | 155(36.2) | 27( 6.3) | 428(100.0) |
| W.B. | 32(12.9) | 78(31.3) | 110(44.2) | 29(11.6) | 249(100.0) |
| Total | 224(17.1) | 282(21.5) | 706(53.9) | 97( 7.5) | 1,309(100.0) |

If status is not salient for opinion on this issue, what about state differences? As the above table shows, support for bringing all industries under government control and management is highest in Punjab (76.37 per cent) and lowest in U.P. (36.22 per cent). If we keep in mind the fact that the faster rate of industrialization in Punjab is due primarily to small-scale industrial entrepreneurs, this high support for the elimination of private enterprise is surprising. It is also surprising to find only moderate support (44.18 per cent) for nationalization of industries in West Bengal where left tendencies of extreme sorts seem to be quite deep-rooted. Further, even if both Bihar and U.P. are mainly agricultural states, the variation in response on this issue is remarkable. If 64.12 per cent of respondents in the former prefer complete nationalization, only 36.22 per cent do so in the latter. It may perhaps be due to the fact that the alternative to the Congress party in U.P. is mainly centrist or rightist, whereas in Bihar it is leftist. As a consequence, this differential political development is reflected also in general public opinion.

The very high support to nationalization of industries is beyond doubt. One question can, however, be raised: Is it possible that since the nationalization of industries affects to any significant degree only a small part of the populace, our respondents can afford to be radical because it does not cost them anything? How will they respond if they were asked to express their opinion about the necessity of abolishing private property? Table 6:4 presents information in this regard. It can be readily seen that there is no consensus among the respondents on this issue inasmuch as opinion is almost equally divided among all three alternatives. Note also that only a little over a quarter of our respondents are in favour of abolishing private property. Also, the socio-economic status of the respondents has only a slight influence on the opinion about the question of the abolition of private property. Worth mentioning in this regard is the fact that as compared to 30.8 per cent of low-statused respondents, 37.6 per cent of high-statused

TABLE 6 : 4

**SES and Issue-Orientation: Private Property (Entire Sample)**

(Q: What about private property? On the whole, would you say that private property should not at all be touched, only part of it should be allowed, or should be abolished?)

| SES | Responses | | | | |
|---|---|---|---|---|---|
| | Should not be touched at all | Only part be allowed | Complete abolition | D.K., N.A. | Total |
| High | 103(37.6) | 110(40.1) | 59(21.5) | 2( 0.8) | 274(100.0) |
| Medium | 204(33.8) | 210(34.8) | 158(26.3) | 31( 5.1) | 604(100.0) |
| Low | 129(30.8) | 113(27.0) | 130(31.0) | 47(11.2) | 419(100.0) |
| NA | 5(41.7) | 2(16.7) | 4(33.3) | 1( 8.3) | 12(100.0) |
| Total | 441(33.7) | 435(33.2) | 352(26.8) | 81( 6.2) | 1,309(100.0) |

respondents oppose any action by the government in regard to private property. Similarly, only 21.5 per cent of high-statused respondents as against 31.0 per cent of low-statused respondents favour complete abolition of private property. Given this, however, there is quite a considerable support for any government action purporting partial abolition of private property. Here again, a larger proportion of higher-statused respondents as compared to lower-statused respondents favour this.

The very low support for the abolition of private property as compared to very high support to the nationalization of industries underlines the fact that any government action meant to substantially affect the economic condition of the common man is unlikely to be supported. It is only in Punjab that a majority of our respondents will welcome the idea of the government taking full control of private property. In West Bengal, only

| SES | Responses | | | | |
|---|---|---|---|---|---|
| | Should not at all be touched | Only part be allowed | Complete abolition | D.K. | Total |
| Bihar | 109(32.1) | 91(26.8) | 114(33.3) | 26(7.8) | 340(100.0) |
| Punjab | 61(20.9) | 46(15.8) | 170(58.2) | 15(5.1) | 292(100.0) |
| U.P. | 243(56.8) | 113(26.4) | 51(11.9) | 21(4.9) | 428(100.0) |
| W.B. | 28(11.3) | 185(74.3) | 17( 6.8) | 19(7.6) | 249(100.0) |
| Total | 441(33.7) | 435(33.2) | 352(26.8) | 81(6.3) | 1,309(100.0) |

about seven per cent of our respondents approve of complete abolition of private property although a large majority (74.3 per cent) would not mind partial take-over by the government. In Bihar, opinion seems to be equally divided between complete abolition of private property and complete exemption from government control. It is in U.P., that a large number of respondents (56.8 per cent) are positively against any takeover of private property by the government. It seems, then, that Punjab and U.P. constitute the two extremes of the "statism" continuum with Bihar and West Bengal occupying different positions on it.

Having discussed the relationship between the socio-economic status of the respondents and their position on a particular issue and the variations in the pattern of their responses from one state to the next, we now turn to presenting a summary measure of what, in the lack of a better term, we characterize statism. This labelling is quite appropriate even if inelegant. It is appropriate since a syndrome of attitudes supporting enlarged jurisdiction for the government means a preference for social rather than individual action. Our index of left orientation[6] is at once a measure of our respondents' willingness to allow greater powers to the government as well as a tendency towards left. In Table 6:5 we juxtapose the tendency towards left against the socio-economic level of our respondents.

At the very first glance it becomes apparent that our expectation of finding consistency of attitude in our respondents on items relating to different issue areas is unrealistic. As we have already seen, when each item is considered singly, a sizeable number of respondents seems to be in favour of granting greater powers to the state. However, it does not seem necessary that if a respondent favours a particular course of action in one particular issue area he will in all likelihood tend to favour a similar course of action in another but related issue area. In other words, attitudinal consistency on issues can be expected to be present in only a small proportion of voters; in the case of the rest, we should not be surprised if a voter prefers strong government action in one issue area and no action in other related areas. It is because of this that we find only a small proportion of our respondents manifesting a high degree of left orientation: Bihar 22.6 per cent, U.P. 7.6 per cent and West Bengal 21.3 per cent. It is only in Punjab that 40.1 per cent of our respondents seem to be highly oriented towards the left. Otherwise, most of the respondents fall in the medium category of the index indicating favourable attitude on one and unfavourable attitude on other items included in the index.

Leaving aside state variations in left orientation, the

---

6. Derived from the three items discussed in the preceding pages.

TABLE 6 : 5

SES and Leftist Orientation (in per cent)

| States | Bihar | | | | Punjab | | | | U.P. | | | | W.B. | | | |
|---|---|---|---|---|---|---|---|---|---|---|---|---|---|---|---|---|
| Left Orientation \ SES | High | Medium | Low | Total | High | Medium | Low | Total | High | Medium | Low | Total | High | Medium | Low | Total |
| High | 30.3 | 60.5 | 9.2 | 76 100.0 | 37.7 | 60.7 | 1.6 | 61 100.0 | 15.8 | 72.4 | 11.8 | 76 100.0 | 24.6 | 70.5 | 4.9 | 61 100.0 |
| Medium | 23.9 | 66.2 | 9.9 | 142 100.0 | 43.9 | 53.4 | 2.7 | 148 100.0 | 8.0 | 64.0 | 28.0 | 89 100.0 | 23.2 | 69.6 | 7.2 | 125 100.0 |
| Low | 16.8 | 74.0 | 9.2 | 119 100.0 | 34.1 | 65.9 | — | 82 100.0 | 8.9 | 63.1 | 28.0 | 157 100.0 | 11.5 | 83.6 | 4.9 | 61 100.0 |
| NA | 33.3 | 66.7 | — | 3 100.0 | 100.0 | — | — | 1 100.0 | — | 67.7 | 33.3 | 6 100.0 | 100.0 | — | — | 2 100.0 |
| Total | 77 22.6 | 231 68.0 | 32 9.4 | 340 100.0 | 117 40.1 | 170 58.2 | 5 1.7 | 292 100.0 | 41 9.6 | 279 65.2 | 108 25.2 | 428 100.0 | 53 21.3 | 181 72.7 | 15 6.0 | 249 100.0 |

socio-economic status of the respondent does not seem to make much difference in the kind of opinion he may hold on these issues. However, except in the case of Punjab, there is some ground to suggest that higher the status, the likelihood of respondents being favourable to the idea of increase in the powers of the state is somewhat greater. Note, for example, that 30.3 per cent of high-statused respondents as against only 16.8 per cent of low-statused respondents in Bihar are high on the index of left orientation. A similar tendency can be observed in U.P. and West Bengal also. In Punjab, on the other hand, it is the respondents at the medium level of status that constitute the largest proportion of those who manifest a high degree of left orientation.

The low salience of socio-economic status for inclining the respondents one way or the other on the ideological continuum is very well reflected in our data. Our data also show that there is available a large degree of support to government if it wanted to increase taxes and nationalize industries. However, the magnitude of support varies from one state to another and from one social stratum to the next. Also, only a very small proportion of our respondents seems to be consistently radically left in respect of all the three issue areas. It is only in the case of private property that opinion seems to be equally divided between no control, partial control and complete control. This is enough to show that even though a large number of our respondents would very well like many people to show no interest in politics, they would, however, be willing to permit the government to take on more powers and actively intervene in spheres that have been conventionally treated as private.

Given this orientation, the question arises: How do the respondents view the institutional framework that functions both as mediating structures of articulating policy alternatives and making decisions? The success of a democratic form of government does not so much depend on the quantum of power that the people are willing to allow to the state, as on the acceptability of mediate, intermediate and ultimate institutions involved in policy making and policy executing processes as not only legitimate but also as necessary instruments. It is to this aspect of our enquiry that we now turn.

We present in Table 6:6 responses of our respondents in

regard to their opinion about the necessity of democratic institutions for better government as against their socio-economic status. The first thing we note is that higher the development of a state, more likely it is that a larger proportion of voters would appreciate the necessity of democratic institutions like parties, assemblies and elections for good government. Note, for example, that 65.5 per cent of our respondents in West Bengal and 62.7 per cent in Punjab think that government in this country cannot be run better if there were no parties, assemblies and elections. In contrast, only 48.8 per cent in U.P. and 47.7 per cent of respondents in Bihar think so. Equally important is the fact that 38.1 per cent of the respondents in U.P. and 30.7 per cent in Bihar feel that the government can be run better without these institutions.

Given the salience of level of development for favourable orientation towards democratic institutions, the socio-economic status of the respondent also seems to be a potent factor in disposing the respondent favourably towards these institutions. Note, for example, that with every drop in the level of socio-economic status, the proportion of those who consider democratic institutions necessary for a better government also drops in each of the states. Similarly, the proportion of those who believe that the government can be run better without these institutions gradually increases particularly in Bihar and Punjab as we go down the status hierarchy. In the case of U.P. and West Bengal, the respondents falling in the medium-status category seem, as can be noted, to be persuaded of the uselessness of democratic institutions in larger proportions than those falling in other status categories.

Our data, then, suggest that, on the whole, a majority of our respondents (54.9 per cent if we take the entire sample into consideration) consider parties, assemblies and elections as necessary components of a good government. Further confirmation of the crucial importance of democratic institutions comes from the responses of the voters in our sample to other questions. We discuss here just one other question that relates to the necessity of political parties. Responding to the question "Do you think political parties are necessary or not in India?", 79.2 per cent of our respondents said that they were necessary. This is, then, enough to show acceptance on the part of the

TABLE 6:6

## SES and Acceptance of Democratic Institutions (in per cent)

(Q: Do you think that the government in this country can be run better if there were no parties, assemblies and elections?)

| States | Bihar | | | | Punjab | | | | U.P. | | | | | W.B. | | | | |
|---|---|---|---|---|---|---|---|---|---|---|---|---|---|---|---|---|---|---|
| Responses SES | Yes | Undecided | No | Total | Yes | Undecided | No | Total | Yes | Undecided | No | NA | Total | Yes | Undecided | No | NA | Total |
| High | 19.7 | 14.5 | 65.8 | 76 / 100.0 | 13.1 | 13.1 | 73.8 | 61 / 100.0 | 30.3 | 7.9 | 60.5 | 1.3 | 76 / 100.0 | 8.2 | 6.6 | 85.2 | — | 61 / 100.0 |
| Medium | 31.7 | 19.7 | 48.6 | 142 / 100.0 | 14.2 | 18.9 | 66.9 | 148 / 100.0 | 40.2 | 9.0 | 49.8 | — | 189 / 100.0 | 24.8 | 12.0 | 61.6 | 1.6 | 125 / 100.0 |
| Low | 37.8 | 26.1 | 36.1 | 119 / 100.0 | 17.1 | 36.6 | 46.3 | 82 / 100.0 | 38.9 | 17.2 | 42.0 | 1.9 | 157 / 100.0 | 14.8 | 31.1 | 54.1 | — | 61 / 100.0 |
| NA | — | 33.3 | 66.7 | 3 / 100.0 | — | — | 100.0 | 1 / 100.0 | 33.3 | — | 66.7 | — | 6 / 100.0 | 50.0 | — | 50.0 | — | 2 / 100.0 |
| Total | 105 / 30.9 | 72 / 21.2 | 163 / 47.9 | 340 / 100.0 | 43 / 14.7 | 66 / 22.6 | 183 / 62.7 | 292 / 100.0 | 163 / 38.1 | 50 / 11.7 | 209 / 48.8 | 6 / 1.3 | 428 / 100.0 | 46 / 18.5 | 38 / 15.3 | 163 / 65.5 | 2 / 0.7 | 249 / 100.0 |

voter of democratic institutions as necessary instruments of a popular government.

It can, however, be argued that the mere acceptance of democratic institutions, say, political parties, is not enough. Even though the common man is persuaded to consider political parties as necessary, he may perceive no difference between them, may dislike the idea of competition among them and, even more important, strongly feel that the existence of more than one party is undesirable in order to avoid unpleasant consequences of party competition. In other words, once the desirability of popular government and its components is established, we have to further explore whether or not the voters relate, either vaguely or clearly, the phenomenon of party competition and, as a consequence, the necessity of the existence of more than one party differentiated on the basis of policies and programmes to the working of the popular government. We, therefore, now turn to these aspects of our enquiry.

We present in Table 6:7 the perception of differences in parties by our respondents and then proceed on to discuss other aspects. As will be seen from the table, in each of the states, more than 60 per cent of our respondents claim to find differences in the policies and programmes of various parties. In Punjab, for example, 84.2 per cent of respondents find policy and programmatic differences in various parties and in West Bengal 62.7 per cent. Given the fact of the awareness of party differences in a large number of respondents, the socio-economic status of voters seems to be a very crucial conditioning factor in promoting this awareness. In each state, for example, the larger proportion of those who perceive policy and programmatic differences among various parties comes from the high-status group. Also, the proportion of those who find no such differences invariably increases as we go down the status hierarchy. The influence of socio-economic status on the awareness of party differences is quite obvious. However, the fact remains that this awareness spills over status boundaries and a large proportion of respondents from each social stratum claim to have the awareness of party differences.

If the awareness of party differences is quite widespread, the idea of political parties competing among themselves for power

TABLE 6:7

SES and Perception of Party Differences (in per cent)

(Q : Do you think that there are important differences in the policies and programmes of various parties?)

| State | Bihar | | | | | Punjab | | | | | U.P. | | | | | W.B. | | | | |
|---|---|---|---|---|---|---|---|---|---|---|---|---|---|---|---|---|---|---|---|---|
| Responses / SES | No | Undecided | Yes | | Total | No | Undecided | Yes | | Total | No | Undecided | Yes | NA | Total | No | Undecided | Yes | NA | Total |
| High | 5.3 | 7.9 | 86.8 | | 76 100.0 | 3.3 | 1.6 | 95.1 | | 61 100.0 | 3.9 | 6.6 | 89.5 | — | 76 100.0 | 13.1 | 9.8 | 75.5 | 1.6 | 61 100.0 |
| Medium | 16.9 | 8.5 | 74.6 | | 142 100.0 | 7.4 | 2.7 | 89.9 | | 148 100.0 | 18.5 | 18.5 | 61.9 | 1.1 | 189 100.0 | 20.0 | 16.8 | 63.2 | — | 125 100.0 |
| Low | 31.1 | 7.6 | 61.3 | | 119 100.0 | 28.0 | 6.1 | 65.9 | | 82 100.0 | 28.0 | 10.8 | 58.6 | 2.6 | 157 100.0 | 31.1 | 21.3 | 47.6 | — | 61 100.0 |
| NA | 33.3 | — | 67.3 | | 3 100.0 | — | — | 100.0 | | 1 100.0 | — | 50.0 | 50.0 | — | 6 100.0 | — | — | 100.0 | — | 2 100.0 |
| Total | 66 19.4 | 27 7.9 | 247 72.7 | | 340 100.0 | 36 12.3 | 10 3.4 | 246 84.3 | | 212 100.0 | 82 19.2 | 58 13.6 | 282 65.9 | 6 1.3 | 428 100.0 | 52 20.9 | 40 16.1 | 156 62.7 | 1 0.3 | 249 100.0 |

does not seem to be that desirable. Responding to the question, "Would you agree that it is not desirable to have political parties compete with each other for power?", as much as 40.8 per cent of our respondents agree and 47.5 disagree. In other words, opinion on this issue is divided. However, the majority opinion is decidedly in favour of competition. It should be noted that the use of the phrase "competition for power" vitiates the interpretation of the responses. Power in itself is a word that is normatively looked down upon. When we add to it the term competition—another normatively undesirable word—the situation becomes all the more unpredictable.

To get away from the difficulties created by the use of these unfortunate words, we asked our respondents another question. The responses are presented in Table 6:8. It is interesting to note that only 6.2 per cent of our respondents think that no party is necessary for the good of the country. Similarly, only 8.5 per cent of the voters feel that there should be more than two parties to assure a good government in our country. In contrast, half of our respondents prefer the existence of only one party and 29.8 per cent of two parties. In other words, our finding that a sizeable number of our respondents is not convinced of the desirability of party competition for power in spite of our use of the phrase "competition for power" holds good. This is so for the reason that this same attitude is again reflected in their preference for one party which in the ultimate analysis means lack of competition or, at least, lack of a vigorous party competition.

Given this preference for the playing down of party competition, it does, however, seem that higher the status of a the respondent, more likely it is that he will show the awareness of necessity of party competition as a means of assuring good government. Note, for example, that only 42.7 per cent of high-statused respondents as against 56.6 per cent of low-statused respondents prefer one party. Similarly, only 20.8 per cent of our respondents falling in the low-status category as compared to 41.2 per cent of high-statused respondents opt for the existence of two parties. Furthermore, the percentages of "do not know" cases increase as we move down the status hierarchy. All these factors strongly indicate that there is some definite association between the socio-economic status of a respondent and his

## TABLE 6 : 8

### SES and the Perception of the Necessity of Parties : Entire Sample (in per cent)

(Q : What will assure a good government in this country : one party for the whole country, two parties, more than two parties, or no party at all?)

| Status level | Responses | | | | | |
|---|---|---|---|---|---|---|
| | No party | One party | Two parties | More than Two parties | DK | NA | Total |
| High | 13(4.7) | 117(42.7) | 113(41.2) | 27(9.9) | 3(1.1) | 1(0.4) | 274(100.0) |
| Medium | 44(7.3) | 304(50.3) | 186(30.8) | 53(8.8) | 14(2.3) | 3(0.5) | 604(100.0) |
| Low | 23(5.5) | 237(56.6) | 87(20.8) | 30(7.2) | 39(9.3) | 3(0.7) | 419(100.0) |
| NA | 1(8.3) | 5(41.7) | 5(41.7) | 1(8.3) | — | — | 12(100.0) |
| Total | 81(6.2) | 663(50.5) | 391(30.0) | 111(8.5) | 56(4.3) | 7(0.5) | 1,309(100.0) |

awareness of the necessity of party competition as a means of assuring good government.

Having discussed some of the issues related with democratic institutions, we now turn to explore the voters' understanding of the legislator's role in the complex institutional set up of a popular government. The first item that we wish to discuss in this regard pertains to the acceptance of the rules of the democratic game by the voters. After the dust of electoral battle raised sky-high by heightened partisan passion and fury settles down, the fact that one side has lost becomes painfully clear to the partisans of the defeated candidate. If this defeat leads the supporters of a defeated candidate to withdraw from the system and express their hurt feelings in overt or covert acts of defiance and alienation, it is certain, then, that the rule of the democratic game that prescribes acceptance of defeat in a good humour has not been learned. To the extent that the rules are either not accepted as legitimate or are broken frequently, the foundation of democratic politics will be weakened. One of the democratic rules suggests that once a majority opinion has settled upon the choice of a representative, he should be universally accepted as such. What do our respondents have to show in this regard?

As will be seen from Table 6:9, as much as 71.8 per cent of our respondents express their readiness to consider a person as their representative even if they did not vote for him. As against this, only 21.5 per cent of the voters in our sample say that they would refuse to treat a person as their representative if they did not vote for him. Also interesting in this regard is the fact that the acceptance of this aspect of the democratic game is not conditioned by the socio-economic status of the respondent. Note, for example, that there is no significant difference in the distribution of responses between one status level and another. In other words, the idea that once a person has been chosen by majority opinions as the representative, he must be treated so, has seeped down even to the people who inhabit the lowest rung of social hierarchy. That is to say, this rule of the game is widespread and diffused over all social stratum.

Given the acceptance of this rule of the game, one might raise the question that this acceptance does not, however, reflect the voters' acceptance of the usefulness of the functional

### TABLE 6 : 9

**SES and Acceptance of the Rule of the Game: Entire Sample**
**(in per cent)**

(Q: Suppose the person you did not vote for gets elected, would you consider him the representative of your area?)

| Status | Responses | | | | |
|---|---|---|---|---|---|
| | Yes | Undecided | No | NA | Total |
| High | 194(70.8) | 10( 3.6) | 69(25.2) | 1(0.4) | 274(100.0) |
| Medium | 447(74.0) | 33( 5.5) | 124(20.5) | — | 604(100.0) |
| Low | 286(68.3) | 45(10.7) | 88(21.0) | — | 419(100·0) |
| NA | 11(91.7) | — | 1 (8.3) | — | 12(100.0) |
| Total | 938(71.7) | 88( 6.7) | 282(21.5) | 1(0.1) | 1,309(100.0) |

status that a representative occupies in a democracy. It is quite possible that the common man treats him as simply a functionary who is there to demonstrate the functioning of the democratic system of government in a formal sense but devoid of any substantial role. That this is not so is demonstrated by our data. Responding to the question, "How useful are MLAs and MPs in managing the affairs of the nation well?" 60.1 per cent of our respondents said that they are useful and only 9.4 per cent said that they are not useful; 25.7 per cent of the respondents said they are only somewhat useful.

Our data, then, indicate a wider acceptance of the role of the representative as being useful. But what notion of the role of the representative do our respondents have? Do the voters in the four states consider the representative a trustee or an agent? Table 6:10 presents pertinent information in this regard. As can be seen, as much as 52.1 per cent of our respondents think that the representative should follow the wishes of the people who have elected him even when he thinks them to be mistaken. As against this, 44.3 per cent of our respondents are willing to grant autonomy to the representative's role. In other words, given a somewhat wider acceptance of the agent role of the representative, his trustee role is also accepted

## TABLE 6: 10

**SES and Voters' Concept of Representatives' Role: Entire Sample (in per cent)**

(Q: Do you think a representative should follow the wishes of the people who elect him even when he thinks the people are mistaken?)

| Status | Responses | | | | |
|---|---|---|---|---|---|
| | Yes | No | DK | NA | Total |
| High | 137(50.0) | 134(48.9) | 1(0.4) | 2(0.7) | 274(100.0) |
| Medium | 312(51.7) | 279(46.2) | 8(1.3) | 5(0.8) | 604(100.0) |
| Low | 237(56.6) | 161(38.4) | 15(3.6) | 6(1.4) | 419(100.0) |
| NA | 6(50.0) | 6(50.0) | — | — | 12(100.0) |
| Total | 692(52.1) | 580(44.3) | 24(1.8) | 13(0.8) | 1,309(100.0) |

by a sizeable number of our respondents. Also worth noting in this regard is the fact that persons inhabiting lower status levels tend to be comparatively more inclined towards the agent role than those who belong to higher status groups. Note, for example, that not only the proportion of those who opt for the agent role of the representative increases as we go down the status hierarchy but also the proportion of those who incline towards the trustee role increases as we go up the status hierarchy. In terms of overall percentages, this difference is not very marked; nonetheless, socio-economic status does seem to have some influence on the concept the voters may hold about the role of the representative.

That there is greater acceptance of the agent role of the representative can be verified from a different angle. In order to check up on the item just discussed, we asked another question of our respondents. Responding to the question, "Do you think that a representative should do what he thinks right even if it is different from what the electorate expects?" only 31.1 per cent of our respondents endorsed the statement. As against

## TABLE 6 : 11

### SES and Voters' Concept of Representatives' Role: Entire Sample
(in per cent)

(Q: Do you think that a representative should do what he thinks right even if it is different from what the electorate expects?)

| Status | Responses | | | | |
|---|---|---|---|---|---|
| | Yes | No | DK | NA | Total |
| High | 81(29.6) | 189(69.0) | 2(0.7) | 2(0.7) | 274(100.0) |
| Medium | 191(31.6) | 402(66.5) | 7(1.2) | 4(0.7) | 604(100.0) |
| Low | 131(31.3) | 267(63.7) | 13(3.1) | 8(1.9) | 419(100.0) |
| NA | 4(33.3) | 8(66.7) | — | — | 12(100.0) |
| Total | 407(31.1) | 866(66.1) | 22(1.6) | 14(1.2) | 1,309(100.0) |

this, 66.1 per cent of the voters expressed their conviction in favour of the representative acting according to the expectations of his constituents rather than doing what he himself thinks right. Note also the fact that differences in socio-economic status are only slightly reflected in the opinions of our respondents in this regard. It is, therefore, indicative of the wide diffusion of the notion that the representative should perform his role according to the expectations of his constituents.

This is enough to show the widespread acceptance of the agent role of the representative. This does not, however, mean that our voters are not persuaded to allow autonomy to the representative; as a matter of fact, more than one-third of the voters in our sample recognize the relevance of the trustee role of the representative. Yet the fact remains that the agent role dominates the thinking of a large majority of the voters.

We have been upto now considering the voters' conception of the relationship between the representative and his constituents. This relationship is mediated by a very important democratic institution, namely, party. Considering the fact that it is the party that sponsors the candidate, mobilizes votes for his election and keeps disciplinary control over him, it is important to examine what role the voters attribute to the party vis-a-vis the representative. In order to ascertain the opinion of the voters on this issue we asked them: "Suppose an important issue is being discussed in the Assembly and the MLA thinks one thing, his party another and the people yet another. What should the MLA do in such a situation? Should he do what he himself thinks best, what his electorate wants him to do, or what his party wants him to do? The result is tabulated in Table 6:12.

As will be seen from the table, in each of the states a large number of respondents is unwilling to allow the representative complete freedom to decide for himself. 70.6 per cent of respondents in Bihar, 66.8 per cent in Punjab, 64.3 in U.P. and 47.8 per cent in West Bengal think that, when faced with a situation where no consensus obtains about what he should do, the representative must act according to what his constituents expect of him. This unequivocal expression of the view that the representative's principal responsibility is towards his constituents whose interests he has been elected to serve is remarkably consistent. Given the primary of the agent role of the representative, what also appears interesting is the fact that very few of our respondents seem to be persuaded of the autonomous role of the representative. Second in importance is the party. In a situation of conflict between the view points of the representative and his party, the voter in our sample would opt for the party thinking as the best guide for the representative's conduct. Note, for example, that only 4.7 per cent as against 19.1 per cent in Bihar, 8.6 per cent as against 24.3 per cent in Punjab, 13.1 per cent as against 20.1 per cent in U.P. and 18.5 per cent as compared to 22.5 per cent in West Bengal feel that the representative should act according to what he himself thinks best.

Our data, then, fully substantiate the finding that the dominant popular thinking favours the agent role of the representative. As a second preference, the voters would like the MLA to be guided by his party's thinking. We shall note here one other interesting facet of this. It seems that voters belonging to lower status group express their preference for the agent role of the representative more than those who fall in higher status

## TABLE 6 : 12

### SES and Voters' Concept of Legislator's Role (in per cent)

(Q : Suppose an important issue is being discussed in the Assembly and the MLA thinks one thing, his party another and the people yet another. What should the MLA do in such a situation? Should he do what he himself thinks best, what his electorate wants him to do, or what his party wants him to do?)

| Responses | Bihar | | | | | Punjab | | | | | U.P. | | | | | W.B. | | | | |
|---|---|---|---|---|---|---|---|---|---|---|---|---|---|---|---|---|---|---|---|---|
| SES | E | H | P | DK | Total | E | H | P | DK | Total | E | H | P | DK | Total | E | H | P | DK | Total |
| High | 64.5 | 11.8 | 23.7 | — | 100.0 142 | 55.8 | 13.1 | 31.1 | — | 100.0 148 | 63.2 | 13.2 | 22.4 | 2.2 | 100.0 189 | 52.5 | 11.5 | 29.5 | 6.5 | 100.0 125 |
| Medium | 69.7 | 9.2 | 19.7 | 1.4 | 100.0 119 | 68.3 | 8.1 | 23.6 | — | 100.0 82 | 59.8 | 14.8 | 23.8 | 2.6 | 100.0 157 | 50.4 | 21.6 | 21.6 | 6.6 | 100.0 61 |
| Low | 75.6 | 9.2 | 15.1 | 0.1 | 100.0 | 72.0 | 6.1 | 20.7 | 1.2 | 100.0 1 | 69.4 | 11.5 | 14.6 | 4.5 | 100.0 6 | 57.7 | 13.0 | 18.0 | 26.3 | 100.0 2 |
| NA | 66.7 | — | 33.3 | 3 | 100.0 | 100.0 | — | — | — | 100.0 | 66.7 | — | 33.3 | — | 100.0 | 50.0 | 50.0 | — | — | 100.0 |
| Total | 240 70.6 | 33 9.7 | 65 19.1 | 2 0.6 | 340 100.0 | 195 66.8 | 25 8.6 | 71 24.3 | 1 0.3 | 292 100.0 | 275 64.3 | 56 13.1 | 86 20.1 | 11 2.5 | 428 100.0 | 119 47.8 | 46 18.5 | 56 22.5 | 28 11.2 | 249 100.0 |

Note : E = Electorate; H = the MLA himself; and P = Party.

groups. This trend operates consistently in all states except West Bengal where it is completely reversed.

Considering the fact that a large number of respondents are not willing to allow any autonomy to the representative in his role performance, cannot it be expected that a majority of our respondents will also view with disfavour the phenomenon of what has been called "defections"? Defection can take place because of two reasons. In the first place, there may be a genuine difference of opinion and conviction between the MLA and his party and the MLA may decide to leave the party in order not to compromise his conscience. In the second place, the MLA may, either for pecuniary reasons or for improving his power position, leave one party and join another and leave it again. Whatever may be the reason, his constituents may not be interested in what motivates him to defect and disapprove of his act. Or, again, the electorate may not be concerned with what the MLA does once he has been elected. We want to find out, in very general terms, as to how the electorate does view the phenomenon of defection. In the next two tables we present information on this issue.

As Table 6:13 reveals, 61.0 per cent of our respondents say that the MLA cannot be permitted to decide for himself whether or not he should leave a party and join another after the elections. As against this, only 26.7 per cent of our respondents would like this issue to be left to the discretion of the MLA. In other words, a large majority of our respondents look with disfavour at the phenomenon of defection. And, as our data suggest, this viewpoint is conditioned by the socio-economic level of the respondent. Note, for example, that the proportion of the high-statused respondents disagreeing with the statement is considerably larger than that of their counterparts falling in lower status groups. Similarly, as we move towards higher status groups in the "agree" response category, the proportions fall. Note also the fact that the proportion of "do not know" cases are larger in lower status groups. This strongly suggests that voters belonging to higher status groups are much more likely to be critical of the phenomenon of defection than those in the lower status groups.

It is thus clear that for a large number of voters the MLA must continue to owe his allegiance to the party on whose ticket

## TABLE 6 : 13

### SES and Voter's View on Defection : Entire Sample (in per cent)

(Q : It is said that MLA are the best judges to decide which party to leave and which to join after elections. Do you agree?)

| Status | Responses | | | | | |
|---|---|---|---|---|---|---|
| | Agree | Partly agree | Disagree | DK | NA | Total |
| High | 49(17.9) | 17(6.2) | 203(74.1) | 3(1.1) | 2(0.7) | 274(100.0) |
| Medium | 149(24.7) | 41(6.8) | 393(65.1) | 17(2.8) | 4(0.7) | 604(100.0) |
| Low | 148(35.2) | 35(8.4) | 195(47.5) | 35(8.4) | 6(1.4) | 419(100.0) |
| NA | 3(25.0) | 1(8.3) | 8(66.7) | — | — | 12(100.0) |
| Total | 349(26.7) | 94(7.2) | 799(61.0) | 55 | 12 | 1,309(100.0) |

he gets entry to the assembly. However, the question might be asked as to what will the voters think when they find their representative changing party labels even while he serves his constituents well? Cannot it be argued that since most of the voters are concerned with the furtherance of their own interests through the office of the representative, they should shut their eyes to the crossing of floor by the MLA if he serves his constituents well? We are raising, in effect, the question of whether or not the electorate perceives in the phenomenon of frequent floor-crossing the implications for the political system as against the parochial interest of the constituents. In other words, we are interested in finding out whether or not the electorate looks beyond the mere serving of its own interests and relates the phenomenon of defection to larger political processes, to the prior claim of the party over the representative and to the necessity of maintaining the dignity of democratic institutions. In order to explore this aspect of our enquiry, we asked our respondents this question: "Many say that as long as an MLA works for his constituents, it does not matter whether he remains in the party on whose ticket he was elected or changes his party. Do you agree?" The results are tabulated in Table 6:14.

As will be seen from the table, even when the respondents are confronted with a situation which juxtaposes their own interest as against that of the party, only 38.0 per cent of the voters in our sample say that if the MLA serves the interests of his constituents well, it is immaterial whether he continues to remain in the sponsoring party or leaves it. As against this, 46.4 per cent of our respondents categorically affirm that, even in such a stuation, the MLA is not free to cross the floor. Even in this case we note the association of socio-economic status with the kind of opinion a particular respondent is likely to hold on this issue. As in the previous case, voters in higher status groups are more likely to incline towards the subservient status of the MLA as against those who are placed in the lower status groups.

Our discussion then amply underlines the fact that a large majority of our respondents consider their representative more of an agent than of a trustee. This has repeatedly been brought out by our data. Even more important in this regard is the fact that most of the voters in our sample disapprove of the

## TABLE 6 : 14

### SES and Voter's Views on Defection : Entire Sample (in per cent)

(Q : Many say that as long as an MLA works for his constituents, it does not matter whether he remains in the party on whose ticket he was elected or changes his party. Do you agree?)

| Status | Responses | | | | | |
|---|---|---|---|---|---|---|
| | Agree | Partly agree | Disagree | DK | NA | Total |
| High | 87(31.7) | 18( 6.6) | 159(58.0) | 7( 2.6) | 3(1.1) | 274(100.0) |
| Medium | 233(38.6) | 50( 8.3) | 186(47.3) | 26( 4.3) | 9(1.5) | 604(100.0) |
| Low | 174(41.5) | 51( 9.8) | 156(37.2) | 43(10.3) | 5(1.2) | 419(100.0) |
| NA | 4(33.3) | 2(16.7) | 6(50.0) | — | — | 12(100.0) |
| Total | 498(38.0) | 121( 8.4) | 507(46.4) | 76( 5.9) | 17(1.3) | 1,309(100.0) |

phenomenon of defection. They would rather like the MLA to continue to owe his allegiance to the party on whose ticket he was elected to the assembly. In other words, for a large number of voters, party as an institution occupies a primary position than the MLA in the whole complex of democratic institutions.

To sum up our discussion, then, we have shown that a sizeable number of our respondents does not favour involvement in politics of a large number of people. This perhaps reflects their antipathy to the undesirable way politics has been conducted in this country. This is also reflected in the fact that relatively more persons evaluate the President's rule favourably in comparison to popular government. This is symptomatic of the common man's disgust with politics that thrives on the sacrifice of decency, principles and higher values.

Given this, however, a large number of voters would not oppose formulating and implementing left-of-the-centre policies by the government. The political development in the course of the last two decades and so much talk about socialism are reflected in the new, emerging consensus that underscore the desirability of pursuing left-of-the-centre policies. The willingness of the electorate to enlarge the functions of the government and to allow it to intervene into spheres that have traditionally been treated as private is well matched by its understanding of the necessity and usefulness of various democratic institutions. However, when it comes to defining the role of the representative in relation to his constituents, a large number of our respondents, favour the agent role. This does not, however, mean that they are unaware of the crucial role that parties play in influencing this relationship. Given the primacy of the agent role of the representative, most of our respondents are definitely against any action on the part of the representative that is likely to endanger the institutional fabric of Indian democracy.

# CHAPTER SEVEN

# The Voter and the Political System

"THE stability of any given democracy," writes S.M. Lipset, "depends not only on economic development but also upon the effectiveness and the legitimacy of its political system,"[1] Its effectiveness lies not only in the extent to which it can fulfil the basic needs of its citizens but also in its capability to effectively utilize its unitary sovereignty for maintaining the precarious balance between the necessity of realizing systemic goals and the aspirations of various groups to achieve through private and public activities whatever value they hold. To put it differently, recognizing that political authority cannot completely eliminate conflicts that arise out of incompatible group interests, the effectiveness of the political regime depends on its capability to facilitate the institutionalization of conflict and bargaining in ways that optimize consensus and values.[2]

In contradistinction to the effectiveness of the political regime to contain and resolve conflict, legitimacy pertains to the way people evaluate the political system in terms of congruence between their own values and those which the regime endeavours to uphold. "Legitimacy involves the capacity of the system to engender and maintain the belief that the existing political institutions are the most appropriate ones for the society."[3] The concept of legitimacy is thus a compound of two elements: evaluation and affect. The functioning of the system is frequently subjected to a critical evaluation by the people who assess its worth in fulfilling their felt needs including symbolic ones. When the system is adjudged to be serving these needs effectively, it is endowed with an element of sanctity making it a desirable instrument of public action. It should be noted here that the sense of legitimacy, that is, willingness of the

---

1. S.M. Lipset, *Political Man* (Garden City, New York : Doubleday & Co., Inc., 1960), p. 77.
2. See H.L. Nieburg, "Violence, Law, and the Informal Polity", *The Journal of Conflict Resolution*, XIII : 2 (June 1969), p. 196.
3. Lipset, *op. cit.*

people to obey its *dictats*, is like a stock of goodwill which must be replenished by acts that enhance people's confidence in the system. Whether this stock continues unabated or has been depleted is discovered when widespread acts of public defiance increase to highlight "misconceived" government actions. Therefore, "any exercise of authority depends upon the willingness of officials and the public to respond positively to commands or rules (or at least not too negatively), hence ultimately the official relies on the existence of goodwill."[4]

In point of fact, these two phenomena—effectiveness and legitimacy—are interrelated. One cannot talk of the one without the other. The effectiveness of the political regime depends on the extent to which it is supposed by the public as a legitimate instrument of public action. Similarly, legitimacy comes to be reinforced by the degree to which the regime is effective in satisfying the basic needs of the populace. The fluctuating stock of legitimacy is one of the clearest indications of the relationship that at any particular moment obtains between those who have the mandate to rule and those who habitually and willingly submit themselves to their rule.

The depletion of the stock of legitimacy is, therefore, indicative of the negative reactions of crucial segments of the society to the commands and rules of political authority. This is most likely to happen when there grows a vast gap between the normative elements centralized in the unitary sovereignty of the state and the factual order that shapes interest. This symbolizes a crisis of consensus. The prevailing legal norms based on some previously arrived consensus prove to be inadequate in coping with the ever-growing demands channelled into political process and, as a result, the necessity of forging a new consensus arises, a consensus that will take into account the surfacing conflicts. We should, in this regard, accept the distinction that Neiburg makes between legality and legitimacy in order to better appreciate the role of political institutions, especially the government, in forging a consensus out of incompatible group demands. The phenomenon of conflict symbolizes a changing configuration of political forces intimating the rise of new

---

4. R. Bendix, *Nation-Building and Citizenship* (New York: John Wiley & Sons, Inc. 1964), p. 19.

forces groping for accommodation and political power. The insistence on legality as a means of coping with the emerging situations provokes still more conflict since the antecedent consensus sanctifying the procedural methods of resolving conflict is itself suspect. The government, if it wants to survive, has to take recourse to finding ways and means for accommodating emerging interests. When the legal order takes cognizance of changes in the factual order and undergoes a process of adjustment, the divisive forces are once again integrated at a new level of consensus reinforcing the existing stock of legitimacy of the political order. Legitimacy is then inextricably related with the process through which the political order adapts to the human and physical environment.

The relevance of these two concepts takes on added weight in the developing countries. Not only is a centralized political authority a new element in these countries, but it also impinges more and more and in diverse ways on the life of the common man. Further, with enlarged functions of the government, large-scale politics acquires special significance. It is true that the post-independence governments in many of the developing countries started with quite a high stock of goodwill. But soon, much of it withered in the political heat generated by parochial clamour for greater access to political power and a share in the benefits accruing from economic development. The divisive tendencies observed to be operating in the political system seem, to many, to tear apart its fabric. Moreover, inexperienced in the management of politics but firm in their resolve to hold on to political power even though losing popular support, the ruling elites in many of the developing countries obstruct the accommodation of politically rising groups. This necessarily affects the legitimacy of the political order. Thus, the concept of legitimacy, as Lipset points out, "is related to the ways in which different societies handle the 'entry into politics' crisis—the decision as to when new social groups shall obtain access to the political process."[5]

The concept of legitimacy thus provides a useful tool for assessing and evaluating the relationship that obtains between the rulers and the ruled. However, in order to identify this

---

5. Lipset, *op. cit.*, p. 78.

phenomenon as a prerequisite of any operating political system and to be able to describe the magnitude of its stock, one has necessarily to take into account the cognitive, the perceptual and the evaluative orientation of the common man towards the political order. On the surface, the political system may look quite calm giving the false impression of durability. But below the surface, things may be changing and the people may be getting restive and disaffected. It is, therefore, necessary to delve deeper into the psychological make-up of the common man and explore the degree to which he is favourably or unfavourably oriented towards the political regime.

It should, however, be pointed out that legitimacy is an attribute of all political regimes irrespective of the structure of political authority. A monarchy, a dictatorship and a democratic regime—all types of government require legitimacy to function effectively. An exclusive focus on the phenomenon of legitimacy is not, therefore, enough to illumine the distinctive structuring of political authority in a democratic polity where the common man is the source of authority as well as its object. To put it differently, the common man in a democratic regime is both a subject and a citizen; in his subject role he complies with the commands and the legal norms of the political order. As a citizen, he influences the course of political decision-making, participates in establishing certain legal and political norms and, if need be, modifies them in order to adapt them to changing situations. As a subject, he is usually required to unquestioningly obey the commands without participating in the decisions that influence his life; but as a citizen, he participates in political process and, even if he is one of the many, his views make some impact on public policies when aggregated with similar other views.

The participation in political processes for determining public policies is, therefore, the most important distinguishing characteristic of a democratic polity. And in such a polity "the role of citizen represents in some sense the highest form of democratic participation. It is through such participation that the ordinary man gains influence over the course of governmental affairs."[6] In order, however, to participate in political

---

6. Gabriel A. Almond and Sidney Verba, *Civic Culture* (Princeton, New Jersey: Princeton University Press, 1963), p. 214.

process, the citizen must feel competent to do so. "As competent citizens, they perceive themselves as able to affect governmental decisions through political influence: by forming groups, by threatening with the withdrawal of their vote or other reprisals."[7] In other words, the concept of citizen competence is one of the means through which diffusion of democratic values in otherwise a traditional society can be measured.

The importance of this concept as an analytical tool for studying a traditional society making a concerted bid to modernize itself is enhanced for three reasons. In the first place, it helps us to determine the character of the transition from subject orientations to citizens orientation. By tapping this dimension we will be able not only to ascertain the magnitude of this transition but also identify the parameters that govern the process of transition. In the second place, the enlarged role of the state in the economic transformation of the society invests too much power in the hands both of political leaders and bureaucrats. If citizens are not alert and lack confidence to check arbitrary use of power, democracy may turn out to be a disguised oligarchy.[8] In the last place, as Inkeles argues, one of the attributes of modernism is that people show strong interest and take active part in civic and community affairs and local politics as well as feel efficacious in coping with life's problems.[9] Given the crucial role of efficacy and participation in acquiring modernity, the examination of the extent to which citizens feel politically efficacious in influencing the course of governmental affairs helps us in understanding the process of change undergoing in Indian society.

We, then, argue that legitimacy and efficacy are two additional attributes that must be explored in order to determine

---

7. *Ibid.*, p. 217
8. Cf. Bruce Russett, "Without a widespread sense of citizen competence in a democracy the controls over policy-making in the government are too weak. In a developing country furthermore, getting people involved in the process of government to the effect that they think they can influence policy, may be very important in building among the citizens a broadbased sense of control over their destinies in both political and economic spheres. "Social Change and Attitudes on Development and the Political System in India," *Journal of Politics*, XXIX : 3 (August 1967), p. 499.
9, "Making Men Modern," *American Journal of Sociology*, LXXV : 2 (September 1969), p.210.

the extent to which the ordinary citizens have come to accept and work through various democratic institutions both in instrumental and symbolic senses; and (b) the degree to which they feel competent to influence the working of these institutions. In short, we are interested in finding out whether or not our respondents endow democratic institutions with legitimacy and feel confident in influencing, through participation, the working of these institutions. This chapter is devoted to a discussion of these two important themes.

Our discussion in preceding chapters has underlined more or less the close relationship between the socio-economic status of an individual and the probability of his greater exposure to the outer world, greater interest in politics and public affairs and greater involvement in political activities. While empirical evidence supports the positing of such an association, it will not be out of place to recapitulate the theoretical underpinning of this relationship. As a general rule, caste in India determined not only the social status of a person but also his economic position and very frequently his political influence. When under the British rule modern education spread and held key to various administrative and other services, the combination of status and wealth enabled persons inhabiting higher social status to take advantage of these benefits. With politics assuming a significant role in shaping societal decisions, individuals in privileged positions turned to politics. As a result, a higher proportion of high caste, economically well-off, educated persons came to be exposed to the outer world, and started taking more interest and engaging themselves in politics. It is true that the waves of freedom movement in the pre-1947 period and consecutive general elections after 1947 inducted individuals from under-privileged social strata into politics. However, this was not sufficient to equip them with capabilities that go with informed, sustained and active interest in politics.

Given this frame of reference, it is natural to suppose that respondents from higher strata of society will manifest a greater sense of legitimacy and efficacy. This, however, does not take into account the cumulative impact of demoeratic processes working for about a generation now on the political orientations of the common man. The phenomenon of the dispersal of inequality induced by economic development, the rising opposition to privileges and its reflection in politics, the frequent exposures to politics and, above all, the experience of democratic processes at various levels—all these factors can be legitimately expected to have diffused democratic values in the last twenty years. It is true that the privileged social sectors still continue to remain at a higher level of political interest and understanding. However, if diffusion of democratic values has, in fact, taken place, the expectation that they must also have seeped down to lower levels of social organization and infused in the common man a sense of legitimacy and efficacy is not overly unrealistic. In view of these considerations, we intend in this chapter to explore the extent to which our respondents manifest the sense of legitimacy and efficacy. Furthermore, if our observations have any relevance, our data should reflect a greater manifestation of these attributes in respondents in higher status categories. However, if the diffusion of democratic values has really taken place, persons in lower status categories should also manifest these attributes in varying degrees.

It will be recalled that we discussed in the last chapter the extent to which our respondents reflect political comprehension. However, we demonstrated the acceptance of democratic institutions as legitimate instrument of public action only indirectly. We present more direct and detailed evidence to suggest that the democratic institutions adopted some twenty years ago have come not only to be accepted but also considered desirable where institutionalized inequality and ascriptive leadership held sway. We begin, first, with a discussion of how our respondents perceive and evaluate the role of elections in a democratic polity. Since it is mainly through elections that the common man can influence the course of public affairs, the voters' conception and understanding of the role of elections retains a high theoretical interest. We then proceed on to examine the voters' sense of legitimacy in respect of other democratic institutions.

Responding to the question, "Do you think elections are or are not necessary in this country?" 86.4 per cent of our respondents said that they are necessary. It is interesting to note that only 7.5 per cent of the respondents felt that they are not necessary and only 0.5 per cent failed to express any opinion. It may be that the overwhelming majority of our respondents feels only the symbolic necessity of elections. Over and above this, they should also be aware of the fact that election is the only suitable means of electing the rulers in a democracy. That there exists this awareness is reflected in their response to the question: "Do you think elections are the best means to determine/decide who should run the government?" While responding to this question, only 7.9 per cent of the respondents said that elections were not the best means of deciding who should form the government. As against this, 88.5 per cent were positive about elections being the best means. Even the socio-economic status of the respondents does not seem to make much difference for the respondents' opinion in this regard. It can be mentioned, for example, that 85.7 per cent of our respondents in the low-status category as against 93.1 per cent in the high-status are convinced of the elections as being the best way to select rulers. If status does not condition this orientation, state differences on this count are also insignificant.

Elections may be considered as the best means of selecting rulers, but this does not necessarily mean that this opinion reflects in any way its effectiveness in relating public opinion with public policy. The voters may, while responding to our questions, be influenced by the consideration of the worth of alternative means of selecting rulers in a democracy rather than by its substantive role. This role consists of truly reflecting the effective balance of public opinion and influencing the course of public affairs. Our data show that our respondents are convinced that elections in this country do perform these two substantive roles.

As will be seen from Table 7:1, between 47.4 per cent of respondents in U.P. and 64.1 per cent of respondents in Bihar say that, to a very great extent, election victories are really decided by the wishes of the people. Note also that only 8 to 20 per cent of our respondents feel that election victories do not really reflect people's wishes. The proportion of those who think that election victories reflect to a great extent the people's wishes is highest in Bihar (64.1 per cent) and lowest in U.P. (47.4 per cent). Given the state differences, however, socio-economic status does seem to play an important role in conditioning respondent's opinion on this count. Note, for example, that in each state the proportion of those who say that election victories are to a very great extent decided by the wishes of the

TABLE 7:1

SES and Election Victory Reflecting People's Wishes (in per cent)

(Q: To what extent election victories are really decided by the wishes of the people?)

| States | Bihar | | | | | Punjab | | | | | U.P. | | | | | W.B. | | | | |
|---|---|---|---|---|---|---|---|---|---|---|---|---|---|---|---|---|---|---|---|---|
| Responses | Great deal | Somewhat | No | NA | Total | Great deal | Somewhat | No | NA | Total | Great deal | Somewhat | No | NA | Total | Great deal | Somewhat | No | NA | Total |
| SES | | | | | | | | | | | | | | | | | | | | |
| High | 73.7 | 13.2 | 11.8 | 1.3 | 76 100.0 | 63.9 | 23.0 | 13.1 | — | 61 100.0 | 52.6 | 22.4 | 22.4 | 2.6 | 76 100.0 | 67.2 | 23.0 | 6.6 | 2.2 | 61 100.0 |
| Medium | 61.3 | 17.6 | 20.4 | 0.7 | 142 100.0 | 56.1 | 27.0 | 16.2 | 0.7 | 148 100.0 | 47.6 | 27.5 | 22.8 | 2.1 | 189 100.0 | 65.6 | 18.4 | 9.6 | 6.4 | 125 100.0 |
| Low | 60.5 | 20.2 | 15.1 | 4.2 | 119 100.0 | 51.2 | 22.0 | 25.6 | 1.2 | 82 100.0 | 43.9 | 36.3 | 15.9 | 3.9 | 157 100.0 | 29.5 | 44.3 | 6.6 | 19.6 | 61 100.0 |
| NA | 100.0 | — | — | — | 3 100.0 | 100.0 | — | — | — | 1 100.0 | 33.3 | 33.3 | 33.3 | — | 6 100.0 | — | 50.0 | 50.0 | — | 2 100.0 |
| Total | 218 64.1 | 59 17.4 | 56 16.5 | 7 2.0 | 340 100.0 | 165 56.5 | 72 24.7 | 53 18.2 | 2 0.6 | 292 100.0 | 203 47.4 | 127 29.7 | 86 20.1 | 12 2.8 | 428 100.0 | 142 57.0 | 65 26.1 | 20 8.0 | 22 8.9 | 249 100.0 |

people decreases as we go down the status hierarchy. The greatest difference can be discerned in West Bengal where 67.2 per cent of high-statused respondents as compared to 29.5 per cent of low-statused respondents say that elections in reality reflect the people's wishes a good deal.

That a large majority of our respondents are convinced that elections truly represent people's wishes is clear. Can the same be said of their perception of elections as a means of making the government responsive to what the people wish? To ascertain this, we asked our respondents the question: "How much does having election from time to time make the government pay attention to the people?" In response, 44.7 per cent of our respondents say that it makes the government pay a great deal of attention, 34.3 per cent somewhat and 16.0 per cent not much.

Our data then suggest that for a large majority of our respondents, elections are not only necessary but also the best means of electing rulers as well as of making the government responsive. In other words, they have come to be recognized as one of the essential institutional arrangements for recording public opinion and making the government pay its attention to the people. We have further evidence to suggest that most of our respondents see a direct relationship between how people vote and what the government does. Note, for example, that responding to the question, "How much effect does the way people vote have on what the government does?" 56.4 per cent of our respondents claimed that it has a lot of effect on what the government does. Only 12.8 per cent of the voters in our sample said that it had no effect, while 25.9 per cent said that it had only some effect. Responding to yet another question, "Do you feel that the way people vote is the main thing that decides how things are run in this country?" 83.2 per cent of our respondents said 'yes' while 11.2 per cent said 'no'.

Without producing more evidence in this regard, it is sufficient to demonstrate the general acceptability of elections as the most effective means of influencing the course of public affairs. Similarly, our data also indicate that similar voter orientations exist in respect of political parties. In response to the question, "Do you think political parties are necessary or not necessary in India?" 79.2 per cent of our respondents said that they are quite necessary. Only 12.7 per cent of the voters in our sample said that they are not necessary, while 6.7 per cent claimed that they are necessary only to a certain extent. As a further evidence of the recognition of the crucial role of political parties in a democracy, we present the responses of our respondents to yet another question. Through this question we wanted to know whether or not the voters thought political parties instrumental in making the government responsive to the people's needs.[10] As much as 37.5 per cent of our respondents feel that political parties help a great deal in making the government pay attention to the people, 35.6 per cent somewhat and 20.9 per cent not much.

A question may in this regard be raised about the desirability of elections and political parties if they lead to political instability. This question gains added significance particularly in the context of a political system where programmes of economic development are likely to be thrown into jeopardy if political instability continues for long. The quick turn-over of popularly elected governments brought about by frequent floor-crossing has created an unfavourable impression in many quarters about the suitability of democracy as an appropriate political arrangement for tackling the problems faced by developing countries. As a result, democracy is maligned and condemned and the need for a strong government unabashedly stressed. It is, therefore, quite essential to find out whether attitudes unfavourable to democracy characterize our respondents or not.

We asked two questions of our respondents in order to ascertain the degree of their attachment (affect) to democratic institutions. One question was: "Do you think that parties and elections are necessary even if they lead to unstable government?" In response to this question, 61.3 per cent of our respondents said that they are necessary, 21.2 per cent said not necessary and 16.7 per cent somewhat necessary. The second question reads: "Do you think that the present system of government is worth keeping even if it delays action?" The result is presented in Table 7:2. As can be seen from this table, more than 60 per cent of our respondents in each state say that the present system of government is worth keeping even if it delays action. The

---

10. The question reads: "How much do political parties help to make government pay attention to the people—a great deal, somewhat or not much?"

## TABLE 7 : 2
### SES and Legitimacy (in per cent)

(Q: Do you think that the present system of government is worth keeping even if it delays action?)

| States | Bihar | | | | | Punjab | | | | U.P. | | | | | W.B. | | | | |
|---|---|---|---|---|---|---|---|---|---|---|---|---|---|---|---|---|---|---|---|
| SES / Responses | Yes | Undecided | No | NA—DK | Total | Yes | Undecided | No | Total | Yes | Undecided | No | NA—DK | Total | Yes | Undecided | No | NA | Total |
| High | 77.6 | 10.5 | 7.9 | 4.0 | 76  100.0 | 75.4 | 9.8 | 14.8 | 61  100.0 | 78.9 | 7.9 | 10.5 | 2.7 | 76  100.0 | 65.6 | 8.2 | 26.2 | — | 61  100.0 |
| Medium | 72.5 | 20.4 | 5.6 | 1.5 | 142  100.0 | 64.2 | 20.3 | 15.5 | 148  100.0 | 75.1 | 12.2 | 12.2 | 0.5 | 189  100.0 | 60.0 | 14.4 | 24.8 | 4.8 | 125  100.0 |
| Low | 52.9 | 38.7 | 7.6 | 1.8 | 119  100.0 | 46.4 | 45.1 | 8.5 | 82  100.0 | 66.2 | 12.1 | 18.5 | 3.2 | 157  100.0 | 54.1 | 32.8 | 13.1 | — | 61  100.0 |
| NA | 100.0 | — | — | — | 3  100.0 | — | — | 100.0 | 1  100.0 | 66.7 | — | 33.3 | — | 6  100.0 | — | — | 100.0 | — | 2  100.0 |
| Total | 228  67.1 | 83  24.4 | 23  6.8 | 6  1.7 | 340  100.0 | 180  61.6 | 73  25.0 | 39  13.4 | 292  100.0 | 309  72.2 | 48  11.2 | 63  14.7 | 8  1.9 | 428  100.0 | 150  60.2 | 43  17.3 | 55  22.1 | 1  0.4 | 249  100.0 |

proportion of those who unfavourably evaluate the democratic system of government is a little over one-fifth of the voters in our sample. Also worth mentioning is the fact that the lower the socio-economic status, the lower is the proportion of those who favourably evaluate the present system of government. Note, for example, that the difference between the high-statused respondents and the low-statused respondents, favouring the present system of government is 29 percentage points in Punjab, 20 in Bihar, 12 in U.P. and 11 in West Bengal. Note, also, that as we go down the status hierarchy the proportion in each state of those who fail to express any opinion in this regard increases. It is only in West Bengal that both favourably and unfavourably oriented respondents can be found in largest proportions in the high-status category.

If a large majority of our respondents favourably evaluate the present system of government, it can also be expected that they will be prepared to willingly abide by and comply with its command and rules. For, the readiness to comply with the commands and rules of the government is one of the surest signs of the legitimacy of the regime. That a vast majority of our respondents do in fact think it necessary to obey the government is confirmed by the data presented in Table 7:3. This table is based on response to the question: "Once the Parliament has fully debated and passed a law, the law should be observed in all circumstances. Do you fully agree, partly agree, or disagree?"

As the table reveals, except in West Bengal, in all the three states more than 80 per cent of our respondents agree that the law should be fully observed. It is only in West Bengal that only 69.1 per cent of our respondents agree to this statement. It can also be seen that status difference does not in any significant way (West Bengal again seems to some extent to be an exception) seem to affect responses to this question.

Our data, then, unequivocally underline the high legitimacy enjoyed by democratic institutions in the four states. But, as we pointed out earlier, legitimacy does not distinguish between a democratic and a non-democratic regime. It only tells us that the government is strongly entrenched and receives the affection of those who are subject to its rule. In a democratic system, however, citizen competence, that is, the confidence of the citizen in his own capability to influence public decisions, is one of the

## TABLE 7 : 3

### SES and Obedience to Law (in per cent)

(Q: Once the Parliament has fully debated and passed a law, the law should be observed in all circumstances. Do you fully agree, partially agree or disagree?)

| States | Bihar | | | | | Punjab | | | | | U.P. | | | | | W.B. | | | | |
|---|---|---|---|---|---|---|---|---|---|---|---|---|---|---|---|---|---|---|---|---|
| Responses SES | Agree | Partly agree | Disagree | NA | Total | Agree | Partly agree | Disagree | NA | Total | Agree | Partly agree | Disagree | NA | Total | Agree | Partly agree | Disagree | NA | Total |
| High | 85.5 | 13.2 | 1.3 | — | 76 100.0 | 85.2 | 8.2 | 6.6 | — | 61 100.0 | 85.6 | 13.2 | 1.2 | — | 76 100.0 | 72.1 | 18.0 | 8.2 | 1.7 | 61 1.000 |
| Medium | 88.8 | 6.3 | 4.9 | — | 142 100.0 | 87.2 | 5.4 | 7.4 | — | 148 100.0 | 82.2 | 13.2 | 3.2 | 1.6 | 189 100.0 | 70.4 | 21.6 | 5.6 | 2.4 | 125 100.0 |
| Low | 86.6 | 6.7 | 5.9 | 9.8 | 119 100.0 | 80.5 | 11.0 | 6.1 | 2.4 | 82 100.0 | 86.0 | 6.4 | 4.5 | 2.5 | 157 100.0 | 63.9 | 14.8 | 9.8 | 11.5 | 61 100.0 |
| NA | 100.0 | — | — | — | 1 100.0 | 100.0 | — | — | — | 1 100.0 | — | 50.0 | 50.0 | — | 6 100.0 | — | 50.0 | 50.0 | — | 2 100.0 |
| Total | 297 87.4 | 27 7.9 | 15 4.4 | 1 0.3 | 340 100.0 | 248 84.9 | 22 7.5 | 20 6.8 | 2 0.8 | 292 100.0 | 360 84.1 | 43 10.0 | 16 3.7 | 9 2.2 | 428 100.0 | 172 69.1 | 48 19.3 | 18 7.2 | 11 4.4 | 249 100.0 |

hall-marks of a well-functioning democratic system. To what extent do Indian voters feel politically efficacious? It is to this aspect of our enquiry that we now turn. We present first a composite index of political efficacy[11] and proceed on to discuss some relevant factors associated with political competence.

In Table 7:4 we present the level of our respondents' political efficacy against their caste background. As is apparent from the table, in all states other than Punjab, only one-fourth to one-fifth of our respondents are high on efficacy. In Punjab, however, 45.2 per cent of the respondents score high on the index of political efficacy. This does not, however, mean that the proportion of those low on efficacy is very high. As a matter of fact, only 7 to 25 per cent of respondents are low on efficacy with the rest of the respondents scoring medium. Given this overall picture, state differences are interesting. That close to one-half of the respondents in Punjab should be high on political efficacy is not surprising. What is surprising is the fact that only 21.7 per cent of the respondents in West Bengal are high on this index. Also interesting is the fact that in West Bengal, again, the proportion of those low on efficacy is greater than those high on it. Given the state differences, what also seems interesting is the fact that relatively larger proportion of respondents located in higher castes as compared to their counterparts in lower castes is high on this index.

As we indicated earlier, due to their economic well-being, men in upper castes have been endowed with the resources to take advantage of modern education. Inasmuch as higher education equips an individual with capabilities to cope with problems and effectively handle environmental pressures, it can be expected that higher the education of the individual, higher will be his level

---

11. Our index of political efficacy is derived from a set of five questions. 1. How much effect do you think people like you have on what the government does? Do you have no effect, some effect or a great deal? 2. How much effect does the way people vote have on what the government does? Does it have no effect, some effect, or great deal? 3. Do you think that politics and government are so complicated that a person like you cannot really understand what is going on? 4. Do you feel that government officials do not care much about what people like you think? 5. Do you feel that the way people vote is the main thing that determines how things are run in this country?

TABLE 7 : 4

Caste and Political Efficacy (in per cent)

| States | Bihar | | | | Punjab | | | | U.P. | | | | W.B. | | | |
|---|---|---|---|---|---|---|---|---|---|---|---|---|---|---|---|---|
| Caste \ Efficacy | High | Medium | Low | Total | High | Medium | Low | Total | High | Medium | Low | Total | High | Medium | Low | Total |
| Upper Castes | 31.0 | 64.8 | 5.0 | 100 100.0 | 53.3 | 46.7 | — | 30 100.0 | 31.6 | 53.2 | 15.2 | 79 100.0 | 28.8 | 54.5 | 16.7 | 66 100.0 |
| Middle Castes | 24.0 | 61.1 | 14.9 | 121 100.0 | 50.0 | 45.1 | 4.9 | 162 100.0 | 14.5 | 70.0 | 15.5 | 193 100.0 | 24.7 | 48.3 | 27.0 | 89 100.0 |
| Lower Castes | 20.9 | 64.2 | 14.9 | 67 100.0 | 37.7 | 52.5 | 9.8 | 61 100.0 | 20.0 | 55.6 | 24.4 | 45 100.0 | 13.9 | 54.2 | 31.9 | 72 100.0 |
| Scheduled Castes & Tribes | 21.6 | 52.9 | 25.5 | 57 100.0 | 30.8 | 46.2 | 23.1 | 39 100.0 | 16.5 | 67.0 | 16.5 | 109 100.0 | 13.6 | 59.1 | 27.3 | 22 100.0 |
| NA | — | — | — | — | — | — | — | — | — | — | — | — | — | 100.0 | — | 100.0 |
| Total | 85 25.0 | 209 61.5 | 46 13.5 | 340 100.0 | 132 45.2 | 137 46.9 | 23 7.9 | 292 100.0 | 81 18.9 | 276 64.5 | 71 16.6 | 428 100.0 | 54 21.7 | 131 52.6 | 64 25.7 | 249 100.0 |

of political efficacy. This is considerably borne out by the information presented in Table 7:5. As we learn from this table, the higher the level of education, the larger is the proportion of those who are high on efficacy. Note also that as the level of education decreases, the proportion of those who are low on the index of efficacy increases. Given this general picture, there is significant difference from one state to the next. Notice that it is in **Punjab** that the largest proportion of highly educated respondents (77.8 per cent) is high on efficacy while in West Bengal only 30.7 per cent of highly educated respondents score high on this index. In Bihar also the proportion of highly educated respondents high on efficacy is lower than those educated only up to primary school.

Given the fact that lower the caste and education of our respondents, lower is the level of their sense of political efficacy, it is not unexpected that the same relationship should also obtain between the level of their socio-economic status and that of their sense of political efficacy. In view of the fact that our index of socio-economic status includes both caste and education, the operation of the tendency towards higher socio-economic status associated with a high level of political efficacy is quite natural. However, being summary measures, the index of political efficacy juxtaposed against that of socio-economic status gives a concise idea of the relationship between the two.

As will be seen from Table 7:6, the general pattern of high status leading to a greater sense of political competence obtains in all states. If in Bihar 31.6 per cent of high-statused respondents as against 18.5 per cent of low-statused respondents are high on the index of political efficacy. In Punjab this difference mounts up to 36 per cent, that is, 60.7 per cent of high-statused respondents, as against 24.4 per cent of low-statused respondents. A similar pattern obtains in U.P. and West Bengal too.

We have so far restricted our discussion to demonstrating the effect of the givens of an individual's socio-economic background on his sense of political efficacy. The feeling of competence in influencing the course of public affairs is not simply the function of socio-economic background but also the function of experience gained and interests developed during the life's journey. In the course of interacting with this environment, the individual forges new loyalties and identifications, develops

TABLE 7 : 5

Education and Political Efficacy (in per cent)

| States | Bihar | | | | Punjab | | | | U.P. | | | | W.B. | | | |
|---|---|---|---|---|---|---|---|---|---|---|---|---|---|---|---|---|
| Efficacy / Education | High | Medium | Low | Total | High | Medium | Low | Total | High | Medium | Low | Total | High | Medium | Low | Total |
| Illiterate | 16.7 | 61.1 | 22.2 | 162 100.0 | 23.6 | 61.8 | 14.6 | 144 100.0 | 11.2 | 69.8 | 19.0 | 242 100.0 | 22.8 | 55.3 | 36.8 | 76 100.0 |
| Upto Primary | 33.3 | 58.6 | 8.1 | 99 100.0 | 57.6 | 41.2 | 1.2 | 85 100.0 | 21.3 | 62.0 | 16.7 | 108 100.0 | 22.8 | 54.4 | 22.8 | 57 100.0 |
| Matriculation & above | 32.1 | 65.4 | 2.5 | 78 100.0 | 77.8 | 20.1 | 2.1 | 63 100.0 | 40.8 | 51.3 | 7.9 | 76 100.0 | 30.7 | 49.1 | 20.2 | 114 100.0 |
| Total | 85 25.0 | 209 61.5 | 46 13.5 | 340 100.0 | 132 45.2 | 137 46.9 | 23 7.9 | 292 100.0 | 81 18.9 | 276 64.5 | 71 16.6 | 428 100.0 | 54 21.7 | 131 52.6 | 64 25.7 | 249 100.0 |

## TABLE 7 : 6

### SES and Level of Political Efficacy (in per cent)

| States / Political Efficacy | Bihar | | | | Punjab | | | | U.P. | | | | W.B. | | | |
|---|---|---|---|---|---|---|---|---|---|---|---|---|---|---|---|---|
| SES | High | Medium | Low | Total | High | Medium | Low | Total | High | Medium | Low | Total | High | Medium | Low | Total |
| High | 31.6 | 64.5 | 3.9 | 76 100.0 | 60.7 | 39.3 | — | 61 100.0 | 36.8 | 52.6 | 10.5 | 76 100.0 | 34.4 | 49.2 | 16.4 | 61 100.0 |
| Medium | 27.5 | 62.0 | 10.6 | 142 100.0 | 50.7 | 43.2 | 6.1 | 148 100.0 | 15.3 | 66.1 | 18.5 | 189 100.0 | 21.6 | 54.4 | 24.0 | 125 100.0 |
| Low | 18.5 | 58.0 | 23.5 | 119 100.0 | 24.4 | 58.5 | 17.1 | 82 100.0 | 14.6 | 68.8 | 16.6 | 157 100.0 | 9.8 | 50.9 | 39.3 | 61 100.0 |
| NA | — | 100.0 | — | 3 100.0 | — | 100.0 | — | 1 0.3 | 16.7 | 50.0 | 33.3 | 6 1.4 | — | 100.0 | — | 2 100.0 |
| Total | 85 25.0 | 209 61.5 | 46 13.5 | 340 100.0 | 132 45.2 | 137 46.9 | 23 2.9 | 292 100.0 | 81 18.9 | 276 64.5 | 71 16.6 | 428 100.0 | 54 21.7 | 131 52.6 | 64 25.7 | 249 100.0 |

certain interests, works for realizing these interests and acquires certain capabilities. In other words, it is through his interaction with the environment that he is most likely to be aware of the necessity to make his weight felt in certain circumstances. As a matter of fact, the resources acquired by the individual through the givens of his socio-economic background remain dormant as long as he is not confronted by certain circumstances and forced to use these benefits endowed to him by these resources. In a nutshell, then, apart from the socio-economic variables as conditioning factors, there are certain other determinants that are equally important in influencing the level of the individual's political efficacy. For the purposes of our analysis, we identify three sets of factors, such as, level of party identification, political interest and electoral involvement. We now turn to discuss the relationship between these and political efficacy.

In Table 7:7 we present information on political efficacy against the level of party identification of our respondents. A quick glance at the table reveals that as the strength of party identification becomes weaker, the proportion of those who are high on the index of political efficacy becomes smaller in all states. Note, for example, that the proportion of those who are high both on identification and political efficacy in Punjab is 64.2 per cent as against 25.6 per cent of those who are low on both these indexes. The corresponding figures for other states are: Bihar 34.6 per cent high—high as against 16.9 per cent low—low; U.P. 46.9 per cent high—high as against 6.1 per cent low—low and West Bengal 36.6 per cent high—high as compared to 14.1 per cent low—low. It should also be mentioned that as the strength of party identification becomes weaker, the proportion of respondents low on political efficacy becomes larger.

Given the salience of party identification as promoter of polical efficacy, the fact, however, remains that even among the strong party identifiers only 34 to 47 per cent of respondents are high on efficacy. It is also interesting to note that, as our data show, it is not necessary that a person who is high on efficacy will also be high on party identification. As a matter of fact, the strength of party identification seems to be more potent in promoting a greater sense of political efficacy. The size of contigency coefficient attests to a close relation between the level of identification and that of efficacy.

TABLE 7:7

Party Identification and Political Efficacy (in per cent)

| States | Bihar | | | | Punjab | | | | U.P. | | | | W.B. | | | |
|---|---|---|---|---|---|---|---|---|---|---|---|---|---|---|---|---|
| Efficacy → <br> Identification ↓ | High | Medium | Low | Total | High | Medium | Low | Total | High | Medium | Low | Total | High | Medium | Low | Total |
| High | 34.6 (31.8)* | 60.3 (22.5) | 5.1 (8.7) | 78 100.0 | 64.2 (46.2) | 34.7 (24.1) | 1.1 (4.3) | 95 100.0 | 46.9 (46.9) | 45.7 (13.4) | 7.4 (8.5) | 81 100.0 | 36.6 (27.8) | 51.2 (16.0) | 12.2 (7.8) | 41 100.0 |
| Medium | 24.6 (51.7) | 62.6 (53.6) | 12.8 (50.0) | 179 100.0 | 38.6 (46.2) | 50.6 (58.4) | 10.8 (73.9) | 158 100.0 | 13.9 (48.1) | 69.8 (71.0) | 16.4 (64.8) | 281 100.0 | 21.5 (51.9) | 56.9 (56.5) | 21.5 (43.8) | 130 100.0 |
| Low | 16.9 (16.5) | 60.2 (23.9) | 22.0 (41.3) | 83 100.0 | 25.6 (7.6) | 61.6 (17.5) | 12.8 (21.7) | 39 100.0 | 6.1 (4.9) | 65.2 (15.6) | 28.8 (26.8) | 66 100.0 | 14.1 (20.4) | 46.2 (27.5) | 39.7 (48.4) | 78 100.0 |
| Total | 85 100.0 | 209 100.0 | 46 100.0 | 340 100.0 | 132 100.0 | 137 100.0 | 23 100.0 | 292 100.0 | 81 100.0 | 276 100.0 | 71 100.0 | 428 100.0 | 54 100.0 | 131 100.0 | 64 100.0 | 249 100.0 |
| | C=0.203 | | | | C=0.287 | | | | C=0.347 | | | | C=0.254 | | | |

*Figures in parentheses denote percentages calculated from column totals.

TABLE 7 : 8

Political Interest and Political Efficacy (in per cent)

| States | Bihar | | | | Punjab | | | | U.P. | | | | W.B. | | | |
|---|---|---|---|---|---|---|---|---|---|---|---|---|---|---|---|---|
| Efficacy → Interest ↓ | High | Medium | Low | Total | High | Medium | Low | Total | High | Medium | Low | Total | High | Medium | Low | Total |
| High | 36.6 | 63.4 | — | 41 100.0 | 65.8 | 32.9 | 1.3 | 76 100.0 | 48.1 | 42.6 | 9.3 | 54 100.0 | 38.8 | 51.0 | 10.2 | 49 100.0 |
| Medium | 31.2 | 61.6 | 7.2 | 125 100.0 | 46.2 | 52.9 | 1.0 | 104 100.0 | 17.9 | 68.4 | 13.7 | 212 100.0 | 21.7 | 58.3 | 20.0 | 115 100.0 |
| Low | 17.8 | 60.9 | 21.3 | 174 100.0 | 30.4 | 50.9 | 18.8 | 112 100.0 | 10.5 | 66.7 | 22.8 | 162 100.0 | 11.8 | 45.9 | 52.4 | 85 100.0 |
| Total | 85 25.0 | 209 61.5 | 46 13.5 | 340 100.0 | 132 45.2 | 137 46.9 | 23 7.9 | 292 100.0 | 81 18.9 | 276 64.5 | 71 16.6 | 428 100.0 | 44 21.7 | 131 52.6 | 64 25.7 | 249 100.0 |
| | C=0.260 | | | | C=0.363 | | | | C=0.298 | | | | C=0.313 | | | |

A more or less similar pattern obtains in the case of the relationship between the level of political interest and that of political efficacy. As can be seen from Table 7:8, the higher the level of political interest, the higher also seems to be the level of political efficacy. In Punjab, for example, if 65.8 per cent of the respondents, high on the index of political interest, are also high on political efficacy, only 17.8 per cent of the respondents low on political interest are high on efficacy. Similarly, the difference (in percentage points) between those high both on interest and efficacy and those low on interest but high on efficacy is 19 per cent, in U.P. about 38 per cent and in West Bengal about 27 per cent. Looking at it from another angle, the lower the level of interest, the larger becomes the proportion of those who are low on political efficacy. This relationship gains further confirmation by the size of contingency coefficients.

The almost identical distribution of cell frequencies that we observe in respect of relationship between the strength of party identification and political efficacy, on the one hand, and between level of political interest and that of political efficacy, on the other, underlines the fact that, taken singly, none of them is the best determinant of the feeling of political efficacy. Furthermore, to identify with a party or to show interest in politics and public affairs does not necessarily mean that an individual will have the necessary confidence in his own capability to influence the course of public affairs. It may perhaps be that the sense of political competence is acquired not through evincing strong interest in politics nor through any partisan identification but through acquiring experience by actively involving oneself in public activities. The reason for thinking so is simply this that when an individual is actively engaged in bringing about a certain state of affairs, he is most likely to exert his energy, try to overcome the impediments and, through doing so, may develop capabilities to effectively handle inter-personal relations. If this be true, it can, then, be expected that those who are high on any index of activity will also be high on political efficacy. To test this, we present in Table 7:9 information on political efficacy juxtaposed against the index of electoral involvement.

As will be seen from Table 7:9, the picture does not improve anyway. Except for Bihar, the pattern that we observed earlier obtains here also. That is to say, if a respondent is high

TABLE 7:9

Electoral Involvement and Political Efficacy (in per cent)

| States | Bihar | | | | Punjab | | | | U.P. | | | | W.B. | | | |
|---|---|---|---|---|---|---|---|---|---|---|---|---|---|---|---|---|
| Efficacy / Involvement | High | Medium | Low | Total | High | Medium | Low | Total | High | Medium | Low | Total | High | Medium | Low | Total |
| High | 26.5 | 73.5 | — | 49 100.0 | 59.2 | 39.4 | 1.4 | 71 100.0 | 51.0 | 43.1 | 5.9 | 51 100.0 | 32.0 | 60.0 | 8.0 | 50 100.0 |
| Medium | 28.4 | 64.1 | 7.5 | 67 100.0 | 46.7 | 50.6 | 2.7 | 75 100.0 | 23.6 | 59.7 | 16.7 | 72 100.0 | 27.5 | 52.9 | 19.6 | 51 100.0 |
| Low | 23.7 | 58.0 | 18.3 | 224 100.0 | 37.7 | 48.6 | 13.7 | 146 100.0 | 12.5 | 69.1 | 18.4 | 305 100.0 | 16.2 | 50.0 | 33.8 | 148 100.0 |
| Total | 85 25.0 | 209 61.5 | 46 13.5 | 340 100.0 | 132 45.2 | 137 46.9 | 23 7.9 | 292 100.0 | 81 18.9 | 276 64.5 | 71 16.6 | 428 100.0 | 54 21.7 | 131 52.6 | 64 25.7 | 249 100.0 |
| | C=0.202 | | | | C=0.245 | | | | C=0.306 | | | | C=0.250 | | | |

on the index of electoral involvement, there is a greater likelihood that he will also be high on the index of political efficacy. In Punjab, U.P. and West Bengal, as the table reveals, the higher the level of electoral involvement, the larger the proportion of those who are high on the index of political efficacy. Very definitely this pattern does not obtain in Bihar. It is also true that when the strength of involvement goes down, the proportion of those who are low on efficacy also increases. Given this, however, electoral involvement does not seem to be a better determinant of political efficacy when compared either to party identification or to political interest. Except in the case of U.P. where 51.0 per cent of the respondents are high both on electoral involvement and political efficacy, the proportions in the equivalent cells in other states record decrease. In other words, then, the hypothesis that experience gained through active participation in some activities—electoral in our case—breeds a greater confidence in one's capability to influence the course of public affairs is only partly borne out by our data.

We can now raise a question pertaining to the concept of political efficacy as well as to our finding that only about one-fourth of our respondents are high on the index of political efficacy. It should be pointed out that no matter how one defines the concept of political efficacy,[13] empirical studies underscore that, relatively, a small porportion of the citizenry scores high on civic competence. If the attribute of civic competence were to be measured with reference to the level of government in respect of which the individual feels competent to exert influence, the proportion of fully efficacious citizens would further go down.[14] However, since a widespread sense of civic competence

---

13. Almond and Verba talk of civic competence by which they mean the capability of individual members of a polity to bring political influence to bear on governmental actions. Under this broad rubric, they make a distinction between citizen competence and subject competence. The former points to the citizen role in forming general policy, the latter indicates just an awareness on the part of individuals of their rights under the rule rather than the necessity to participate in the making of the rule. *Civic Culture*, chaps. 7 and 8.
14. While constructing their scale of subjective competence, Almond and Verba used attitudes towards local rather than national government, "because there is a substantially higher level of subjective competence in

is supposed to be a crucial component of democratic political life, the smaller proportions of competent citizens in other democracies should give us little comfort.

These considerations lead us to raise questions about our own instrument of political efficacy, in particular, and the relevance of the concept of political efficacy as a tool for measuring the diffusion of democratic values, in general. To take the latter first, the sense of political competence has been given a central place in the complex of democratic values. As Almond and Verba observe:

> In many ways, then, the belief in one's competence is a key political attitude. The self-confident citizen appears to be the democratic citizen. Not only does he think he can participate, he thinks that others ought to participate as well. Furthermore, he does not merely think he can take a part in politics: he is likely to be more active. And, perhaps most significant of all, the self-confident citizen is also likely to be the more satisfied and loyal citizen.[15]

This is self-explanatory. And to question and raise doubts about the almost universal verdict of social scientists in respect of the pertinence of the concept of political efficacy seems sacrilegious. However, for the sake of clarity and, therefore, understanding, we must examine the concept in its manifold aspects. To begin with, we must make a distinction between what an individual actually does and what he may potentially do when faced with a situation that provokes him to take certain action. It will at once be apparent that this distinction pertains to the amount of influence an individual wields as reflected in his actual behaviour, on the one hand, and his influence potential without any reference to behaviour, on the other. It may be recognized that to the extent to which the individual perceives himself to be capable of influencing the course of public affairs when needs arise, his commitment and loyalty to the values the political regime upholds is strengthened. However, belief in influence

---

relation to the local government in all countries.... If a scale based on the national government had been used, too many respondents would have fallen into the lower categories of subjective competence and the scale would not have been useful to discriminate about various types of citizens. *Civic Culture*, p. 232.

15. Almond and Verba, *o;. cit.*, p, 257.

potential by itself is not sufficient to insure democratic participation in formulating public policies. As a norm signifying that in democracy all citizens should be able to influence governmental action in certain situations, the concept of political efficacy does not encounter any difficulty. But trouble starts when we seek to explore its empirical foundation.

It does not need to be demonstrated that an average citizen neither takes a sustained interest in nor is equipped to understand the complexity of public issues to take an informed position and act accordingly. For most of the citizens, periodical elections provide the opportunity of not only participation in politics but also of exposure to hotly debated public issues. Their stand in respect of these issues is shaped usually by their identification with some party or candidate or by their need to conform to opinions articulated in primary and secondary groups. Their contacts with bureaucratic functionaries and other public officials are usually few and far between. Even more important, their rare moments of contact with the officials are usually motivated by the furtherance of personal gain or removal of personal difficulty. We do not mean to suggest that individuals are not moved by the considerations of bureaucratic impropriety or some anomaly threatening public welfare.

In addition to two types of actions meant to influence administrative policies and decisions—one originating from private and the other from public motive—yet a third kind of action can be identified that has its genesis in certain personality traits— a syndrome of attributes that can be termed action-propensity. Given favourable opportunities and proper institutional structures to mobilize and canalize the energies of persons manifesting these traits, they turn out to be the activists who concern themselves with public issues, mobilize support for their view-points and direct their own and others' energies towards influencing public policies. Needless to say that the way it is handled as an instrument for measuring the diffusion and distribution of democratic values, the concept of political efficacy does not isolate these elements from the horde of common men so that the level of political efficacy of the activists and the non-activists can be differentiated.

When the concept is used indiscriminately, it encounters certain difficulties. As we indicated earlier, the attempt to influence administrative decisions or wider public policies may originate either from private or from public motive. If it is private, it may involve either personal gain or deprivation. Whatever the case, the individual concerned may either attempt to circumvent certain legitimate administrative rules and procedures for achieving his personal ends; or, he may, in fact, be greatly concerned over the existence of some unjust rules and regulations and, learning from his own experience, may either seek to remove them or, at least, seek redress of his own inconvenience caused by them. No matter what the case, the individual in order to cope with the emerging situation, may take recourse to one or all of the three alternatives that are available to him. He may personally approach the official concerned and try to make him see his point of view. He may approach others who, he thinks, can influence the official concerned. Or, he may make a public issue of it, organize support and pressurize the official to take necessary action.

If the objective is some illegitimate personal gain, the individual can take recourse to only the first two alternatives. That is, he may personally try to influence the official concerned or seek the help of others who may influence the behaviour of the official. This type of attempt to influence public officials cannot properly be included under the rubric of political efficacy inasmuch as such attempts, whether successful or not, are a travesty of democratic principles. Needless to say that the operationalization of the concept of political competence does not always exclude this category of influence. In regard to the second category of action, that is, attempt to remove some unjust regulation or, at least, to seek redressal of personal inconvenience caused by that unjust regulation, the individual must have cognizance of rules and regulations, of the authority structure appropriate for rectifying the mistakes and also have ample confidence in his own ability to move the creaking machinery of administration. Experience shows that only a handful of men are capable of doing all this. In a large majority of cases, men at battle with official impropriety or intransigence need allies, intermediaries and contact men to take up their cause, mobilize reinforcements and see the battle through. In any case, when once the question of administrative impropriety or intransigence is raised and the creaking wheels of bureaucracy moved, it takes an awful lot of time to pursue the matter to the end trying the patience of even the most patient men.

If the individual approach and the approach through influentials are beset with difficulties, one can easily imagine the difficulties that can be encountered when a common man tries to raise an issue of public concern and mobilize support for moving the authorities to do something about it. In the first place, the individual must have the technical abilities of leadership, organization as well as the intellectual capacity to lift up the particular issue from the realm of parochial concerns and transform it into a broad general issue of vital public concern. If an individual succeeds in doing this, he rises above the level of a common man and becomes, in the real sense of the term, an activist. As such, the ability to influence the course of public affairs should no longer be measured by the concept of political efficacy because the activist by definition acts to influence.

Even if we include men of this type, it is very difficult to isolate and measure the exact proportion of the individual's influence inasmuch as actions like this involve a concerted effort of numerous individuals and institutions. In the second place, then, the individual act of influence forms only a miniscule part of other acts of influences made possible by organized group action. When an individual takes recourse to institutional means of influencing the course of public affairs, he is again confronted with the necessity of transforming the particular into general, convincing others of its relevance and setting a complex process of opinion formation into motion in which his own participation amounts to very little and whose course of development he cannot control. In other words, the phenomenon of wielding influence as it relates to political processes is seldom a matter of face-to-face inter-personal relationship; it is primarily a public, institutionalized arrangement involving many people and groups and operating in the complex ways of large-scale social arrangements. The concept of political efficacy as operationalized in the literature on electoral behaviour is not suited to isolate the magnitude of individual influence and even less suited to measure it.

We can now summarize our discussion by underlining four difficulties inherent in the concept of political efficacy. First, the distinction between an average citizen and an activist is generally ignored when the concept of political efficacy is applied to measure the diffusion of democratic values. As V.O. Key has ably demonstrated, it is the activists who are the pace-setters of democratic culture. The classical notion that a citizen in a democratic society must be active and capable of influencing public policies and their implementation is not borne out by empirical studies of voting behaviour. However, the persistence of the notion and the ideological urge to demonstrate its relevance become instrumental in introducing in political analysis the idea of citizen activeness through the backdoor of the concept of political efficacy.

Second, as it is operationalized, the concept of political efficacy does not take into account the changing meaning of influence depending upon the nature of a concrete issue that prompts the individual to attempt to influence the behaviour of public functionaries. Almond and Verba define political influence of a group or individual over a governmental decision as "equal to the degree to which governmental officials act to benefit that group or individual because the officials believe that they will risk some deprivation (they will risk their jobs, be criticized, lose votes) if they do not so act."[16] Two things are immediately clear. In the first place, according to this definition, the quantum of influence is measured in terms of what the official does. As such, whether or not the individual succeeds in influencing the behaviour of the officials can be measured only in terms of official acts. Apart from the confusion that it creates between citizen influence and official responsiveness, there is the additional difficulty in that legitimate role performance on the part of the official, although he is prodded to it, cannot be taken as an index of citizen influence. In the second place, even more important is the fact that such a formulation not only over-simplifies the process of influencing governmental actions but also pays little heed to the objective for which influence is brought to bear on the official's behaviour. To see an official, say, for the resumption of electric supply after due payments have been made, and to see him for asking him to do something about gross irregularity in his department or for providing some public facilities are entirely different things. Also different

---

16. *Op. cit.*, p. 180.

is the request to sanction electric supply out of turn. In all these cases, the nature of influence varies and so does its relevance and consequence for the political system. By grouping all these acts of influence together the concept of political efficacy is bereft of its distinctiveness.

Third, it appears that the delineation of the concept of political efficacy assumes that individuals as citizens are isolates and each of them confronts the state and its functionaries in his sovereign "aloneness". As an isolated sovereign, he oversees the deeds and misdeeds of the rulers and takes steps to rectify the misdeeds. It is usually forgotten that an average citizen has fewer occasions to come into contact with the official. Even when he needs to enter the precincts of officialdom, he is most likely to seek the services of others in order to facilitate the achievement of his end. When there are others to come to his help, why should he himself bother to devote his energies to change the world he least understands? If the process of influencing the official's behaviour operates through numerous identifiable and non-identifiable channels, we cannot really talk of subjective civic competence of individual citizens. And, lastly, it is through a complex institutional set up mediating between the citizen and the state that the attempt at influencing the course of public affairs becomes meaningful. Without the existence of such institutions, the individual would be utterly helpless in front of the leviathan which the state is.

In sum, then, to determine the extent to which an individual citizen is capable of influencing governmental action is not a simple matter. This strongly indicates the necessity of distinguishing between a widespread belief in the common man's influence potential and the empirical manifestation of it. The wider diffusion of the norm that in a democracy the common man can influence public decisions is sustained by the existence of a network of intermediary structures—peer groups, associations, parties, etc. The concept of political efficacy should, therefore, mean no more than a reflection of the actual distribution of this norm. To seek its validation in individual acts of influencing the official's behaviour is to insist that every norm must have its behavioural counterpart. The concept of political efficacy taps simply the perceptual, not the behavioural influence potential.

We can now appreciate why so small a proportion of citizens appears to be politically efficacious. When operationalizing the concept, it is customary to mix both perceptual and behavioural items. When it is so done, many respondents who score high on perceptual items, score low on behavioural items. As a result, the law of averages pulls down the proportion of efficacious citizens when a composite index or scale of political efficacy is constructed. This is also true of our instrument. In view of this, we present, in the remainder of this chapter, some data that illustrate the considerations delineated above.

We shall first adduce some evidence to indicate that the need to contact public functionaries through some "middlemen" is widely felt suggesting the inference that the notion of the isolated sovereign citizen is misconceived inasmuch as very few citizens either feel capable of or are convinced of the advantages of direct approach. Through this we want to emphasize the salience of intermediate structures of action for individual efficacy. We then show that when the respondents are asked to indicate the extent of influence they personally can wield, only a smaller proportion of them owns to have greater influence. However, when the personalized "you" is transformed into a group "you", the pattern changes. This underscores the difference between personal influence potential and efficacy as an essential trait of a group.

To return to the first of our concerns, we asked our respondents three questions in order to ascertain whether or not they felt the necessity of using connection in contacting different public functionaries. The responses to one of the questions are presented in Table 7:10 set against the SES level of the respondents. As will be seen from the table, between one-half and two-thirds of our respondents concede that it is necessary to approach an MLA through some personal connection. Also, it is in U.P. and Bihar that we find the largest proportions of the voters in our sample—72.9 and 64.7 per cent, respectively—expressing the necessity of using connections. This suggests that lower the level of economic development, somewhat greater the necessity of using connections in approaching a public functionary. Also interesting is the fact that as the level of socio-economic status drops, the proportion of those approving the use of connection increases.

## TABLE 7:10

### SES and Sense of Political Efficacy (in per cent)

(Q : Suppose you had some problems to take up with the MLA of your area but you did not personally know him. Would it be necessary to approach him through some personal connection or would you approach him directly?)

| States | Bihar | | | | | Punjab | | | | | U.P. | | | | | W.B. | | | | |
|---|---|---|---|---|---|---|---|---|---|---|---|---|---|---|---|---|---|---|---|---|
| Responses SES | Connection | Depends | Direct | NA | Total | Connection | Depends | Direct | NA | Total | Connection | Depends | Direct | NA | Total | Connection | Depends | Direct | NA | Total |
| High | 44.7 | — | 55.3 | — | 76 100.0 | 36.1 | 6.6 | 57.3 | — | 61 100.0 | 44.7 | — | 55.3 | — | 76 100.0 | 13.1 | 3.3 | 83.6 | — | 61 100.0 |
| Medium | 64.1 | 3.5 | 31.7 | 0.7 | 142 100.0 | 49.4 | 7.4 | 43.2 | — | 148 100.0 | 76.2 | 0.5 | 22.8 | 0.5 | 189 100.0 | 53.6 | 0.8 | 44.8 | 0.8 | 125 100.0 |
| Low | 77.4 | 0.8 | 21.8 | — | 119 100.0 | 70.7 | 11.0 | 15.9 | 2.4 | 82 100.0 | 82.2 | — | 14.6 | 3.2 | 157 100.0 | 82.0 | — | 16.4 | 1.6 | 61 100.0 |
| NA | 100.0 | — | — | — | 3 100.0 | 100.0 | — | — | — | 1 100.0 | 83.3 | — | 16.7 | — | 6 100.0 | — | — | 100.0 | — | 2 100.0 |
| Total | 220 64.7 | 6 1.8 | 113 33.2 | 1 0.3 | 340 100.0 | 154 52.7 | 24 8.2 | 112 38.4 | 2 0.7 | 292 100.0 | 321 72.9 | 1 0.2 | 109 25.5 | 6 1.4 | 428 100.0 | 125 50.2 | 3 1.2 | 119 47.8 | 2 0.8 | 249 100.0 |

We asked similar questions in respect of district officials and local (panchayat or municipal) officials. Since we have already shown the salience of socio-economic status, we need not repeat it. As is evident from Table 7:11, fewer respondents admit of using connection for contacting local officials than district officials. However, the fact remains that even in the case of local officials, about half of our respondents feel the necessity of approaching local officials through intermediaries.

TABLE 7 : 11

**Whether Connection Necessary for Contacting Officials**
(in per cent)

| Contacting officials | Neces-sary | Depends | Not necessary | D K | N A | Total |
|---|---|---|---|---|---|---|
| District officials | 65.1 | 3.9 | 30.2 | 0.2 | 0.6 | 1,309 (100.0) |
| Local officials | 49.2 | 2.8 | 47.2 | 0.2 | 0.6 | 1,309 (100.0) |

Our data, then, forcefully establish the fact that using connections for contacting public functionaries has wider support. Let us now turn to discussing our respondents' capability to understand politics as well as to influence its course. Through the question, "Do you think that politics and government are so complicated that a person like you cannot really understand what is going on?" we explore the former. In Table 7:12 are presented the responses of our respondents against their socio-economic status. It is apparent that more than 60 per cent of respondents in each state admit that politics and government are so complicated that they cannot understand what is going on. Also, the highest proportions of such persons are again to be found in U.P. (78.3 per cent) and Bihar (66.8 per cent). Given state differences, what also seems to be interesting is the influence of socio-economic status on the understanding of politics. With the exception of Bihar, in all the other states, the proportion of those who admit of their inability to comprehend the complexity of politics sharply increases as the level of socio-economic status drops. As a matter of fact, the percentage point difference

TABLE 7:12

## SES and Voter's Understanding of Politics (in per cent)

(Q : Do you think that politics and government are so complicated that a person like you cannot really understand what is going on?)

| States / Status | Bihar | | | Punjab | | | | U.P. | | | | W.B. | | | |
|---|---|---|---|---|---|---|---|---|---|---|---|---|---|---|---|
| Responses | Yes/D.K. | No | Total | Yes/D.K. | No | NA | Total | Yes/D.K. | No | NA | Total | Yes/D.K. | No | NA | Total |
| High | 64.5 | 35.5 | 76 100.0 | 54.1 | 45.9 | — | 61 100.0 | 57.9 | 40.8 | 1.3 | 76 100.0 | 45.9 | 49.2 | 4.9 | 61 100.0 |
| Medium | 68.3 | 31.7 | 142 100.0 | 57.4 | 41.9 | 0.7 | 148 100.0 | 79.9 | 19.6 | 0.5 | 189 100.0 | 60.8 | 37.6 | 1.6 | 125 100.00 |
| Low | 66.4 | 33.6 | 119 100.0 | 86.6 | 13.4 | — | 82 100.0 | 86.0 | 10.8 | 3.2 | 157 100.0 | 80.3 | 19.7 | — | 61 100.0 |
| NA | 66.7 | 33.3 | 3 100.0 | 100.0 | — | — | 1 100.0 | 66.7 | 33.3 | — | 8 100.0 | 100.0 | — | — | 2 100.0 |
| Total | 227 | 113 | 340 100.0 | 190 | 101 | 1 | 292 100.0 | 335 | 86 | 7 | 428 100.0 | 155 | 89 | 5 | 249 100.0 |

between high-statused and low-statused respondents admitting of the complexity of politics is very large. It is only in Bihar that the SES level does not make any difference.

If a large majority of our respondents admit of their inability to understand politics, it is also true that a large number of them also feel that they have no influence on the policies and actions of the panchayat or municipality. This can be ascertained from Table 7:13. Note, for example, that 59.1 per cent of our respondents in Bihar, 55.1 per cent in U.P., 45.0 per cent in West Bengal and 31.2 per cent in Punjab say that they have no influence on the policies and actions of the local government— i.e., panchayats in the rural areas and municipalities in the urban areas. The level of economic development or the status also seems salient here. Also, it is only in the case of Punjab that the highest proportion (39.4 per cent) of respondents admitting of wielding a lot of influence can be located. As in other cases, the level of socio-economic status also appears to be an important conditioning factor. Except in the case of West Bengal, in all other states, high status carries with it a greater influence potential in regard to policies and actions of the local government. In West Bengal, however, this trend is completely reversed; the lower the status, the higher is the perception of influence potential.

That very few individuals perceive that they are so equipped as to have greater comprehension of politics as well as be able individually to influence local governmental decisions is amply reflected in our data. It does not, however, mean that there is no widespread diffusion of the belief that the people can change the government or influence its decisions. Our data, as we shall presently show, leave no doubt about the wide currency of such a belief. This suggests that even if at the individual level the voters feel least efficacious, at the collective level their confidence in influencing the behaviour of the rulers sharply increases. In other words, even if the behavioural manifestation of individual influence potential is very low, at the normative level and at the group level where anonymous individuals through joining hands with others gain much more potency, the perception of influence potential is very high.

This phenomenon is amply reflected in the responses of the respondents to two of our questions. One question asked them

TABLE 7 : 13

### SES and Sense of Political Efficacy (in per cent)

(Q : How much influence do you think you can have on policies and actions of the Panchayat/Municipality : a lot of influence, some influence, or none at all?)

| States | Bihar | | | | | Punjab | | | | | U.P. | | | | | W.B. | | | | |
|---|---|---|---|---|---|---|---|---|---|---|---|---|---|---|---|---|---|---|---|---|
| Responses / SES | None | Some | A lot | NA | Total | None | Some | A lot | NA | Total | None | Some | A lot | NA | Total | None | Some | A lot | NA | Total |
| High | 51.3 | 18.4 | 28.9 | 1.4 | 76 100.0 | 13.1 | 26.2 | 60.7 | — | 61 100.0 | 39.5 | 28.9 | 30.3 | 1.3 | 76 100.0 | 52.5 | 27.9 | 13.1 | 6.5 | 61 100.0 |
| Medium | 57.7 | 26.8 | 14.8 | 0.7 | 142 100.0 | 22.3 | 32.4 | 45.3 | — | 148 100.0 | 57.7 | 23.3 | 18.5 | 0.5 | 189 100.0 | 47.2 | 24.8 | 22.4 | 5.6 | 125 100.0 |
| Low | 66.4 | 19.3 | 14.3 | — | 119 100.0 | 61.0 | 23.2 | 13.3 | 2.4 | 82 100.0 | 59.2 | 27.4 | 10.2 | 3.2 | 157 100.0 | 34.4 | 32.8 | 21.3 | 11.5 | 61 100.0 |
| NA | 66.7 | 33.3 | — | — | 3 100.0 | — | 100.0 | — | — | 1 100.0 | 66.7 | 16.7 | 16.7 | — | 6 100.0 | — | 50.0 | 50.0 | — | 2 100.0 |
| Total | 201 59.1 | 77 22.6 | 60 17.6 | 2 0.7 | 340 100.0 | 91 31.2 | 84 28.8 | 115 39.4 | 2 0.6 | 292 100.0 | 236 55.1 | 110 25.7 | 75 17.5 | 7 1.7 | 428 100.0 | 112 45.0 | 69 27.7 | 50 20.1 | 18 7.2 | 249 100.0 |

to indicate whether the people have any means to influence the government. The other question asked them to say whether or not it is possible for the people to change the government if they so willed.[17] The result is presented in Table 7:14. Note the fact that as much as 57.3 per cent of our respondents think that the people have some means to influence the government.

TABLE 7:14

**Voter's Perception of Influence Potential of the People**
(in per cent)

| Questions | Yes | DK/NR | No | NA | Total |
|---|---|---|---|---|---|
| Do people have any means to influence the government? | 57.3 | 13.8 | 27.1 | 1.8 | 829 100.0 |
| Is it possible for them to change government if they so willed? | 84.0 | 6.9 | 8.2 | 0.9 | 829 100.0 |

This is quite different from what we find from the responses of our respondents to a similar but differently phrased question. Responding to the question, "How much influence do you think people like you have on what the government does?" only 23.7 per cent of the voters in our sample said that they can influence it a lot, 27.2 per cent somewhat and 46.1 per cent not at all. The difference between the frequencies on this and the previous question is remarkable and due, in all likelihood, to the fact that when the respondents evaluate their influence potential as an individual they perceive it to be very low as against that of the people treated as an abstract—an aggregate and collectivity. This is further substantiated by the fact that as much as 84.0 per cent of our respondents claim that it is possible

---

17. These two questions could be administered to only 829 of the 1309 respondents.

for the people to change the government if they so willed. Our data, then, amply support our contention that basing on the evaluation of individual influence capability very few people would seem to be highly politically efficacious. However, when it comes to attributing political efficacy to an abstract and aggregate category like people, the widespread belief that people have some influence on the course of public affairs is reflected in our data.

We can now sum up our discussion. As our data show, democratic polities of more than two decades now has percolated below and seems to have persuaded the people of the usefulness of democratic institutions. A large number of voters are also convinced of the necessity to comply with the rules and commands of the government. In other words, the legitimacy of democratic institutions is a widely held value. Our discussion brings this out quite emphatically. Next, we discussed the extent to which voters in the four states perceive themselves to be politically efficacious. It is true that higher social background, political interest, strong party identification and greater electoral involvement do, to some extent, influence the degree of political efficacy. However, the very low proportion of highly efficacious voters, on the one hand, and the low salience of both the background and the intervening variables for political efficacy, on the other, led us to critically examine this concept. As our discussion underlines, we cannot consider the individual as an isolate nor can we ignore the fact that the process of influence is mediated through a complex social arrangement. We, therefore, concluded that we cannot, by the help of this concept, really measure the behavioural manifestation of influence potential. It is, therefore, desirable to separate the behavioural from the normative. When both are combined, the result is the low proportion of highly efficacious voters. And yet at the perceptual level a large number of voters seems to be highly politically efficacious. If what matters is the widespread belief in the people's capacity to influence the course of public affairs, the voters in the four states, then, are highly efficacious even though they may individually feel ineffective.

# CHAPTER EIGHT

# *Varieties of Electoral Behaviour*

THE discussion in the preceding chapters underscores the differential pattern of the political attributes of voters in the states under study. While we have deliberately discussed these at some length in the body of this book, it would be wrong to suppose that these attributes behave in any discrete or disjointed fashion. We have repeatedly stressed their inter-relatedness and sought to discern the interaction pattern among various components of electoral behaviour. And yet our discussion has been too wide-ranging to allow an easy comprehension of the totality of the phenomenon under study.

It is time now to pull together the various strands of our enquiry and try to construct a coherent picture of the world of the electorate in the four states as it relates not simply to their voting behaviour but, even more importantly, to the larger political system. While the delineation of the determinants of voting behaviour is theoretically quite interesting, implications of the voting act as well as its determinants for the political system at large need also to be examined and specified. Needless to say, one of the ways in which the common man expresses his judgements on the political system and plays a role in effecting changes in it is through the act of voting. We say "one of the ways" because even though democratic practice provides for systematic change only through occasional elections and through established procedures, other ways are not automatically excluded. In varying degrees people in various democracies do resort to these other ways—both peaceful and violent—to express their dissatisfaction, anger and even opposition in respect of the political regime. However, elections offer the only means through which important changes can systematically be brought about.

And yet the fact remains that the extent to which other means are used reflects not only the degree of effectiveness and sensitivity of a particular government in power but also the salience of democratic norms that influence the working of political institutions. Democracy exists both in its normative elements and in their manifestation in the behaviour of people and institutions. When the gap between norms and practice widens and frustrations generated by unredeemed hopes and aspirations accumulate, political processes have to contend with anomic and aggressive behaviour. The preservation of the intricate balance between norm and practice is difficult everywhere. For, the difficulty in changing the structure of the "factual order" by constant reference to the "normative order", the rigidity of institutional work-ways, and the domination of certain vested interests make it extremely unlikely that an automatic adjustment between the normative order and the demands arising from changing perceptions of the factual order will always take place. This may, in turn, add to frustrated aspirations gradually eating away the vitals of democratic political life.

It should, however, be noted that established democracies can claim to have a somewhat better chance in comparison to new democracies in coping with the contingencies that grow out of the increasing divergence between the normative and the factual. It is not only that democratic institutions are more firmly rooted in the former; it is also the case that the social order and the political order, far from being alien to each other, are well synthesized and adjusted to each other. Democratic values are well diffused among the people and firmly anchored in their orientation. In contradistinction to this, in the new democracies, not only are democratic institutions new but they are also prone to come into direct conflict with the antecedent social order. To the extent that democratic norms and those embodied in the antecedent social order are incompatible, people are exposed to two different standards of evaluation and judgement. This creates an anomalous situation fraught with ambivalences that often lead to anomic behaviour. When hopes are aroused and promises made by politicians who have their own short-term gains in mind, and when the democratic structure fails to give effect to them, the very legitimacy of these institutions is thrown into doubt.

Influenced by these considerations, we set for our enquiry a task more comprehensive than the simple concern of "why people vote the way they do." Of course, this question is in itself interesting and we have tried to answer it by delineating some of the crucial parameters of voting. But it constitutes only one part of our enquiry, and not the major part. We are more interested in exploring differential configurations of other dimensions in respect of basic attitudes of people situated in different socio-economic environments, and the implications of these configurations for the working of democratic institutions in the different states. To be specific, our interest lies not only in ascertaining the degree to which democratic values have come to be accepted by the common man but also in specifying the differential patterns of the various components of these values in different states, and in tracing the implications of these patterns for the sustenance and preservation of democratic institutions in these states.

How are we to interpret and evaluate the differential implications of what are in fact political attributes of *individuals* for the political development of *states?* Since sustained political development is linked up to a considerable extent with the possibility of political stability, how do we measure and compare the situation in the four states? Robert Dahl defines the stability of a political system as the persistence of six characteristics: well-nigh universal suffrage, a moderately high participation in elections, a highly competitive two-party system, opportunity to criticize the conduct and policies of officials, freedom to seek support for one's views among officials and citizens, and surprisingly frequent alterations in office from one party to the other as electoral majorities have shifted.[1]

Viewing from another perspective, V.O. Key considers the manner in which leadership interacts with mass opinion to provide room for innovation, creativity and change in the making of public policy as a corner-stone of a democratic polity.[2] Expressing a similar theme in a different way, Schattschneider argues that "the problem is not how 180 million Aristotles can run a democracy, but how we can organize a community of 180 million ordinary people so that it remains sensitive to their

---

1. Robert A. Dahl, *Who Governs* (New Haven: Yale University Press, 1961), p. 311.
2. V.O. Key, Jr., *Public Opinion and American Democracy* (New York: Alfred A. Knopf, 1961), Ch. 21.

needs. This is a problem of *leadership, organization, alternatives, and systems of responsibility and confidence.*"[3]

These three examples[4] are enough to show how different students of democracy (all of them eminent) articulate the necessary conditions for sustaining and preserving democratic institutions. How does one discriminate between them and arrive at one's own criteria? We can unhesitatingly dismiss conditions stipulated by Dahl as not only being rooted in the experience of a particular country but also as being excessively formalistic and hopelessly narrow. It does not need to be emphasized that only few democracies have "a highly competitive two-party system"; that a particular configuration of political forces may retard "frequent alterations in office"; and that the "freedom to criticize the conduct and policies of officials" may fail to achieve anything in want of appropriate supportive institutional structures and elite orientations. Moreover, the set of conditions prescribed by Dahl, in addition to being inadequate, touches only those factors that relate to obvious, easily identifiable, and highly visible characteristics that are commonly associated with a democratic polity. We are not told how these conditions come into being; what pattern of interaction among the common man's image of and expectations from democratic institutions, leadership norms and structures, and a particular institutional framework is conducive to democratic political processes; and what predispositions, attitudes, and orientations should the common man evince to insure the continued vigour of democratic institutions and processes.

In view of these considerations, the formulation of Key and Schattschneider is more relevant for understanding the complex reality represented by democratic political structures. It should be recognized that both Key and Schattschneider put an emphasis on the centrality of the stratum of what Key calls "political activists" for the effective functioning of democratic institutions. Key argues that it is this stratum that represents

---

3. E.E. Schattschneider, *The Semi-Sovereign People* (New York: Holt, Rinehart and Winston, 1960), p. 138 (Italics in original).

4. The literature on democracy is too rich to be summarized here. These examples are only illustrative.

the political subculture of a society, transmits appropriate values and offers checks and balances. It must in fairness be said that while the political sub-stratum is a key component for Key, he nevertheless argues that the population must exhibit certain qualities, attitudes and expectations that enable the leaders to maintain democratic consensus and commitment among themselves.

The crucial role of political leadership in preserving democracy should undoubtedly be accepted. However, it cannot be assumed that the wider diffusion and acceptance of norms of political behaviour appropriate to the functioning of democratic institutions is dependent exclusively on political leadership—its structure, orientations and behaviour. Nor can it be assumed that the mass of citizens is nothing more than an "echo chamber" whose essential characteristics are determined by inputs that the political sub-stratum chooses to channel into it. Also worth considering is the fact that, although it is recognized that the population must exhibit certain attributes, it does not help us to isolate and identify particular mixes or configurations of these attributes that can be said to be functional for the preservation of democratic values and, through them, democratic institutions.

That the survival of democracy is associated not alone with the characteristics of the political sub-stratum, not even with a particular institutional framework, but also with the attributes of the entire populace can be readily conceded. This, however, raises the difficult and thorny question of what kind of "civic culture"[5] is appropriate and proper for democracy to succeed. If "civic culture" is just a part of culture affecting not only the political but also other aspects of organized living, how can it be distinguished and separated? If it can be so distinguished—even if only analytically—how can we arrive at the proper mixes or configurations of its diverse components that may confidently be identified as being functional to democratic political processes? Not only is the concept of culture very vague and wide-ranging, the question of relevance too is not an easy nut to crack. The easiest way out of this difficulty seems to be in the selection of

---

5. A term coined by Edward Shils and discussed in greater detail in Almond and Verba, *op. cit.*, Ch. 15.

some theoretically relevant attributes and the examination of the implication for the political system of their particular distribution and configuration. We shall return to this point later on. Meanwhile what does the existing literature suggest?

Elaborating upon the suggestive formulation of Harry Eckstein, Almond and Verba emphasize that a democratic political system requires a blending of apparent contradictions or "balanced disparities". Expanding this theme, they argue that:

> On the one hand, a democratic government must govern; it must hove power and leadership and make decisions. On the other hand, it must be responsible to its citizens...The need to maintain this sort of balance between governmental power and governmental responsiveness, as well as the need to maintain other balances that derive from the power responsiveness balance—balances between consensus and cleavage, between affectivity and affective neutrality—helps explain the way in which the more mixed patterns of political attitudes associated with the civic culture are appropriate for a democratic political system.[6]

But how are these balances maintained? Or, to go back a little to the beginning of this process, how do these balances come into being? Clearly these are two different questions dealing with two different aspects of the same process. While the first question draws our attention to the necessary conditions that prevail *now* and that have an important bearing on the maintenance of these balances, the second question pertains to the factors that help the emergence of these balances. To put it differently, the latter is concerned with a longitudinal view of emergence of these balances and is, therefore, pertinent for evaluating the prospects of democratic institutions in a country where such institutions are only of recent origin. The former, on the other hand, takes a cross-sectional view of the working of democratic institutions and attempts to identify conditions that facilitate their working.

Almond and Verba attempt to provide some answer to the first question. It is true that while doing so they also touch, to some extent, upon the latter. This is, however, neither conscious nor adequate. In fairness, we should also note that their

---

6. Almond and Verba, *op. cit.*, p. 476.

primary concern lies with the former; we cannot, really, expect a longitudinal sketch of the conditions affecting effective functioning of democracy, although such a sketch is essential. As we have already indicated, they consider "balanced disparities" as an essential condition for the stability of democratic institutions. In successful democracies these disparities are reflected at both the systemic and the individual levels. They argue that while at the systemic level conflicts must be cross-cutting and political issues very mild, at the individual level there must exist a wide gap between democratic norms and behaviour. To quote them again:

> Within the civic culture, then, the individual is not necessarily the rational, active citizen. His pattern of activity is more mixed and tempered. In this way he can combine some measure of competence, involvement, and activity with passivity and non-involvement. Furthermore, his relationship with the government is not a purely rational one, for it includes adherence—his and the decision-maker's—to...the democratic myth of citizen competence.[7]

These disparities, then, become instrumental in allowing the elite to rule effectively. "If elites are to be powerful and make authoritative decisions, then the involvement, activity and influence of the ordinary man must be limited." Since the ordinary man cannot himself rule, he must "turn power over to elites and let them rule". The need for elite power requires that the ordinary citizens be relatively passive, uninvolved, and deferential to elites. It is these characteristics that assure the effective functioning of democracy. Accepting the importance of these characteristics, they conclude that "the democratic citizen is called on to pursue contradictory goals: he must be active, yet passive: involved, yet not too involved; influential, yet deferential".[8]

It is important to bear in mind that what the authors of *Civic Culture* prescribe for maintaining the stability of democratic regime is supported by a mass of empirical data. And yet we do not seem to be any closer to comprehending the complex phenomenon, that is, democratic stability. It must be

---

7. *ibid.*, p. 487.
8. *ibid.*, p. 479.

emphasized that a cross-sectional analysis may provide us with some insight about how the system works. It cannot, however, illuminate the way the manifold facets of a complex reality have, through interaction among themselves, succeeded in producing conditions that assure the system to function in a particular way. Admittedly this calls for a developmental perspective which must take into consideration a particular configuration of diverse components or reality at a particular point in time. Proceeding from there, we must ascertain the way these diverse components interact and, through this, give rise to a new configuration which again, through interaction and changes in strategic components, undergoes further transformation. Given this perspective, a delineation of the interaction between different components, their variability and changing configurations has to be placed into a longitudinal, temporal frame of reference.[9]

At the very outset, it must be emphasized that, to quote Louis Hartz, "the symbols of monarchy are the symbols of popular submission, while those of democracy are the symbols of popular participation."[10] In spite of the fact that popular participation[11] ranges between ritualistic to destructive participation, it nevertheless remains a key impulse in a democratic society. Even more important, popular participation is never a goal in itself; through it is attempted to change the content and implementation of policies and the elite that formulates and implements particular policies. We cannot, therefore, agree with Almond and Verba when they say that once the ordinary man has delegated his power to the elite, he must let the elite rule. It need not be emphasized that how the elites rule is itself

---

9. To elaborate such a perspective requires drawing heavily on the literature on political development and comparative politics. It is not our intention here to offer a full-blown theory that incorporates such a perspective. Our purpose here is primarily to articulate a perspective that helps us to interpret the implications of differential configurations of political attributes for political development in the states under study.
10. Louis Hartz, "Democracy: Image and Reality" in William N. Chambers and Robert H. Salisbury, eds., *Democracy in the Mid Twentieth Century* (Saint Louis: The Washington University Press, 1960), p. 24.
11. For a systematic discussion of political participation, see Lester Milbraith, *Political Participation* (Chicago: Rand McNally and Co., 1965).

a matter of popular scrutiny, and this has an important bearing on how the ordinary man perceives and evaluates the performance of the rulers. Leaving it aside for the moment, if popular participation is to bring into being some desired state of affairs, we must take into account three sets of factors: manifest reality, subjective reality and intentionality.[12]

This specification postulating three layers of reality is not arbitrary. As Berger and Luckmann point out, "Society is a human product. Society is an objective reality. Man is a social product."[13] This involves the simultaneous working of three processes of "externalization, objectivation, and internalization" which link all the three layers of reality. The manifest reality, or the environmental aspect, including both the natural and the social surroundings, cannot, due to "its temporal and spatial complexities...be fully grasped in an objective manner". The common man therefore..."utilizes highly subjective images of this reality to help him in finding his way around".[14] This image constitutes the subjective reality and colours the ordinary man's interpretation of the vast and only partially known world around him. Interposing between the two—manifest and subjective reality—is the human intention that "provides a link between what is imagined as real and what is manifestly real... Man pre-interprets the outcome of his actions, the anticipated results, while his means of arriving at them are largely pre-interpreted". Thus "both the anticipated outcome and the means to arrive at the outcome have reference to the individual's 'reflective reality' and to the extent to which an individual in society typifies the social group of which he is a member, his action is motivated within the meaningful aspect of that group."[15]

It is through constant interplay among these different types of reality that continuity and change in a social order are assured.

---

12. This section draws heavily on Gerald A. Gutenschwager, "Social Reality and Social Change", *Social Research*, XXXVII: 1 (Spring 1970), pp. 48-70.
13. Peter L. Berger and Thomas Luckmann, *The Social Construction of Reality: A Treatise in the Sociology of Knowledge* (Garden City, Doubleday and Co. Inc., 1966), p. 61.
14. Berger and Luckmann, *op. cit.*, p. 56.
15. *ibid.* p. 57.

If there occurs a great divergence between what is manifestly real and what is supposed to be, the individual or a group of individuals engages in intentional action to modify or change the manifest reality. The divergence between the manifest reality and the subjective image of it may occur either because the environment has greatly changed leaving the subjective reality unaffected or only partly affected; or, subjective reality has, due to the pressure of external forces, itself changed while the manifest reality remains static or changes only partially. "Thus, social change arises out of the nexus of changing environment and a continuous re-interpretation of that environment by the human actors whose combined actions produce the environmental changes in the first place."[16]

Given this perspective, it should be clear that the nature of environment has a great salience for both the subjective reality and intentionality. It is also to be kept in mind that while environmental characteristics change only slowly, subjective reality may be drastically changed through a large input of influences in the environment from external sources or through increasing contacts with the outside world. Whatever it may be, one of the consequences of planned social change in the developing countries is to change the character of subjective reality through a deliberate change in the environment. However, acceleration of the social change creates tensions and traumas. It can be argued that tensions and traumas attending the process of change can, to a considerable extent, be mitigated if there is no sharp and wide divergence between the manifest reality and the subjective reality, on the one hand, and there is no sharp break with tradition and all that it implies, on the other.

It will be readily conceded that the accent on social change and the requisite social mobilization to bring about desired changes creates a climate of high expectancy that treats change as good, beneficial and desirable. While no one doubts the necessity of change to assure a better life for the people, the fact should not be lost sight of that the magnitude as well as the rate of desired change cannot be brought about if impediments to change are not either neutralized or eliminated. The necessity

---

16. *Ibid.* p. 70.

to loosen the rigidities of social order and to socialize men in new ways of thinking and doing by removing psychological and cultural constraints, on the one hand, and transmitting appropriate ideas and creating relevant structures, on the other, is generally recognized as basic to change.

In this process, a profound dilemma confronts the developing countries. Once expectations have been aroused and traditional norms have been weakened, impulse to chaotic change becomes very strong. If this impulse is not checked, restrained and channelled into constructive directions, it will lead to disorder. If, on the other hand, this impulse is utilized to give a fillip to the process of change, the scarcity of appropriate resources will soon widen the gap between expectation and achievement threatening the very basis of political community. This threat becomes all the more potent when a fragmented sense of nationality prevails among the people. One of the basic problems in any developing country is, therefore, to bring change without excessively disrupting order and reinforcing order without impeding the tempo of change.

This can, to a considerable extent, be assured if the change in the manifest reality is adequate to prevent an excessive rise in the level of relative deprivation. This is however, difficult to attain. Two other conditions have, therefore, to be met. In the first place, not only sufficient material and nonmaterial goods have to be generated to satisfy rising expectations but also their distribution must insure the satisfaction of the aspirations of at least the emerging socio-economic interests. In the second place, if the rising level of relative deprivation cannot be kept under control, the centralized political authority must be capable of keeping under control the anomic manifestation of frustrated aspirations. While the role of the centralized political authority in maintaining the balance between change and order is very crucial, what is also necessary is the existence at the micro-level of the social order of strategic social elements that can keep the impulse to chaotic change within manageable limits. We refer here specifically to the necessity of the continuity of tradition, the resilience of normative elements and the robustness of elite class.

In view of these considerations, it is legitimate to suggest that if the nature of manifest reality varies from one milieu to the next, the constituents of subjective reality will also vary not only in their individual characteristics but also in their configuration. For our purposes, manifest reality shapes the characteristics of the subjective reality in two different ways. First, it represents an unequal distribution of resources and status and through it promotes differential capabilities and perspectives. In the second place, the changes undergoing in the environment determine the magnitude of relative deprivation. It is important to note here that if the gap between expectations and achievement takes the form of what Gurr calls "incremental deprivation", that is, along with the rise in the aspiration level achievement capability also rises, the legitimacy of the normative element is not seriously affected unless there is a sharp reversal.[17] If, on the other hand, the rise in the level of deprivation is due either to decline in achievement capability with aspiration level remaining unchanged or to rising aspirations, with the level of achievement capability remaining unchanged, an unfavourable evaluation of the manifest reality is most likely to occur.

These two elements taken together will have much influence on not only the way certain political attributes are distributed and sequentially ordered but also the way in which they are activated to endow certain content and direction to political participation. If the differential access to social resources and status makes for differential manifestation of political attributes, the level of relative deprivation affects the way political attributes are sequentially ordered as well as activated. We cannot, however, assume that a perfect relationship between socio-economic status and the level of political attributes obtains. Given the salience of socio-economic status, other factors, such as, diffusion of certain values through mass media, political mobilization, exposure to outside influence, mobility, etc., intervene to shape these attributes. And yet, in a society just beginning to feel the first impact of social change, the impact of status differences on differential distribution of political attributes remains largely unaltered or is weakened very slowly.

---

17. Tedd Gurr, *Why Men Rebel* (Princeton: Princeton University Press, 1970), p. 48.

Socio-economic status does not simply imply a particular pattern of the distribution of material and non-material societal resources. It also represents a particular normative system that legitimizes and justifies that particular distribution of societal resources. However, the emphasis on social change strikes at the very root of this legitimacy rendering the unequal distribution of social resources unjust and unjustifiable. If we add to it the fact of escalation of the sense of relative deprivation, the growing sense of alienation from the social order can be better appreciated.[18] In such a situation, privilege comes under severe attack and the privileged ones turn to be suspect and a butt of thwarted disorientation.

Thus a combination of these two factors has a profound impact not only on how certain political attributes are distributed in the population but also on how they combine in different configurations to incline different sectors of the population to grasp the obtaining reality, to evaluate its relevance, and to engage in action in different ways. This is true not only of people living in different environments but also of people placed in the same milieu but differentiated on the basis of differing life situations.[19]

Given the differential distribution of political attributes, it can also be assumed that their sequential ordering will vary

---

18. We are not sure whether this can be treated as an invariant relationship. As Boulding demonstrates, this situation may take alternate courses: ambivalence, apathy—alienation, and rational resolution. See *Conflict and Defense : A General Theory* (New York: The Harper Torchbooks, 1963), Ch. 5. Also, if the traditionally privileged social sector suffers from a sense of deprivation, the most likely reaction would be conservatism. If, on the other hand, it is the emergent social sector labouring under a sense of deprivation, the most likely reaction would be alienation and radicalism.
19. If this is accepted, one cannot, then, legitimately assume that there is a unitary stream of national profile of political attributes. To attempt to construct a national profile of voters on the basis of averages, central tendencies and sample means estimated, calculated and derived from a sample of individuals located in different milieus, brought up in different kinds of political climate and confronting different problems is, therefore, not likely to yield satisfactory result. We cannot, if we accept the validity of these observations, legitimately talk of national profiles of voters unless our sample is drawn from contextual units carefully stratified on the basis of some theoretically relevant criteria.

from one milieu to the next. For example, it is quite possible that in an environment characterized by a mild phenomenon of incremental deprivation, involvement in political activities will grow out of sustained interest in politics and public affairs. In contrast, in an environment characterized by an acute sense of deprivation, involvement will precede interest, information, and identification. We should also add that the relationship among these variables is never invariant. As Goldberg has shown, changing external stimuli affect political awareness and, through it, the vote.[20] It is thus apparent that a temporal element enters into the shaping as well as the ordering of these attributes.

To sum up, the manifest reality at any particular point represents a balance of satisfaction-dissatisfaction and a particular distribution of resources and capabilities. If the subjective reality diverges sharply from what is manifestly real, it gives rise to intentional action through which a balance between satisfaction-dissatisfaction is attempted to be restored by changing or modifying the characteristics of the environment. Through a continuous process of interpretation and reinterpretation of the environment, the content and direction of intentional action are determined. This, in turn, brings about a variation in the level of political attributes as well as in their sequential ordering. This is a continuous process in which some components are more or less invariant but some others quite variable.[21]

We can now turn to the question we raised earlier. To repeat, our problem is to identify conditions that insure stability of a democratic regime. As we indicated earlier, the basic impulse in a democratic polity is participation. Now, this participation is meant to affect both the composition of the ruling elite and policies and programmes espoused by it. This impulse to let continue or change a particular set of ruling elite is not whimsical nor purposeless; it has its genesis in the favourable or unfavourable image that voters have of the manifest

---

20. Arthur S. Goldberg, "Discerning a Causal Pattern among Data on Voting Behaviour," *American Political Science Review*, LX : 4 (December 1966).
21. This raises the important question of which components should be treated as isomorphous and which are highly variable across societies and cultures.

reality as well as in their perception and evaluation of the extent to which those in power are able or unable to insure for the voters a favourable balance of value over disvalue in relation to their environment.

In short, participation, as Milbraith points out, involves two components; action or inaction and direction of action.[22] These, in turn, are linked up with choices and understanding. While the former relates, in part, to systemic attributes, such as, availability of alternatives, structures, etc., and, in part, to individual psychological make-up, the latter is primarily individual. It involves the individual voter's level of information, degree of opinionatedness, intensity of feeling, strength of political identification, etc. Depending upon what interpretation a voter puts on his environment as well as the role performance of the centralized political authority, his action-propensity and the direction of his action will be greatly influenced by his own individual characteristics and the available structures of action and their effectiveness.

For participation to be constructive, it must avoid two extreme poles of apathy and anomie. If a large section of the population is apathetic, it offers excellent opportunities to self-seeking demagogues to turn the instruments of power to their own advantage. If, on the other hand, an equally large proportion of voters is alienated, it may pave the way for mass mobilization characterized by high interest and involvement in political processes culminating in "rigid fanaticism that could destroy democratic processes if generalized throughout the community".[23] It does not, however, mean that apathy and high participation are undesirable in all conditions. Apathy can be dangerous only when it originates from helplessness rather than from a feeling of satisfaction with the way things are run. Similarly, high participation, as Medding points out, can be quite dangerous "if it is dogmatic, fanatical, anomic, prone to violence, or makes demands that cannot be met and that are not given to compromise." He further suggests that "high participation could be highly beneficial if based upon political awareness, on sophistication, and on ability to relinquish one's

---

22. Milbraith, *op. cit.*, p.6.
23. Bernard Berelson, Paul F. Lazarsfeld, and William McPhee, *Voting* (Chicago: University of Chicago Press).

particular view in some compromise that approaches the general good or the public interest more closely."[24]

We can now appreciate why a simple determination of the distribution of certain political attributes in the population even if expressed in terms of "balanced disparities" is inadequate. We can also now hypothesize about the relationship that should obtain between various components that we have argued are relevant for our enquiry. This, in essence, requires specification of the complex process of interaction between socio-economic conditions, individual characteristics, political processes and public policies.

If the argument developed in the preceding pages has any validity, it can be safely hypothesized that when the manifest reality is not interpreted as excessively unfavourable to the individual's attempt to reduce the magnitude of relative deprivation, it will insure continued commitment to the value symbolized by the political system. To put it differently, if the gap between aspirations and achievement takes the form of incremental deprivation, this will bring into being a trend towards dispersal of inequality. This will, in turn, facilitate greater access to societal resources and acquisition of requisite capabilities to participate in political processes. Informed interest and sober involvement keep political processes on an even keel and make political leadership responsive to public opinion. The political system, assured of the continuing support of the citizenry, can then be rendered effective in performing its functions. This, in turn, reinforces citizen capability to effectively participate in political processes. In addition, with growing experience with democratic politics, political understanding and maturity increase; with it also develops a sense of efficacy that becomes instrumental in controlling the public conduct of political leadership. Also, the experienced voter functions as a reference group offering appropriate behavioural guides to young voters. In short, such a system develops capacity for reinforcing agreement, encouraging moderation, and maintaining social peace.

The obverse of this can also be stated. If the magnitude of relative deprivation is quite high as well as characterized by

---

24. Medding, *op. cit.*, p. 651.

the phenomenon of cumulative inequality, the acceleration of the rate of social change and the intensification of the process of political mobilization induct into the political process a large section of the population, with the result that diverse demands channelled into the political process cannot be met because of the lack of resources. This initiates the process of alienation which, in turn, is likely to promote high participation without the moderating influence of informed interest and sober involvement. One of the consequences of this situation is that experienced voters, though highly informed and interested, become apathetic while the highly volatile and emotionally more unstable young voters become greatly involved in political processes. This lends capricious overtones to electoral outcome. The growing political unrest gets reflected in unstable coalitions adversely affecting the capacity of the government to perform its role effectively. Thus a vicious circle is created in which a high degree of relative deprivation leads to anomic participation; anomic participation renders government ineffective; and governmental incapacity adds to relative deprivation.

We have sketched two polar models which try to specify the relationship between socio-economic conditions, individual characteristics, political processes and public policies as it relates to democratic political development. Needless to say that they supply only a broad outline of an analytic framework that should inform the exploration of the problem of the stability of democratic regime in a developing country. No claim is made that the models suggested are either adequate or complete. However, they serve to illustrate the underlying patterns in our data. It is to developing these patterns that we now turn.

As we have already shown, both Punjab and West Bengal are fairly industrialized, urbanized, prosperous in terms of per capita income, and high on literacy. And yet it is Punjab that spends most on developmental activities as compared to West Bengal where developmental expenditure is very low. Also, the distribution of economic resources is more unequal in West Bengal than is the case in Punjab. Furthermore, the higher concentration of upper castes in West Bengal and the large proportion of middle castes in Punjab mean that the gap in social status is wider in West Bengal than in Punjab. Given the very close relationship between social status and access to economic and other resources the differential configuration of these factors in the two states is highly suggestive. In West Bengal, for example, the greater diversification of occupational structure promoting physical mobility has raised the level of people's aspirations and expectations. However, the insufficiency of resources and the rigidity of the social system precludes both social mobility and realization of aroused aspirations. In contrast, in Punjab a high degree of economic development and the relative openness of the social order make for a greater satisfaction of aspirations. In short, then, while Punjab is characterized by a small gap between aspiration and achievement as well as a tendency towards dispersal of inequality, in West Bengal the level of relative deprivation is higher and the cumulative inequality a dominant tendency.

The differential configurations of socio-economic conditions are associated also with differential configuration of individual political attributes. It is interesting to note that more than three-fourths of respondents in Punjab as against about one-half of respondents in West Bengal are highly politically informed. Also interesting is the fact that the impact of socio-economic status on the level of information is quite slight in Punjab and considerable in West Bengal. One other difference lies in the fact that in Punjab, young voters, i.e., voters in age cohorts below 40, are more informed than older voters. No such distinction can be discerned in West Bengal. It is true that the impact of socio-economic status on the level of political interest is considerable in all the four states. However, such an association is strongest in Punjab ($C=0.411$) and not that strong in West Bengal ($C=0.306$). Again, the proportion of interested voters increases with advancing age in Punjab but decreases in West Bengal. More or less similar is the case with electoral involvement but with one significant difference. Socio-economic status retains its impact on the level of electoral involvement but, in terms of age, voters in West Bengal tend to be less and less involved in electoral activities as they advance in age. In contrast, in Punjab advancing age does not have this influence; the proportion of involved voters rises steadily as voters gain more and more experience of electoral process.

In terms of political comprehension and issue-orientation, Punjab and West Bengal again present different patterns. Note, for example, that while only 39 per cent of respondents in Punjab disapprove of wider popular participation, 44.2 per cent do so in West Bengal. Again, 84.2 per cent of respondents in Punjab as against 62.7 per cent in West Bengal differentiate parties on the basis of policies and programmes. It is interesting to note that as far as support to political regime is concerned, it is high in both the states. However, higher socio-economic status seems to be a prime inducing factor in this regard. Even more interesting is the fact that voters in Punjab seem to be more consistent in terms of issue-orientation than their counterparts in West Bengal. Our respondents in Punjab consistently opt for greater state control and power in different issue areas. In contrast, voters in West Bengal manifest moderate statism stand in spite of the operation of extreme left tendency there. Moreover, this stand is less consistent than is the case in Punjab. Another important difference lies in the fact that as compared to 22 per cent of respondents in West Bengal, 45 per cent of respondents in Punjab feel highly efficacious in political matters. Apart from this, only 20 per cent of respondents in West Bengal as compared to about 40 per cent in Punjab claim to have very much influence on the policies and programmes of local government. While in Punjab a large proportion of respondents in high status category feel politically efficacious at the grass roots, such voters come from low status group in West Bengal.

Also interesting in this regard is the differential patterns of sequential ordering of relevant individual political attributes in these states.[25] As is shown in Fig. 8.1, we treat political efficacy as a dependent variable. It can be seen that in Punjab

---

25. This is based on a preliminary exercise in causal modelling on the lines suggested by Herbert A. Simon and elaborated by Hubert M. Blalock. The Simon-Blalock model is essentially hierarchical in character and assumes unidirectionality of causal chains in order to avoid the problems created by interaction and collinearity among variables, particularly the independent variables. See, for example, Simon, *Models of Man: Social and Rational* (Chapel Hill: The University of North Carolina Press, 1964). For an application of this model to voting behaviour, see Arthur S. Goldberg, *op. cit.* We are quite aware of the imperfections inherent in the model. We are also aware of the very tentative nature of our own findings. However, we present here the results of our preliminary analysis simply as hypotheses. The final result will hopefully be reported later on.

# VARIETIES OF ELECTORAL BEHAVIOUR

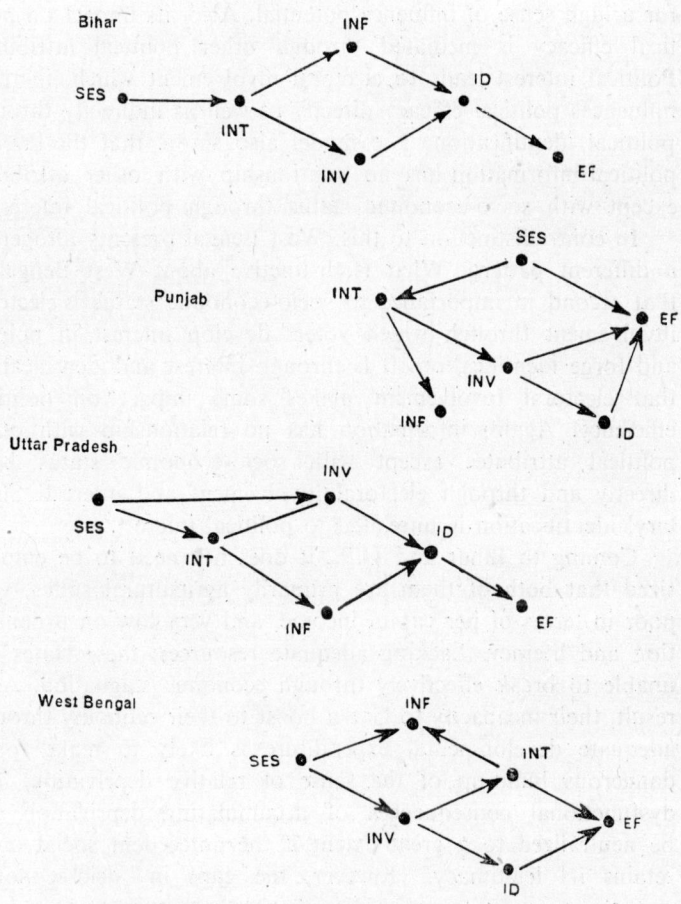

Fig. 8.1: Causal linkages among political attributes

Abbre. :
SES = Socio-Economic Status
INT = Political Interest
INV = Political Involvement
INF = Political Information
ID = Political Identification
EF = Political Efficacy

socio-economic status is the basic conditioning factor that promotes interest in politics and public affairs. It is also a direct cause for a high sense of influence potential. Also, its impact on political efficacy is mediated through other political attributes. Political interest leads to electoral involvement which, in turn, influences political efficacy directly as well as indirectly through political identification. The model also shows that the level of political information has no relationship with other attributes except with socio-economic status through political interest.

In contradistinction to this, West Bengal presents altogether a different pattern. What is distinctive about West Bengal is that second in importance to socio-economic status is electoral involvement through which voters develop interest in politics and forge identification. It is through interest and identification that electoral involvement makes some impact on political efficiency. Again, information has no relationship with other political attributes except with socio-economic status both directly and through electoral involvement and interest. Similary, identification is unrelated to political interest.

Coming to Bihar and U.P., it does not need to be emphasized that both of them are primarily agricultural states, very poor in terms of per capita income, and very low on urbanization and literacy. Lacking adequate resources, these states are unable to break effectively through economic stagnation. As a result, their incapacity to give a boost to their economy through adequate developmental expenditure is likely to make for a dangerous build-up of the sense of relative deprivation. The dysfunctional consequences of accumulating deprivation can be neutralized to a great extent if the antecedent social order retains its legitimacy. However, the gaps in socio-economic status and access to economic resources are very high in both these states.

Socio-economic status has greater impact on political attributes of the voters in U.P. than it has in Bihar. While at the aggregate level, 58.5 per cent of respondents in Bihar as against 51.4 per cent in U.P. are high on political information, the difference between high-and low-statused respondents in terms of political information is higher in U.P. than in Bihar. This is also true in the case of political interest and electoral involvement. Another difference lies in the behaviour of different age cohorts. To put it simply, Bihar is closer to West Bengal and U.P. to Punjab in this regard.

It is also of interest to note that the disapproval of wider popular participation in politics seems to be a function of economic backwardness. This is indicated by the fact that the largest proportions of voters in our sample disapproving wider participation in politics are located in Bihar and U.P. In both the states a large number of voters are able to differentiate parties on the basis of policies and programmes. However, in terms of issue-orientation, U.P. is definitely against greater power to state while voters in Bihar are much more favourably inclined to greater state power. In terms of political efficacy, 25 per cent of respondents in Bihar as against 19 per cent in U.P. feel highly politically efficacious. Given this, however, status-anchored differences are larger in U.P. than in Bihar. A similar pattern is discernible in the case of influence potential *vis-a-vis* local government. In terms of sequential patterning of political attributes, however, both the states, as Fig. 8.1 shows, have similar patterns except for the fact that in U.P. there is an additional causal link between socio-economic status and electoral involvement.

Given these differential characteristics, the salience of obtaining political conditions in each of the states for voting decision should also be taken into consideration. The social diversity obtaining in each state could not be homogenized into a unitary political tendency even while Congress monopolized political power. Being reflected in its factional structure, this diversity brought into prominence a tendency in Congress towards subordination of organizational objectives to individual and sectional interests, fragmentation of power structure and multiplication of factions.[26] These, in turn, made the party extremely vulnerable to vested interests and rendered Congress Governments incapable of sustaining effective development programme and consolidating its hold on the electorate.[27] With the decline

---

26. On this point, see my "Dynamics of One-party Dominance in an Indian State" *Asian Survey*, VIII : 7 (July 1768), pp. 553-575.
27. For an insightful and pioneering study of the consequences of one-party electoral politics for administration, see V.O. Key, Jr., *Southern Politics* (New York: Random House, 1949; a Vintage paperback reprint), especially Ch. 14.

in the Congress dominance, social diversity did finally culminate in multi-polarity of political forces which now functions as a deterrent to the needed emergence of a winning coalition of political forces for assuring political stability and effective implementation of development programmes.

Given this, however, state differences are quite remarkable. While left tendencies dominate in West Bengal, they play only a marginal role in U.P. where right tendencies happen to be dominant. While in Punjab political competition is mainly triangular, it is multi-polar in other states. Also, while in Punjab there is a blurring of ideological differences, they are becoming sharper in other states. Movement of voters across party boundaries does occur in each state, but, with the exception of Punjab, it conforms to ideological differences. This differential pattern of the segmentation of party-system offers, as it were, a variety of political preferences to voters. If the strength of party identification is weak, or political events impinge on it to weaken it, voters may shift their loyalty and will have no difficulty in selecting a party that conforms to their idea.

In terms of the strength of partisanship, Punjab again scores high, followed by other states. Viewed from a different angle, the largest proportion of voters willing to switch to other parties, if candidate choice of the party of their preference is wrong, is located in U.P., followed by Bihar, Punjab and West Bengal in that order. When it comes to the question of the main considerations for voting choice, the strongest force is group pressures in U.P., candidates in West Bengal and party loyalty in Punjab and, to a lesser degree, in Bihar. Yet another dimension in voting decision is the timing of decision. In Punjab, followed by U.P., West Bengal and Bihar, the largest proportion of voters make their voting decision prior to the start of the campaign. Looked at from a different angle, 62 per cent of respondents in Bihar and 49 per cent in West Bengal make up their mind towards the fag-end of the campaign. The corresponding figures for U.P. and Punjab are 40 per cent and 30 per cent, respectively.

Our data, then, suggest that there exists a variety of electoral behaviour. They also suggest that what the mid-term poll produced was only an uncertain verdict—uncertain not in the sense that the voters acted in an uncertain way but in the sense that it produced no certain future. West Bengal, after a stretch of popular ministry, came under President's rule and was, at the time of writing, going to polls again for a fresh electoral verdict. Bihar and U.P. have been alternating between one popular ministry and another with President's rule thrown in for a change. Punjab, too, experienced a brief spell of uncertainty; however, it seems now to have settled down. It is, therefore, of interest to ascertain what indications our data have for the future course of political development in these states.

Our data make it abundantly clear that as far as democratic institutions are concerned, they have acquired a high degree of acceptability and legitimacy. But does it indicate anything more than a widespread diffusion of the fundamentals of both the institutions of democracy and what Arora calls "the language of contemporary politics".[28] It is very clear from our data that there seems to be no clear and universally applicable answer to this question. Configurations of political attributes vary from one state to another. It is only in Punjab that voters seem to have acquired, to a considerable extent, the essential political traits that sustain and support democratic institutions. However, political awareness, activeness and efficacy seem to be the attributes mainly of voters located in the upper stratum of the society. The roots of political instability in Punjab must, therefore, be sought elsewhere, probably in its communal overtones and elite dispositions, orientations and interaction.

In West Bengal, however, the voters cannot be exonerated from the responsibility of producing and reinforcing political instability. Widespread economic distress, the collapse of the traditional social order, the apathy and withdrawal of the aged and experienced voters, the large contingent of unstable but active young voters, the lack of congruence between issue-orientation and political behaviour—all these factors augur continued political instability and confusion in West Bengal. In Bihar and U.P. too, political stability cannot be expected to be reinstated and restored in the near future. In U.P., for example, the greater

---

28. Satish K. Arora, "Exploring Political Predisposition : Efficacy and Cynicism in Rural Andhra Pradesh," *Behavioural Sciences and Community Development*, III : 2 (September 1969), p. 128.

salience of localized group pressures for voting decision is likely to reinforce the tendency towards the fragmentation of political parties. In Bihar, on the other hand, ideological polarization is in progress but must take a long time to consummate. In the meantime, the tortured progression of this tendency must introduce more volatility in the politics of this state.

Also important in this connection is the fact that the existing syndrome of relationships between socio-economic conditions, political process and policy implementation has brought into being a vicious circle of instability producing disorientation at the level of the electorate which, in turn, produces more instability. The only way of breaking this circle is, of course, a faster rate of economic growth and an equitable distribution of economic benefits to keep under control the phenomenon of incremental deprivation. Only a determined and cohesive leadership can attain such a breakthrough.

# Appendix

THE sample for the present study was drawn on the basis of probability proportionate to size. All the districts in each of the four states were grouped into sets on the basis of population size so that districts with various population sizes had equal probability of being included in a particular set. One such set was picked up in each state giving us five districts in U.P., three districts each in Bihar and West Bengal, and two districts in Punjab. From each of these districts, Assembly constituencies and polling stations within Assembly constituencies were randomly picked out and the sample of male electorate randomly selected from polling stations, at each stage following the principle of probability proportionate to size. Out of a total of 1908 targeted interviews, 1309 interviews were completed. The following table presents information of sample size and completion rate in each of the states.

| State | Targeted Interviews | Completed Interviews | Completion Rate |
|---|---|---|---|
| Bihar | 480 | 340 | 70.0% |
| Punjab | 322 | 292 | 90.0 |
| Uttar Pradesh | 625 | 428 | 69.0 |
| West Bengal | 481 | 249 | 52.0 |
| Total | 1908 | 1309 | 69.0 |

Whether the sample represents the parameters in some essential respects is a crucial question. On this depends the validity of generalization based on the data collected through a sample survey about some properties of the universe. It must be pointed out that while our sample conforms to certain attributes of the universe, viz., age structure, it over-represents as well as under-represents the magnitude of voters' preferences in favour of certain parties (See Table attached).

## Age Distribution of Male Adult Population: Sample-Universe

*(Based on 1961 Census for Actuals and 1969 mid-term Election Study for Survey)*

| Age Group (Years) | Bihar | | Punjab | | U.P. | | W.B. | |
|---|---|---|---|---|---|---|---|---|
| | Actual | Survey | Actual | Survey | Actual | Survey | Actual | Survey |
| 21—25 | 18.52 | 15.0 | 18.54 | 22.6 | 18.19 | 19.6 | 18.49 | 18.1 |
| 26—30 | 17.14 | 17.9 | 16.76 | 14.7 | 16.77 | 12.1 | 18.53 | 20.5 |
| 31—35 | 13.86 | 16.5 | 11.88 | 12.0 | 13.03 | 12.1 | 14.08 | 13.7 |
| 36—40 | 12.39 | 11.5 | 11.67 | 8.9 | 12.89 | 11.0 | 13.58 | 14.5 |
| 41—45 | 10.26 | 9.4 | 8.77 | 7.2 | 9.41 | 8.6 | 9.63 | 8.4 |
| 46—50 | 8.63 | 7.4 | 9.61 | 10.3 | 9.63 | 10.0 | 8.29 | 6.4 |
| 51—55 | 6.06 | 4.4 | 5.19 | 4.8 | 5.45 | 7.2 | 5.66 | 7.6 |
| 56+ | 13.07 | 13.5 | 17.47 | 17.8 | 14.54 | 18.2 | 11.69 | 10.8 |

Rural-Urban Breakdown of Sample and Universe

|  | Bihar | | Punjab | | U.P. | | W.B. | |
|---|---|---|---|---|---|---|---|---|
|  | Rural | Urban | Rural | Urban | Rural | Urban | Rural | Urban |
| Actual | 91.6 | 8.4 | 79.9 | 20.1 | 87.4 | 12.6 | 75.5 | 24.5 |
| Sample | 79.4 | 20.6 | 82.2 | 17.8 | 81.5 | 18.5 | 68.3 | 31.7 |

Party Preference: Sample—Universe

| Parties | Bihar | | Punjab | | U.P. | | W.B. | |
|---|---|---|---|---|---|---|---|---|
|  | Sample | Actual | Sample | Actual | Sample | Actual | Sample | Actual |
| Congress | 30.9 | 30.3 | 50.3 | 39.3 | 36.0 | 33.7 | 24.9 | 41.3 |
| Communist | 15.9 | 11.3 | 31.2 | 7.6 | — | — | 28.5 | 27.1 |
| Right | 8.2 | 15.9 | — | 8.8 | 8.9 | 19.2 | — | — |
| Socialist | 23.2 | 19.2 | — | — | 10.5 | 9.5 | 2.37 | 3.2 |
| Regional | 7.9 | 4.0 | 15.4 | 29.6 | 23.2 | 26.9 | 13.2 | 13.0 |
| Independent | — | 21.8 | — | — | 2.8 | 7.15 | 4.0 | 14.5 |

# Bibliography

ALFORD, ROBERT A., AND SCOBIE, HARRY M., "Sources of Local Political Involvement", *American Political Science Review* 62:4 December 1968

ALMOND, GABRIEL AND VERBA, SIDNEY, *Civic Culture*. Princeton: Princeton University Press. 1963

ARORA, SATISH K., "Explaining Political Participation: Efficacy and Cynicism in Rural Andhra Pradesh," *Behavioural Sciences and Community Development* 2:2. September 1969

ATAL, YOGESH, *Local Communities and National Politics*. Delhi: National Publishing House. 1971

BENDIX, RICHARD, *Nation-Building and Citizenship*. New York: John Wiley & Sons. 1964

BERELSON, BERNARD, LAZARSFELD, PAUL P., AND MCPHEE, WILLIAM, *Voting*. Chicago: University of Chicago Press. 1954

BLALOCK, HERBERT M., *Social Statistics*. New York: McGraw-Hill Book Co., Inc. 1960

BOULDING, KENNETH, *Conflict and Defence: A General Theory*. Harper Torchbooks. 1963

BURGER, PETER L. AND LUCKMANN, THOMAS, *The Social Construction of Reality: A Treatise in the Sociology of Knowledge*. Garden City: Doubleday & Co., Inc. 1966

CAMPBELL, ANGUS, "Surge and Decline: A Study of Electoral Change," in Angus Campbell *et al* (eds.), *Election and the Political Order*. New York: John Wiley and Sons Inc. 1966

Centre for the Study of Developing Societies, Delhi. *Party System and Election Studies*. New Delhi: Allied Publishers. 1967

——*Context of Electoral Change in India*. New Delhi: Academic Books. 1970

COLE, STEPHEN, "Teachers' Strike: A Study of the Conversion of Pre-disposition into Action," *American Journal of Sociology* 74 : 5. March 1969

CONVERSE, PHILIP, "Survey Research and Decoding of Patterns in Ecological Data," in Mattei Dogan and Stein Rokkan, (see Dogan below).

——"Information Flow and the Stability of Partisan Attitudes," in Angus Campbell *et al* (eds.), *Elections and the Political Order*.

——"Of Time and Partisan Stability," *Comparative Political Studies* 2 : 2. July 1969

COX, KEVIN R., "The Spatial Structuring of Information Flow and Partisan Attitude," in Mattei Dogan and Stein Rokkan. (see Dogan below).

DAHL, ROBERT A., *Who Governs*. New Haven: Yale University Press. 1961

DAS GUPTA, JYOTIRINDRA, "Language Diversity and National Development," in J.A. Fishman *et al* (eds.), *Language Problems of Developing Nations*. New York: John Wiley & Sons. 1968

DEUTSCH, KARL W., "Social Mobility and Political Development," *American Political Science Review* 55 : 3. September 1961

DOGAN, MATTEI, AND ROKKAN, STEIN (eds.), *Quantitative Ecological Analysis in the Social Sciences*. Cambridge, Mass. : The M.I.T. Press. 1969

DURKHEIM, EMILE, *Suicide*. Glencoe, Illinois: Free Press. 1951

DUVERGER, MAURICE, *Political Parties*. Trans. Barbara and Robert North. London: Methuen & Co. Ltd. 1961

GOLDBERG, ARTHUR S., "Discerning a Causal Pattern among Data on Voting Behaviour," *American Political Science Review* 60 : 4. December 1966

GOYAL O.P. AND HAHN, H., "The Nature of Party Competition in the Five Indian States," *Asian Survey* 6 : 10. October 1966

GURR, TED, *Why Men Rebel*. Princeton: Princeton University Press. 1970

GUTENSCHWAGER, Gerald A., "Social Reality and Social Change," *Social Research* 37 : 1. Spring 1970

HARTZ, LOUIS, "Democracy: Image and Reality," in William N. Chambers and Robert N. Salisbury (eds.), *Democracy in the Mid-Twentieth Century.* Saint Louis: The Washington University Press. 1960

HIMMELSTRAND, ULF, *Social Pressures, Attitudes and Democratic Process.* Stockholm: Almquest and Wicksell. 1960

HOFSTADTER, RICHARD, *The American Political Tradition.* New York: Vintage Books. 1959

HUNTINGTON, SAMUEL P., "Social and Institutional Dynamics of One-party Systems," in Samuel P. Huntington and Clement A. Moore (eds.), *Authoritarian Politics in Modern Society: The Dynamics of Established One-party Systems.* New York: Basic Books Inc. 1970

Indian Oxygen Ltd. *India: Statistical Handbook.*

INKELES, ALEX, "Making Men Modern: On the Causes and Consequences of Individual Change in Six Developing Countries," *American Journal of Sociology* 75 : 2. 1969

KASHYAP, S.C., *The Politics of Defection: A Study of State Politics in India.* Delhi: National Publishing House. 1969

KEY, V.O., *The Responsible Electorate.* Cambridge, Massachusetts: Harvard University Press. 1966

——"Theory of Critical Elections," *Journal of Politics* 17. 1955

——*Public Opinion and American Democracy.* New York: Alfred A. Knopf. 1961

KOTHARI, RAJNI, "Congress 'System' in India," *Asian Survey* 4 : 12. 1964

——*Politics in India.* Boston: Little Brown & Co. 1970—New Delhi : Orient Longman. 1970

LERNER, DANIEL, *The Passing of the Traditional Society.* Glencoe: The Free Press. 1968

LIPSET, S.M., *The Political Man.* Garden City, N.Y.: Doubleday and Co. 1960

LOCKWOOD, DAVID, "Some Remarks on 'the Social System'," in N.J. Demerath and Richard A. Peterson. (eds.), *System, Change and Conflict.* New York: The Free Press. 1967

MARVICK, DWAINE AND BAY, JANE H., "Domains and Universe: Problems in Concerted Use of Multiple Data Files for Social Science Inquiries," in Mattei Dogan and Stein Rokkan (see Dogan above).

MCRAE, DUNCAN, AND MELDRUM, JAMES A., "Factor Analysis of Aggregate Voting Analysis," in Mattei Dogan and Stein Rokkan (see Dogan above).

MEDDING, PETER Y, "Elitist Democracy: An Unsuccessful Critique of a Misunderstood Theory," *The Journal of Politics* 31 : 3. August 1968

MILBRAITH, LESTER, *Political Participation*. Chicago: Rand McNally & Co. 1965

MISHRA, B.B., *The Indian Middle Class: Their Growth in Modern Times*. London: Oxford University Press. 1961

NIEBURG, H.L., "Violence, Law and the Informal Polity," *The Journal of Conflict Resolution* 8 : 2. June 1969

PITKIN, HANNAH F., *The Concept of Representation*. Berkeley: University of California Press. 1967

PUTNAM, ROBERT D., "Political Attitudes and the Local Community," *American Political Science Review* 60. 1966

PYE, LUCIAN, *Aspects of Political Development*. Boston: Little Brown & Co. 1966

RANNEY, AUSTIN, "The Utility and Limitations of Aggregate Data in the Study of Electoral Behaviour," in Austin Ranney (ed.), *Essays on the Behavioral Study of Politics*. Urbana: University of Illinois Press. 1962

ROBINSON, W.S., "Ecological Correlations and Behaviour of Individuals," *American Sociological Review* 15. 1950

ROY, RAMASHRAY, "Election, Electorate and Democracy in India," *Perspective,* a Supplement to *Indian Journal of Public Administration* 17 : 4. October-December 1971

——"Dynamics of One-Party Dominance in an Indian State," *Asian Survey* July 1967

——"Social Diversity, Economic Development and Political Integration," Mimeo.

——"Patterns of Political Instability: A Study of the 1969 Midterm Elections," *Economic and Political Weekly* 6 : 3-5. January 1971

RUSSETT, BRUCE, "Social Change and Attitudes on Development and the Political System in India," *Journal of Politics* 2 : 3. August 1967

SARLVIK, B.O., "Socio-Economic Determinants of Voting Behaviour in the Swedish Electorate," *Comparative Political Studies* 2 : 1. April 1969

SARTORI, GIOVANNI, *Democratic Theory*. Calcutta: Oxford and IBH Publishing Co. 1965

SCHATTSCHNEIDER, E.E. *The Semi-Sovereign People*. New York: Holt, Reinhart and Winston. 1960

SCHEUCH, IRVIN K., "Social Context and Individual Behaviour," in Mattei Dogan and Stein Rokkan (see Dogan above).

——"Cross-National Comparison Using Aggregate Data: Some Substantive and Methodological Problems," in Richard Merritt and Stein Rokkan (eds.), *Comparing Nations*. New Haven: Yale University Press. 1966

SCHUTZ, ALFRED, *Collected Papers*, edited by Maurice Natanson. The Hague: Martinus Nijhoff. 1962

SEGAL, DAVID R., AND MEYER, MARSHALL W., "The Social Context of Political Partisanship," in Mattei Dogan and Stein Rokkan. (see Dogan above).

SHILS, EDWARD, "Primordial, Personal, Sacred and Civil Ties," *The British Journal of Sociology* 8 : 2. 1957

SIMON, HERBERT A., *Models of Man: Social and Rational*. Chapel Hill: The University of North Carolina Press. 1964

WEINER, MYRON, *Party Politics in India*. Princeton, New Jersey: Princeton University Press. 1957

——*Party Building in a New Nation*. Chicago: Chicago University Press. 1967

WILENMANN, HERMANN, "The Interlocking of Nation and Personality Structure," in Karl W. Deutsch and W.J. Foltz. (eds.), *Nation-Building*. New York: Atherton Press. 1963

# Index

f—footnote     t—tables     fig—figures

Age and electoral involvement, 176t, 177t; and partisanship. 168fig, 169, 170t; and party identification, see Party identification; and political efficacy, 237t; and level of political information, 157t, 158, 159t; and political interest, 161t, 162, 163t; and voting behaviour, 64, 75, 105-6fig, 107-9, 110t-12t, 155t, 280

Akali Dal, 34, 36t; losses and gains, 38t, 44; retention capacity of voters, 49t; socio-economic status of voters, 98

Alford, Robert A., 164f

Almond, Gabriel, 15, 222f, 243f 244f, 248f, 263f, 264f

Apathy, 272

Arora, Satish, 281

BKD: see Bharatiya Kranti Dal

Bangla Congress: losses and gains, 38t, 39t, 43

Bays, Jane H., 20, 21

Bendix, Reinhard, 16f, 17f, 220f

Berelson, Bernard, 74, 272f

Berger, Peter L., 22f, 266f

Bharatiya Jan Sangh, 32f; losses and gains, 41t, 42, 43-44; voters, 121; retention capacity of voters, 49t

Bharatiya Kranti Dal, losses and gains, 38t, 41t, 54, 56; voters, 121

Bihar, see under various sub-headings

Blalock, Hubert M., 68f

Building, Kenneth, 69f

CPI, see Communist Party of India

CPI(M), see Communist Party of India (Marxist)

Campaign participation, 144t, 145t, 146t; see also electoral involvement

Campbell, Angus, 99f, 100

Caste, 120, 121; and political efficacy, 236t; and politics, 67, 221, 234t; and voting behaviour, 116, 117t, 118t, 119t, 120-121

Centre for the Study of Developing Societies, 5f, 23f, 61f

Charan Singh, 33

Citizens: civic sense in, 16-17, 19; competence in democracy, 223-224; equality between, 14; participation in democracy, 222; public affairs, interest in, 14

Civic culture, 262, 264

Coalition governments, 13, 33-35, 46

Cole, Stephen, 128f

Communist parties, see also Communist Party of India, Communist Party of India (Marxist): losses and gains, 38t, 43-44; retention capacity of voters, 56-57

Communist Party of India, 54; losses and gains, 38t-41t; retention capacity of voters, 48-49; socio-economic status of voters, 95

Communist Party of India (Marxist), 36; losses and gains, 38, 38t-41t, 42-43; socio-economic status of voters, 95

# INDEX

Congress Party, *see* Indian National Congress
Control over industries, *see* nationalisation of industries
Converse, Philip, 11f, 61f, 99f
Canvassing, 81
Cox, Kevin R., 21f, 101f
Cumulative inequality, *see* inequality, cumulative

Dahl, Robert A., 4f, 261-62
Defections: *see* legislators, defection of; voters, defection of
Democracy, 7, 13, 15, 79, 184-187, 220-225, 230, 231t, 258, 260-263, 282; balanced disparities in, 260; stability of, 272-275; and government, 203
Democratic institutions: *see* democracy, elections, legislators, legislatures, political parties
Deutsch, Karl W., 87f
Developing countries and social change, 268
Dictatorship, 222
Dogan, Mattei, 101f
Durkheim, Emile, 128f
Duverger, Maurice, 10f, 11f

Economic development, 220; *see also* states—economic conditions
Education, 63t, 67, 123t, 126fig, 127-128, 234-236; and political information, level of, 157t; and political interest, 124, 125, 126fig, 127, 128
Election studies, v
Elections, v, 1-3, 202, 203t, 225-228; (1967) 67, 103, 105fig, 106fig, 107; (1969) 103, 109; not as festive occasion 76, 81; victory in, 6, 8, 227t, 228, 229
Electoral involvement, 78t, 79t, 80, 81, 82t, 174t, 175, 176t, 177t, 178, 179t, 180, 181t, 182, 183, 242t, 243, 244, 279; index of, 173f

Elites, ruling, *see* ruling elites
Environmental characteristics, 267, 269-271

Fallacy, ecological, 20
Forward Bloc: losses and gains, 37, 38t, 42

Goldberg, Arthur S., 271
Goyal, O.P., 44
Gurr, Ted, 69f, 269f
Gutenschwager, Gerald A., 22f, 266f

Hahn, H., 44f
Hartz, Louis, 265f
Hatscheck's law, 11
Himmelstrand, Ulf, 100f
Hofstadter, Richard, 10f
Homopolitical selectivity, 100f, 102
Huntington, Samuel P., 5f

Illiteracy: *see* education, (States) literacy
Income and political interest, 126fig, 127-128
Independent candidates: losses and gains, 38t-41t
Indian National Congress, 33-36, 55fig; as a dominant party, 4-5, 32-33, 280-281; losses and gains, 5, 6, 38t-41t, 42, 43-44, 46; opposition to, 45-46; Voters: 56, 57fig; age group, 104, 105fig, 106fig, 107; retention capacity of, 47-48, 56, 57fig; socio-economic status, 94t, 95t, 96; Votes polled: comparison with other political parties, 36; percentage delcine in, 35
Inequality, cumulative, 4, 114; dispersal of, 4
Inkeles, Alex, 133f, 223

Intentionality, 266-267
Interviews, conducted, 283-284

Jana Sangh, *see* Bharatiya Jana Sangh

Kashyap, S.C., 33f
Key, V.O., 8-10, 183f, 248, 260f, 261-262, 279f
Kothari, Rajni, 2f, 3f, 31f

Landholdings and voting behaviour, 63t, 66, 121-122t
Law, obedience of, 231, 232t
Lazarsfeld, Paul F., 272f
Leftism, 200t, 201
Legislative assemblies, *see* legislatures
Legislators, 188, 208, 210t, 217t; defection of, 6, 31, 35, 188-189, 190, 214, 215t, 217t, 218; role of, 208-209, 210t-211t, 212, 213t, 214; and political parties 188-189, 211-212, 213t, 214, 216, 217t; and the voters, 144, 210t, 211-213
Legislatures, 187, 202, 203t
Legitimacy of political regime, 18-19, 219-222, 224-225, 230t, 231
Lerner, Daniel, 15f
Lipset, S.M., 15f, 219f, 221f
Lockwood, David, 12f
Losses and gains by political parties, 37, 38t-41t, 42, 43; *see also* subdivision 'losses and gains' under the names of the individual political parties i.e. Indian National Congress: losses and gains; Bihar, 39t; Punjab, 41t; Uttar Pradesh, 40t; West Bengal, 38t
Luckmann, Thomas, 22f, 266f

M.L.A.'s, *see* legislators
Manifest reality, 22, 266-269, 271-273

Marvick, Dwaine, 20f, 21f
Medding, Peter Y., 152f, 273f
Meyer, Marshall W., 20f, 21f, 101f
Milbraith, Lester W., 265f, 272f
Mishra, B.B., 66f
Monarchy, 222, 265
Multiparty system, 6, 12-13

Natanson, Maurice, 150f
Nation-building, 12-13, 220f
Nationalisation of industries, 193, 195t-196t, 197-198, 201
Nieburg, H.L., 18f, 219f, 220
New voters, 63-64, 66, 75, 104, 108; party affiliation of, 66

Occupations, *see* voters' occupations
Oligarchy, 223
One-party dominance, 2, 11, 12; *see also* Indian National Congress: as a dominant party
One-party system, 32-33, 280
Opposition parties, 32-35, 36, 38

P.S.P., *see* Praja Socialist Party
Partisanship, 98-147, 280; *see also* voters: partisan preference
Party identification, 82t, 83t, 100-101, 120, 129-131, 135, 136t-138t, 139-140, 147, 164-165, 166t, 167-168, 170t, 171, 172t, 178, 179t, 238, 239t, 241; *see also* party preference; index of, 165f
Party loyalty; *see* party identification
Party preference, 67, 94t, 95t, 287t; factors in, 57-58; *see also* party identification
Party system, v, 5, 8, 32, 33, 38, 46-47, 150, 189-190, 206-207t; *see also* multiparty system, one-party system, political parties, two-party system
Philips, Wendell, 10f, 11f
Pitkin, Hanna F., 184-188
Plebiscite, 186

# INDEX

Political activist, 261
Political attributes: causal linkage, among, 277fig
Political efficacy, 233, 234t, 237t, 238, 238t, 240t, 241t, 242t, 243-250, 251t, 255t, 257; *see also* age and political efficacy, caste and political efficacy
Political interest, 101, 126fig, 127-128, 131t, 132t, 133, 134, 150, 159t, 161t, 162, 163t, 164, 165, 171, 172t, 180, 182-183, 190, 191t, 192, 223, 241; *see also* age and political interest, education and political interest, income and political interest
Political parties, 45, 60, 187, 190, 202, 203t, 204, 206; *see also* Akali Dal, Bangla Congress, Bharatiya Kranti Dal, Bharatiya Jana Sangh, Communist Party of India, Communist Party of India (Marxist), Forward Bloc, Indian National Congress; competition in, 31-48, 49t-52t, 53, 55fig, 56-57; necessity of, 206-208t; policies and programmes, 204-205t; role in democracy, 239; and elections, 203t, 230; and legislators, *see* legislators and political parties
Political power, *see* power
Political regime, 222
Political stability, *see* political systems, stability of, 219, 257, 263, 273; *see also* one-party system, two-party system, multi-party system; stability of, 260, 281
Political values, *see* values
Politics, 184-185, 190, 191t; discussion about, in families, 67; as legitimate activity, 187; and caste, *see* caste and politics; and voters, 183-186
Power, 3; arbitrary, 223; in the hands of states, *see* statism; shifts in, 1-4
Praja Socialist Party: losses and gains, 38t, 41t, 42-43

President's Rule, 32-33, 218
Private property, abolition of, 193, 197t-198t, 201
Public affairs, interest in, 164
Public policies, influencing of, *see* voters: influencing of public policies
Punjab, *see* the various subdivisions under the heading 'States'
Putnam, Robert D·, 101f
Pye, Lucian W., 3f

Reality, *see* manifest reality, subjective reality
Rebellion, 71
Representation, 184, 188
Representatives *see* legislators
Respondents, *see* voters
Robinson, W.S., 20f
Rokkan, Stein, 10f, 102f
Roy, Ramashray, v-vi, 8f, 18f, 23f, 30f, 65f, 73f, 101f, 279f
Ruling elites, 1-2, 264-265
Rural voters, 63t, 115t; defection of, 114
Rulers, selection of, 1, 226
Rulers and the ruled, 17-19
Russett, Bruce, 223f

Samyukta Socialist Party: losses and gains, 38t-41t, 42, 43; retention capacity of voters, 48
Sarlvik, B.O., 60f
Sartori, Giovanni, 14f, 74f
Schattschneider, E.E., 261f
Scheuch, Erwin K., 15f, 19f-20f
Scobie, Harry M., 164f
Segal, David R., 21f, 101f
Shift in party preference, *see* legislators: defection of, voters: defection of
Shils, Edward, 22f, 262f
Single party, dominance of, *see* one party, dominance of
Social change, 267-270
Social statistics, 68-69

Social reality, 151-153
Socialist parties: retention capacity of voters, 49t-52t, 56-57fig
States: development expenditure, 25, 26t 27t, 29-30; economic conditions, 24, 25t, 26-30, 58, 60; employment, 29-30; income, per capita, 29; land area, 24; literacy, 24; politics, 30-35, 57, 59; population, 24
Statism, 187, 193-194
Stokes, Donald E., 99f
Subjective reality, 152, 267-268, 270-272
Survey research, criticism of, 19-21
Swatantra Party, 34; decline of, 36

Taxation, reduction in, 193, 194t, 195t, 202
Two-party system, 12-13, 261

United Fronts, *see* coalition governments
Urban Voters, 62t, 97, 115t; defection of, 113
Uttar Pradesh: *see* various subdivisions under the heading 'States'

Value, 184
Verba, Sidney, 14f, 222f, 243f, 244f, 263f, 264f
Voters: *see* new voters, rural voters, urban voters; age, age and voting behaviour; campaign participation, 144t, 145t, 146t; *see also* caste and campaign participation; classification of, 103; contacting the legislators, 250, 251t, 252; contacting the officials, 252t; defection of, 10-13, 45-47, 49t-52t, 53-56, 100, 102, 115, 129-130, 133; democratic norms, awareness of, 153; education of, *see* education; electoral involvement of, *see* age and electoral involvement;
financial conditions of, 68t, 70t, 72t; illiteracy of, *see* education, (States) literacy; income of, 62t, 63t; influencing the administrative decisions, 245-250, 254-255, 256t; influencing the public policies, 228, 245-250, 260; information level of, 155t, 275, about contestents, 77, about ex-M.L.A.'s, 154, about winning candidate in the last elections, 75, 76t, 79, 82, 135, 136t-138t; interest in election, *see* electoral involvement; interest in politics, *see* age and political interest, education and political interest, political interest; issue orientation of, 276-277, *see also* nationalisation, private property abolition, taxation reduction; land owned by, *see* land holdings and voting; occupations of, 63, 68; partisan preference of, 82t, 83t, 85t, 86, 89t, 94t, 95t, 102, 119-122, 147, 149, 150, 166, 183, *see also* age and partisanship; party identification of, *see* party identification; political information, level of, 154, 155t, 157t, 158, 162, 163t, 170t, 171, 172t; political participation of, 191t, 193, 272, 273; politics, understanding of 252t, 254; socio-economic status of, 61, 62t, 63t, 65, 67, 68t, 70t, 72t, 78t, 85t, 89t, 92t, 94t, 95t, 97t, 103, 114, 115t, 115, 123, 125, 149-150, 155-156, 159t, 167t, 173, 174t, 175, 181, 190, 191t, 192-193, 194t, 198t, 200t, 202, 203t, 205t, 207t, 208, 209t, 211t, 213t, 215t, 217t, 229t, 230t, 231, 237t, 251t, 253t, 255t, 269-270, 278; and political interest, *see* political interest; and government policy, *see* public policies; and legislators, *see* legislators and voters; and politics, *see* politics and voting; and representatives, *see* legislators and voters

INDEX

Voters, indifferent, 116, 120, 121
Voting behaviour, 9, 19-23, 61, 257-260, *see also* age and voting behaviour, caste and voting behaviour
Voting decisions, 82-83t, 84-85, 91, 92t-94t, 95t, 98; appropriateness of, 84, 85t, 86; group pressure on, 81-82, 88-90, 91, 152-153, 283; influencing of, 91t, by parents, 66; timing of, 61, 91, 92t, 95, 139, 140t-142t, 280

Weber, Max, 22-23
Weiner, Myron, 8f
Wilenmann, Herman, 16f, 17f
West Bengal, *see* the various subdivisions under the heading 'States'

LIBRARY OF DAVIDSON COLLEGE